THE
VIPER
THE LIFE+ CRIMES
OF MARTIN FOLEY

For Dave Dehora

THE
VIPER
THE LIFE + CRIMES
OF MARTIN FOLEY

MICK
McCAFFREY

Y BOOKS

First published in 2012 by
Y Books
Lucan, Co. Dublin, Ireland
Tel/fax: +353 1 6217992
publishing@ybooks.ie
www.ybooks.ie

Text © 2012 Mick McCaffrey
Editing, design and layout © 2012 Y Books

Photographs © of individuals or institutions listed under each image in the photograph section.

Paperback	ISBN: 978-1-908023-58-2
Ebook – mobi format	ISBN: 978-1-908023-59-9
Ebook – ePub format	ISBN: 978-1-908023-60-5

A CIP catalogue record for this book is available from the British Library.
10 9 8 7 6 5 4 3 2 1

Typeset by Y Books
Cover design by Graham Thew Design
Cover images: Front left courtesy of the *Sunday World*
Printed and bound by CPI Group (UK) Ltd, Croydon, CR0 4YY

Author biography

MICK MCCAFFREY IS an investigative journalist with the *Sunday World*. He has previously worked as News Editor of the *Sunday Tribune* and Security Editor at both the *Sunday Tribune* and the *Evening Herald*. He has specialised in crime journalism for the last nine years. *The Irish Scissor Sisters* was Mick's first book and spent several weeks as a No.1 bestseller in 2007. Mick is also the author of the No.1 bestseller *Cocaine Wars: Fat Freddie Thompson and the Crumlin/Drimnagh Feud*, which was adapted for television by TV3 in 2010.

Praise for *The Irish Scissor Sisters*

'This is a unique insight into the underbelly of a "new" Ireland.
Riveting.'
JOE DUFFY, RTÉ

Praise for *Cocaine Wars*

'Well-researched and authoritative account of
a vicious gang war.'
IRISH INDEPENDENT

'An intimate knowledge of the engagement and a commendable
level of research render this account indispensable for
interested parties.'
SUNDAY BUSINESS POST

'An in-depth exposé.'
IRISH DAILY MIRROR

'Explosive.'
SUNDAY WORLD

Acknowledgements

THANKS TO ALL THE people who have either known or dealt with Martin Foley over the last forty years – friends and foes – for giving their time to help me research this book and for offering their valuable insights.

Thanks to *Sunday World* editor, Colm McGinty, managing editor, Neil Leslie, and news editor, John Donlon, for giving me the time to write this book. Also thanks to picture editor Owen Breslin and photographer Ernie Leslie.

Fellow crime correspondents, Ken Foy of the *Evening Herald*, Nicola Tallant and Niall Donald of the *Sunday World*, Ali Bracken of the *Irish Daily Mail* and Jim Cusack of the *Sunday Independent*, were always happy to offer help and opinions whenever asked. This was much appreciated.

Thanks to Ian Mallon of the *Irish Independent*, and *Evening Herald* photo editor, Jane Last, for helping with photos. Also to *Irish Independent* photographer Mark Condren.

Solicitor Kieran Kelly from Fanning & Kelly has always been on hand to offer sound advice on the various legal missives Martin Foley has sent me over the years. Many thanks for that and for reading this book for libel.

Thanks to Chenile Keogh and Robert Doran from Y books for their support and hard work in getting this book onto the shelves.

Also thanks to Ken Swan, Donal Galvin, Ronan Bent, Dave Dehora, Gareth Curley, Brendan Cronin, Brian Hurl and Maureen Gillespie for happily listening to me complain about deadlines.

Thanks also to my mam and dad and sisters Debi, Caron and Laura and especially to my beautiful fiancée, Jennifer Stevens.

Finally, thanks to all the people who helped me research this book, proofread it and who offered great advice, suggestions and ways to improve it. I cannot name them for various reasons but they know who they are and it wouldn't have been possible without them.

Mick McCaffrey
October 2012

Contents

Introduction

'I'M DEAD, I'M DEAD. Dean did it, Dean did it.'

Martin 'The Viper' Foley mumbled the words to the ambulance staff who had rushed to the entrance of the Carlisle gym on the Lower Kimmage Road, in Dublin. The fifty-six-year-old had been shot just minutes before. He was clearly in a bad way, with multiple bullet wounds to his body and a nasty graze above his right eye, where a bullet had hit him and somehow bounced off his skull. It was the afternoon of 26 January 2008, and after naming the man he believed had set him up to be shot Foley lapsed into unconsciousness. As he was brought to St James's Hospital the situation did not look good.

This was the fourth attempt to assassinate The Viper. Foley suffered seven gunshot wounds and had now been hit by a total of eighteen bullets in his lifetime, which was easily a gangland record. This time he had fallen foul of the man who masterminded the importation of most of the drugs sold on our streets.

As Foley lay in a coma, senior gardaí who had chased him for years, and journalists who had eagerly written about his life of crime over the previous four decades, began to publically consider the legacy Foley would leave behind.

Martin Foley was convicted of his first criminal offence in 1968 and went on to become one of the key members of Martin 'The General' Cahill's gang. From taking part in massive jewellery heists to masterminding daring raids on country houses containing priceless collections of art, Foley embraced his chosen career with gusto. In March 1984 he was snatched from his bed in Crumlin by an IRA active service unit. Bound, gagged and badly beaten, it seemed certain that Foley was about to meet his maker on that occasion. Luckily for him a neighbour noticed the commotion and called the gardaí, who arrested the gang after a shootout in the Phoenix Park.

Foley always moved with the times and in the nineties he became a drug dealer, attracted by the easy money that could be made. He went into business with his trusted pal Seamus 'Shavo' Hogan, but little good came from that enterprise and both men ended up getting shot for their troubles, Foley twice, Hogan fatally.

The Viper's chosen career and frequent brushes with death tormented his family. His beloved wife, Pauline, succumbed to cancer and he was left to bring up two teenage girls singlehandedly.

In 2008 Foley made a fresh start of sorts and he turned his back on drug dealing. Having set himself up as a debt collector, he was now on the straight and narrow. Well, as straight and narrow as he had ever been, anyway. He considered himself a legitimate businessman and was making more money than ever, with little or no risk. The poor suckers he was chasing to pay their debts might have been scared out of their minds when he called to their doors, but he told himself he wasn't doing anything illegal. It wasn't his fault that people were afraid of him and his reputation for violence.

Foley hated the newspapers and blamed the media for many of his troubles. They had built him up to be a fearsome character, portraying him as a godfather of crime, robbing from the rich and the poor, caring about nobody but himself. That was not true. He was a good, family man, a loyal friend, who was misunderstood and misrepresented by the media. They had even blamed him when a hoax bomb was found under the car of a journalist outside his home, as the hack and his family slept in bed. He had been arrested all right, but there was no proof that he was responsible. He believed the cops were trying to stitch him up again, just like they had when the Tango Squad detectives followed him around for six months in the 1980s, causing havoc on the streets of Dublin.

Twelve days after he was shot outside the gym, Martin Foley woke up. Remarkably, there was no long-term damage to his health, save a few more battle scars. Gangland's Rasputin had survived again and the Grim Reaper would have to wait to bring the criminal on his final journey home. Three days after he woke up, two detectives called to see him. They reminded Foley that he had shouted Dean Howe's name as he lay slumped in his car, thinking he was a dead man. 'Sorry, lads, I can't remember a thing,' he told them. The Viper did not make a statement to gardaí; that is not what gangsters like him did. He would sort out his latest problem himself, like he always had.

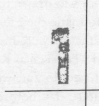

Schooled by The General

MARTIN FOLEY WAS BORN on 24 November 1951, the youngest of five children. When his mother left hospital she brought her newborn son home to the working-class suburb of Crumlin, four miles from Dublin city centre. Foley has never left Crumlin and has become synonymous with the area. His parents hailed from County Derry but they moved to Dublin when they got married, feeling that the capital would be a better place to bring up their family. Martin Foley grew up in relative poverty, but his father always made sure there was a hot meal on the table each night, and both his parents were very loving towards their kids.

As Foley grew into a young adult, he realised that Crumlin was not typical of most neighbourhoods. The close-knit community was very suspicious of authority and outsiders. Local men called door-to-door selling goods that had been stolen from shops and factories, and they always seemed to get a warm welcome. If a garda was walking the beat, word would soon spread, so that anyone on the run from the law or up to no good could quietly slip away undetected.

Foley was drawn to the shadowy thieves and petty criminals who made their living from petty crime and larceny. These characters were more respected in Crumlin than politicians and were seen as Robin Hood type figures who looked after old people and were happy to wait until the next social welfare day before being paid for the stolen goods they supplied. Foley liked what he saw and was attracted to the glamorous lifestyle of the older teens who had money in their pockets and an air of danger about them. He wanted to be like them and he began to hang around with people who were destined for lives of crime.

In Crumlin Foley was surrounded by many like-minded people who had scant regard for the law and who were more than happy to break it in order to line their own pockets. Some of Ireland's most notorious lawbreakers either hailed from the area or gravitated towards it. Such criminal luminaries as Martin 'The General' Cahill, Seamus 'Shavo' Hogan, Joseph 'Jo Jo' Kavanagh, Eamon Daly, Christy Dutton, Larry Dunne and his family, and the Cunningham brothers – John 'The Colonel', Fran 'The Lamb' and Michael – were friends and contemporaries of The Viper.

Crumlin and neighbouring Drimnagh became known as the first 'home of organised crime in Ireland', and short-sighted planning officials have to take the blame for this. In the early 1930s Dublin Corporation began a huge building programme in the area, relocating families from Dublin's inner-city tenements to purpose-built flat complexes in what was then effectively the countryside. There were no facilities for youngsters, and with nothing for them to do, they inevitably drifted towards crime, and later, drugs. Parts of Crumlin and Drimnagh became ghettoised and there was huge unemployment in the areas. Residents developed a hatred of authority figures and they especially hated the gardaí. They would literally cross the street to avoid them. There was an unwritten rule that you could never, ever engage with gardaí; it was more acceptable to be a paedophile than a garda informant, or rat. It was perhaps no surprise that many young men who went on to be the country's most notorious villains came from the Dublin 12 and Dublin 8 areas.

Martin Foley began to rebel at an early age. Although he signed up to learn the trade of a tyre fitter and served his apprenticeship in various service stations around the city, his heart wasn't really in it. He would come home after working a ten-hour day, exhausted and with only an apprentice's wage in his pocket, while his mates were wearing the latest clothes, courtesy of the proceeds of a robbery or some other crime. He quickly became tired of getting up at first light and travelling by bus to break his back for a pittance. Foley came to the conclusion that an honest day's work for an honest day's pay was for mugs, and he became more and more involved with the likes of Seamus Hogan and Martin Cahill. This inevitably led to him drifting into crime. The local criminals were impressed by Foley's physical strength and he was regarded as a local hard man who knew how to use his fists and was very difficult to beat in a fair fight. The young wannabe would be very useful as muscle to frighten and intimidate rival criminals, his new friends thought.

As well as being a tough character, Foley was fun to be around. He was a natural joker who was forever laughing and slagging people and he loved to tell stories and spread gossip. He also had a reputation as a ladies' man and was involved in a number of short-lived relationships with various women from the Crumlin area. They were drawn to his cheeky grin and charming ways and he could often be seen on dates in local pubs.

Foley's criminal career started off innocuously enough. He was given the Probation Act in 1968 for being drunk and disorderly and he was warned by the judge to keep his nose clean unless he wanted another appearance in the dock. The warning went unheeded, though, and two months later he was back before the courts, charged with larceny and receiving stolen goods. He was convicted and from that moment on his job became crime, and he was very good at it.

In April 1972 Foley suffered injuries to his face after he was attacked by a man wielding a petrol bomb, following a row with a local man outside the Blackhorse Inn on Captain's Road in Crumlin. The man, knowing that he would find it difficult to beat Foley with his fists, threw the device at him. Foley was rushed to the Adelaide Hospital, while the other man was arrested. Luckily his injuries were not serious and the attacker was later charged in connection with the assault. Foley never complained about the attack and this reinforced his image as a tough nut. Other criminals were impressed that somebody would have to go to such lengths as to throw a petrol bomb to get the upper hand in a row with Foley.

Martin 'The General' Cahill took a keen interest in the rising criminal's career. The General was the undisputed king of the Crumlin mob. Born in May 1949 in the slums of Dublin's north inner city, Cahill was the second of twelve children. The family moved to Captain's Road in Crumlin in 1960 as part of the government's programme to move people out of the city centre. The Cahill family was poor and Martin often had to go and ask for handouts of food from the local convent. He received his first conviction, for larceny, at the age of twelve and kept getting into trouble after that. He confessed to two burglaries when he was sixteen and was sent to an industrial school in Daingean, County Offaly. By the time he was released a year later, his family had been evicted from Captain's Road for rent arrears and they had moved to the Hollyfield Buildings, which were tenements in the Rathmines area. It was there that he met Frances Lawless, with whom he began a relationship and soon married.

Cahill was heavy set and was known for his love of cream cakes. He had a good sense of humour and a kind and eccentric nature, at least towards his friends. He became an expert burglar and housebreaker and he would bury his loot, often forgetting where he had hidden it. But he was a ruthless criminal and didn't hesitate to have people who did him wrong 'sorted out'. Cahill hated the gardaí and would stare at the wall and refuse to answer a single question when he was being interrogated. Because of his skill as a burglar and armed robber and the fact that he was the eldest lad in a large family of criminals, other hoods around Crumlin and the surrounding areas looked up to Cahill and he became the leader of the pack, acquiring the nickname The General because of the meticulous way he planned his jobs, never leaving anything to chance, much like an army general.

Cahill and his cronies embraced Foley and by the early 1970s he had become a vital cog in the wheel of the mob and a trusted member of The General's inner circle. Cahill was more of a thinker than a fighter and he often used Martin Foley to settle his scores with violence. Foley was more than happy to help out his mentor. From an early age Martin Foley was a fitness fanatic. He loved lifting heavy weights, going on long runs and cycles and generally maintaining a fitness level that an athlete would be proud of. He was a talented boxer and competed at a high level for Crumlin Boxing Club. He had an impressive physique despite being just 5 ft 7". He was square and muscular and definitely not to be messed with.

Foley fit nicely into Cahill's gang and was highly valued as their enforcer, a key role in any criminal organisation. He wasn't the cleverest of criminals but this was more than compensated for by his brawn, and he was very handy to have around when it looked like things might get out of hand or when the threat of violence was in the air. Foley had a distinctive, abundant moustache, which he let grow around both sides of his mouth, right down close to his chin. Cahill used to say that the two tips of Foley's moustache looked like snake fangs and he jokingly called him The Viper. The nickname stuck and when anyone in Crumlin referred to The Viper, it was instantly known that they meant Foley. The nickname was also apt because Foley was a slippery character who was hard to pin down and who was lethal on the attack, much like a snake.

The Viper was devoted to Martin Cahill from day one and he would do anything to keep his boss happy. He was prepared to bully weaker individuals and throw his weight around and threaten man, woman or beast to get what he or Cahill wanted. In short, he was a thug and had no problem throwing a sly dig if he felt the moment demanded it. He was also cunning and had a great ability to escape from sticky situations unharmed.

The advent of the Troubles meant that many gardaí were

moved away from policing the streets as the force was concentrating more on the growth of subversive groups than on ordinary criminals. This meant that there were greater opportunities to carry out serious crimes, and far less chance of getting nabbed. So larceny gave way to armed robbery, with banks, factory payrolls, cash-delivery vans and shops being targeted by The General's crew. They were soon carrying out a heist a week. They ran rings around the gardaí, who were struggling to keep tabs on the IRA and an expanding army of 'volunteers', never mind getting to grips with the young generation of criminals from Crumlin, who were robbing with a gusto never seen before. Serious crime in Dublin in the early 1970s was still relatively rare and it was a while before gardaí caught up with the tactics of The General's mob and longer still before Garda Headquarters in the Phoenix Park developed a plan to take on the growth in armed robberies. The General, Foley and the other gang members knew this and took the attitude that they may as well make hay while the sun shone and trouser as much loot as they could before the boys in blue fought back.

The gang was soon No. 1 on the gardaí's most wanted list. On 19 November 1974 they raided a bank security van that was delivering cash at Rosemount shopping centre, in Rathfarnham. This was the robbery that really catapulted them into the big time. Five armed and masked men attacked two Securicor workers as they were preparing to make a delivery to Quinnsworth. The raiders grabbed four containers of cash and escaped in a waiting car. Cahill and his cohorts made off with £92,000 in cash, an astonishing haul that would be the equivalent of over €1 million in today's money.

Two getaway cars were discovered the following day.

One was found in Harold's Cross, not far from Crumlin. A second car, along with a double-barrelled shotgun, was recovered in Rathfarnham, near where the raid took place. A £9,000 reward, which was immediately offered for the safe return of the money, led to a tip-off from a member of the public. Not long after this breakthrough, Martin Cahill, his brother Eddie and future brother-in-law Hugh Delaney were arrested by gardaí. They were charged almost immediately and Hugh Delaney, obviously not versed in the sacrosanct rule of non-cooperation with the law, made verbal admissions while in custody. He was charged, as were the two Cahill brothers, although the charges against them were later dropped because of a lack of evidence. Delaney soon had second thoughts about his confession and announced that Martin Foley would be the key witness speaking on his behalf. He claimed that Foley would give him a watertight alibi.

The trial for armed robbery was due to begin at the Central Criminal Court in July 1976, but Cahill wasn't about to allow his sister's partner get sent down without a fight. He devised a stroke to get Delaney off the hook. As Martin Foley was about to enter the imposing Four Courts building on Dublin's Inns Quay, he was unceremoniously snatched off the street, seemingly by a gang of criminals or IRA men. Gardaí soon got wind that the kidnapping had been staged by The General's mob so that Delaney would lose his main alibi witness, thereby leaving the judge under pressure to acquit him. Criminals in Crumlin tried to put out a rumour that the IRA had indeed been responsible, but gardaí dismissed this out of hand after investigating the kidnap. They could, however, find no trace of the elusive Martin Foley. Cahill's clever plan had the desired effect.

Delaney's defence counsel applied to have the robbery charge dismissed on the basis that Foley's enforced absence meant the accused man was unable to properly defend himself. The judge agreed and Delaney was set free, but a bench warrant was issued for Foley to explain himself if and when he resurfaced before the court. This was the first time that Foley allowed himself to be used as a public pawn in The General's games with gardaí, but it wasn't the last.

Unsurprisingly Foley re-appeared, healthy and unharmed, two weeks after his 'kidnap ordeal'. In reality he had stayed in a safe house in Dublin and had kept his head down until the heat of Delaney's acquittal had died down. He wasn't exactly forthcoming about what had happened to him when he presented himself at Sundrive Road Garda Station, saying he had been freed. He was taken straight to the Central Criminal Court on foot of the warrant for his arrest, where he told Mr Justice Gannon that he had been kidnapped by the Provisional IRA. Detective Sergeant Brendan Gallagher of Rathfarnham Garda Station told the court that he had arrested Foley at Sundrive Road but that Foley refused to tell him where he had been held for the previous fortnight. Foley told the court that on the first day of the trial into the Quinnsworth robbery he had been accosted by somebody he knew, outside the Legal Eagle pub near the Four Courts. At first Foley thought it was a joke, he said, but he realised it wasn't when the man produced a gun and pressed it to his stomach. The mystery man then ordered Foley into a car, which was driven by an accomplice. There was a third man in the back seat, whom Foley said he also knew. He said he was taken to a luxury flat near the Rendezvous pub on the northside of the city, where he was held for a week. He claimed he was allowed to leave only after the kidnappers had shown him a copy of the *Irish Independent* in which the verdict of the trial was reported. Foley said he knew that Delaney had been acquitted because of his no-show in court. He told the judge that he also knew who had taken him and where he had been held but refused to name his abductor, claiming: 'If I give his name, my life is not worth living.' He also said he didn't know the name of the road where he had been held and that if he did, he would take gardaí there.

Foley said his kidnappers knew he was a key witness in the Delaney trial. He said he didn't know for sure if they were IRA members, but he was adamant that he would not reveal their identities in court. Mr Justice Gannon said, 'You're asking me not to do anything about it because they were the IRA?' The judge also remarked that there had been a rumour that Foley had been paid in exchange for not turning up in court to give evidence on behalf of Hugh Delaney. The Viper maintained that he did not get a penny and was certain that his kidnappers would have used the gun if he didn't agree to get into the car with them. Foley also said that he had been arrested the previous Sunday evening and had spent over twelve hours in a garda cell without so much as a cup of tea. The judge said that this was very wrong. Detective Sergeant Gallagher said he knew the people Foley was talking about and was satisfied that they were 'serious' people. He also admitted that it was possible that events had happened the way Foley had claimed. The garda said that another witness in the Delaney trial who had turned up in court had his garage burned down and £600 stolen from him. Detective Sergeant Gallagher said that if Foley's story was true then the same people had probably been responsible for the two incidents. It later emerged that

The General had organised for the witness's garage to be burned down to add credibility to Foley's story. Mr Justice Gannon said the explanation provided by Foley represented a very serious situation and that 'something should be done about it. I cannot direct what should be done; it is not my function.' He released Foley and dismissed the charge of failing to appear as a witness. Foley made his way back to Crumlin with a smile on his face wider than the River Liffey. He and The General had fought the law and won the battle; but the war would be a long one.

Foley continued to be a key member of The General's gang but he branched out and forged links with the fledgling terrorist group, the Irish National Liberation Army (INLA). The INLA was formed in 1974 in response to the Troubles in Northern Ireland, which had begun in 1968. The organisation recruited heavily in the working class areas of Tallaght and Crumlin and several of Foley's close friends became members. Many senior INLA men lived in the Republic most of the time, as far as possible away from the Royal Ulster Constabulary (RUC). They mostly operated under the radar, plotting armed robberies to fund the purchase of arms to be used in attacks against British targets in the North.

Foley liked to be seen by his fellow criminals as being close to the INLA. Many even suspected that he was secretly a member and he never contradicted them, enjoying the mystery and notoriety it gave him. In reality Foley was never a member but he was close to some of the leadership, most notably Dominic 'Mad Dog' McGlinchey, who was the INLA chief of staff and happened to be a neighbour of

Foley's on Cashel Avenue, where Foley had moved into a Dublin Corporation house, not far from where he had been brought up. McGlinchey, originally from County Derry, was as nasty a piece of work as the Troubles had ever seen and he took pleasure in carrying out murderous acts. He was interned in 1971, when he was just seventeen years old, and he went on to mastermind the INLA's campaign of terror. He had a series of run-ins with both the gardaí and the RUC, who wanted him extradited to face a string of terrorist-related charges.

Foley loved to be seen around Crumlin in the company of McGlinchey because it reinforced his reputation as a hard man who wasn't to be messed with. Foley also associated with Thomas 'Fingers' McCartan, another senior INLA man, who hailed from Belfast and who also lived on Cashel Avenue, which was becoming a haven for on-the-run INLA volunteers. Martin Cahill was mightily impressed with Foley's new friends and the two mobs briefly worked together, planning and carrying out armed robberies. Cahill was happy because his pockets were being lined and the INLA also desperately needed funds to fight what they saw as the British occupation. Foley was the go-between for Cahill and the INLA and he relished his newfound status.

As well as being skilled armed robbers, the INLA had expertise in bomb making, something The General took full advantage of in an incident that shocked the nation. Martin Cahill didn't know it at the time but it would be the biggest mistake he ever made and would put him and his gang at war with the gardaí. In October 1981 Martin Cahill was facing trial for armed robbery and possession of a firearm, at Dublin Circuit Criminal Court. Cahill and fellow gang member Christy Dutton had been caught red-handed following a job at the office of Quintin Flynn Ltd, in an industrial estate in Clondalkin, West Dublin the previous January. They had nabbed nearly £6,000 in cash while threatening staff with a gun. The problem for the two thieves was that over £1,000 of the haul was made up of coins and they struggled to carry it to the getaway motorbike. Their slow getaway gave gardaí time to scramble to the area and the theives were arrested following a high-speed chase. It was a blow to The General and it looked inevitable that he would serve a stretch.

The State forensic scientist, Dr James Donovan, was the country's preeminent forensic expert at the time Cahill and Dutton were arrested for the robbery. Dr Donovan was a highly regarded scientist and had given evidence that had been crucial in securing the prosecution of several members of Martin Cahill's immediate family. He was also vital to Cahill's trial because he was responsible for examining fifty-eight pieces of evidence that linked the two men to the robbery, the stolen money and the motorbike that had been recovered. Essentially the gardaí's case relied on Dr Donovan's expertise.

On the day Cahill was sent forward for trial, he broke into the Chancery Street office of the clerk of the court, found the file on which his prosecution hinged and set it alight. He believed that with no file the State would have no case. But the State simply compiled another book of evidence, and The General responded by ordering the Four Courts to be burned to the ground. Two of his cronies set a large fire, which, although it didn't totally destroy the courts complex, left it closed for over a month.

With his mischievous plans failing, Cahill turned his attention to Dr Donovan. Cahill reckoned that Dr Donovan was an easy target because he did not receive regular garda protection, except when he was giving evidence in cases involving paramilitaries. The criminal decided he would have the forensic scientist murdered in a car-bomb attack so that there would be no option but for the charges against him to be dismissed. He turned to his INLA friends, whom he had got to know very well through Martin Foley. Thomas McCartan was an INLA explosives expert and, being a neighbour of Foley's, he was happy to oblige by preparing a devastating explosive device.

In early December 1981 Cahill and an accomplice placed a petrol bomb underneath Dr Donovan's car, the plan being that the heat from the car's engine would detonate the device, causing the car to be engulfed in flames, hopefully killing the scientist. Luckily the bomb exploded while Dr Donovan was driving at just 20 m.p.h. and did not detonate properly. He was able to park the car on a grass verge and escape. Nobody even realised that there had been a bomb and the accident was put down to a leaking petrol tank.

Cahill was not easily deterred, though, and on 6 January 1982 he struck again. Cahill planted Fingers McCartan's homemade bomb, which had been placed in a shaving foam container, underneath the doctor's car, where the exhaust pipe enters the engine. Dr Donovan had only travelled a mile and a half before the engine heated to the temperature required to detonate the bomb. The blast lifted the car off the road as dozens of motorists in rush hour traffic at Newland's Cross looked on in horror. Dr Donovan somehow survived the impact when the car landed in a crumpled heap, and he was rushed to hospital. He spent several hours in surgery as doctors battled to save his left foot and leg, but Dr Donovan ultimately lost half of his left foot as a result of the attack.

The finger of blame for the bomb was immediately pointed in the direction of the IRA or the INLA but both groups denied responsibility. Gardaí gradually learned of Cahill's involvement and detectives based in Crumlin Garda Station, led by Detective Superintendent Ned 'The Buffalo' Ryan, argued with Garda Headquarters that more attention needed to be paid to the growth of serious crime gangs led by the likes of Cahill and Foley.

Garda top brass divided crime into two categories – Crime Special and Crime Ordinary. Crime Special was the term used for acts involving the IRA and other paramilitary organisations, while Crime Ordinary was all other non-subversive crime. This later led to criminals with no subversive link being called ODCs, or Ordinary Decent Criminals. The attack on Dr Donovan was an attack at the very heart of the State and forced an immediate rethink of policing priorities. Sixty detectives were assigned to the investigation into the bomb attack and, as a result, Cahill was arrested on 9 February. He refused to allow his fingerprints or photograph to be taken and had to be forcibly compelled to do so by frustrated detectives. During his twelve hours in custody he refused to answer a single question and he was released without charge.

Martin Cahill didn't know if the case against Dutton and him would go ahead or not, but he didn't want to take any chances. He needed a nest egg for his family in case he was sent away to serve a stretch. In late 1982 he was approached by John 'The Coach' Traynor, who had an idea for the robbery of all robberies. Traynor was from a middle-class background but he loved the life of the criminal and surrounded himself with hoods like Cahill and Foley. He was an expert planner of crimes and a fencer of stolen goods who was trusted in the criminal underworld. Traynor suggested targeting O'Connor's jewellery factory in Harold's Cross, not far from where Cahill and Martin Foley were based. He said he had an inside man in the factory who told him that over £2 million worth of gold, gems and jewels were stored in a reinforced room there. Cahill discussed the plot with his closest associates, including Foley, and they decided that it should go ahead. A huge amount of planning would have to be done in order for the heist to succeed. Besides the potential for a massive payday, Cahill and Foley liked the idea of being involved in what could potentially be the biggest ever robbery in Irish history. They were also attracted by the notoriety it would bring them.

The Thomas O'Connor and Sons jewellery manufacturing plant had long been a target for criminals. The IRA had carried out a risk assessment for a possible heist at the factory but they concluded that the security system was too elaborate. Henry Dunne, brother of heroin kingpin, Larry, had also planned to rob the place with a gang dressed as gardaí, but he was arrested before he got the chance.

Gardaí got wind that somebody was planning a major job on O'Connor's and armed detectives from the Serious Crime Squad locked themselves into the building each night for a six-month period between the middle of 1982 and the start of 1983, waiting for the would-be thieves to arrive. However, when nothing happened officers assumed that the plan had been called off because it was just too difficult to execute.

Meanwhile Traynor had been working on the problem of the almost impenetrable security system, and he had found a solution. Traynor's inside man gave him and the gang enough concrete intelligence to enable them to breach the system. The mole had been stealing small quantities of jewels and selling them to Traynor, so The General and Foley knew that he could be trusted. All he wanted in return was a share of the spoils from the job.

Cahill was determined that the raid would go like clockwork. It had been planned with military precision for over six months. Cahill was given photographs and plans of the security system during secret meetings with Traynor and the inside man. Most of the gang were kept in the dark until the month before the robbery was due to be carried out, for fear that there would be loose talk. The raid was timed to take place between close of business on 26 July 1983 and early the following morning. Six cars and motorbikes were stolen and fitted with false number plates in the week before the robbery. Ten close and trusted members of the gang would be directly involved, including Cahill himself, Martin Foley, Seamus 'Shavo' Hogan, Jo Jo Kavanagh and Traynor. Thomas 'Fingers' McCartan, the INLA bomb maker, was supposed to take part but he was a last-minute no-show, much to Cahill's annoyance and Foley's embarrassment. Although there were one hundred staff employed at the factory, because of summer holidays and shift work, only twenty-five would be on duty when the raid took place, and this number was manageable to a gang of ten seasoned armed robbers.

At 9 p.m. on 26 July the ten likely lads met at the

Dropping Well pub in Milltown and had a few pints, trying to blend in with the regulars. They were dressed in ordinary clothes, and a couple of them, including Foley, carried sports bags, so that it looked like they were members of a football team. The sports bags contained guns, hand grenades, smoke bombs, balaclavas and everything else you might need to carry out the heist of the century.

Shortly before closing time they piled into a waiting blue Hiace van that had been stolen to order for the job. When they arrived in Harold's Cross, three of the gang, including Shavo Hogan, jumped over the twelve-foot-high wall into the courtyard of the factory and broke into the plant's boiler room, which was not hooked up to the security system. The rest of the gang, including Cahill and Martin Foley, went home for some sleep and made plans to meet up again early the following morning. Shortly before 8 a.m. the company's production manager, Bobby Kinlan, arrived to open up. When he opened the front gates the alarm link to the Garda Metropolitan Headquarters, in Dublin Castle, was automatically deactivated. He noticed nothing unusual and turned off the building's alarm as usual and waited for staff to arrive for the 8 a.m. shift. The general manager, Daniel Fitzgibbon, arrived shortly afterwards. He went into the main office and opened the strong room, where the jewels were kept. Then the gang struck. The Hiace van and another stolen car were driven into the complex, while Cahill stayed on a motorbike at the front entrance, directing the raid through a walkie-talkie, communicating with Foley who was in the van. The three men in the boiler room burst out and held up the staff as they queued to get in the front door to begin work. The gang, using staff members as hostages, burst into the building and made straight for

Kinlan and Fitzgibbon. They forced Fitzgibbon to open the safe and show them where the diamonds were. Fitzgibbon and Kinlan were then brought into the toilets and told to stay there while the robbery went down.

The raid went off without a hitch. Foley, Shavo Hogan and the rest of the gang were pros by this stage. They reassured the terrified staff that they would be fine if they cooperated and didn't cause any trouble. The employees were corralled into a small room and many of them later remarked that the gang seemed to know their way around the factory. Within thirty minutes the entire strong room was stripped bare. The haul included diamonds, other gems, gold bars and thousands of rings. The gang got away with over half a tonne in all, with a value of £2 million. It was a remarkable robbery and it cemented the mob's position as the most important gang in the criminal underworld.

Foley and Cahill supervised the breakdown of the huge haul at a lock-up garage owned by a pal, while they listened in to the garda radio frequency. The divvying up of the valuables took over twelve hours and when it was finished each of the fourteen men who had been involved in the planning or execution of the robbery was given a pile of booty weighing three stone.

Eventually the diamonds were fenced through a London-based man by the name of Les Beavis. Foley and the rest of his cronies received £40,000 each for their loot. It was a massive payday for everyone and the job made them all quite wealthy. This made the gardaí more determined than ever that the criminals should be brought back down to earth with a bang. Most members of the gang who had taken part in the robbery were arrested and questioned, including Cahill and Foley. The gardaí knew they had been involved but proving it was a different matter.

The robbery had a devastating effect on O'Connor's because the factory was under-insured. The company was eventually forced to close, with the loss of one hundred jobs. Cahill liked to portray himself as a Robin Hood type of criminal, but by carrying out the O'Connor's heist, he and his gang consigned dozens of families to the misery of unemployment.

Cahill still had the small problem of the trial for the armed robbery. His plan to kill Dr James Donovan had failed and the dedicated doctor wasn't about to allow the bomb plot deter him from continuing his life's work of putting wrongdoers behind bars. He slowly recovered from his injuries and was determined to face down Cahill in court. Because of the scientist's serious injuries, The General did not stand trial until May 1984. It was the first case at which Dr Donovan would give evidence since the bomb attack.

In court Dr Donovan hobbled past Cahill to the witness box and proceeded to give his evidence, a stand that had nearly cost him his life. Describing having to sit face-to-face in court with the man who had tried to murder him, he later said, 'I was about two feet away from him and I found that quite unnerving. He was a distinctly obnoxious individual. He is one of the few people that I cannot think of any redeeming feature.'

Unfortunately Dr Donovan gave his evidence in vain. The woman who was robbed during the Clondalkin raid refused to give evidence because she feared she would be killed. The judge ordered that Cahill and Dutton be acquitted, much to their jubilation and to the frustration of the gardaí.

Cahill may have left the court happy, but by that time he was under huge strain. By plotting to murder Dr Donovan, he had taken on the State, and garda management had finally decided that Cahill, Martin Foley and the other senior gang members should have the full might of the force brought to bear on them.

On Collision Course

AFTER THE O'CONNOR'S JEWELLERY heist and the murder attempt on Dr James Donovan, Cahill and Foley were under pressure on several fronts.

Because The General and his gang had been carrying out armed robberies with what seemed like virtual impunity, Detective Superintendent Ned Ryan was tasked with drawing up a plan to put manners on them. The targeting of Dr Donovan in particular had led to serious pressure on garda management to regain control. Ryan, a tough and uncompromising police officer who was popular with his colleagues, believed that the best way to take on a criminal was to fight him at his own game. Ryan became linked with a unit that allegedly existed within the gardaí known as the Heavy Gang. The Heavy Gang was a group of officers who were said to have used violence and other controversial tactics to secure convictions against criminals.

Ned Ryan despised Martin Cahill, and the feeling was mutual. Ryan had served in the Rathmines district since 1973 and he knew Cahill as well as any garda. He was in charge of the Central Detective Unit, known as the Flying

Squad, and The General's gang was his main target. Ryan vowed that he would have the two Martins, Cahill and Foley, before the courts on charges that would see them sent to prison for a long time. He suggested to his bosses that the best way to effectively destroy the gang was to keep them under round-the-clock surveillance. Garda management eventually signed off on a budget for special surveillance on the mob's main players. The three principal targets were Martin Cahill, Martin Foley and Seamus Hogan, who had become a very close friend of The Viper. As well as arresting almost the entire gang after the O'Connor's robbery, the gardaí routinely stopped the criminals as they went about their business, following them and watching them so it got to the point where no actual business – i.e. robberies and burglaries – could be done.

The pressure of the surveillance started to get to the gang. Foley wisely thought that it was better to just sit back and wait until the gardaí got tired of following them. Then everything could go back to normal. Cahill, however, became increasingly frustrated and he feared that the cops were going to stitch them up by planting firearms on them to get them prosecuted and taken off the streets.

Cahill devised a scheme that he felt would discredit the gardaí before anything could happen to him or his men, and he roped in The Viper to help him. On 9 October 1983 Martin Foley phoned the newsroom of the *Irish Press* and said he had disturbing information that gardaí were trying to frame Martin Cahill and that they were determined to bring him down by illegal means. He said he had proof of the plot and would meet one of the newspaper's reporters to discuss the matter that night. The reporter arrived at the designated meeting place, the car park of a pub in

Tallaght, and met Foley, who was heavily disguised. The Viper described himself as a petty criminal who had no links whatsoever to the Republican movement and said he was was trying to go straight. He said he did not like what the gardaí were doing to Martin Cahill and brought the reporter to a nearby field, where he handed him two guns – a pistol and a sawn-off shotgun. Foley claimed that he had been forced by two unnamed detectives to plant the weapons on The General and that gardaí planned to arrest Cahill and use the evidence to convict him. Foley said he wanted the story publicised in the newspaper but he was not prepared to disclose his real identity. He felt that an exposé might end the garda harassment of Cahill and his family. It was a bizarre meeting, and if Foley or Cahill ever thought that a respected newspaper would print outrageous allegations against gardaí on the say so of a hooded man with firearms, they were sorely mistaken. However, Cahill and Foley naively believed that if they were ever actually caught with guns in their possession, the newspaper might remember the incident in the pub car park and come to the conclusion that they had been set up.

It was later determined that the two guns held by Foley were stolen from the garda depot on St John's Road in South Dublin. The depot was used to store firearms seized from criminals and subversives and the Cahill gang had broken into it on several occasions and made off with some of the guns. Gardaí were not initially aware that there had been a break-in at the building, such was the skill of The General.

Ned Ryan and his colleagues realised that the gang was under pressure and he put in a request to Garda Headquarters that the surveillance be made permanent. But the budget didn't allow for this and the unit was gradually disbanded. At least the detectives now knew how to make the criminals uncomfortable, and they hoped that if they could mount similar operations in the future, the pressure would cause the gang to make mistakes.

It wasn't just the gardaí paying the gang unwanted attention, though. Word soon got around that Cahill's mob had been responsible for the O'Connor's robbery, and both the IRA and the INLA wanted to get their hands on some of the proceeds to help fund their operations. The two terrorist groups held a meeting to share their intelligence on Cahill. Thomas 'Fingers' McCartan, who was scheduled to take part in the robbery but failed to show up, had still demanded that he be paid his share. But after Cahill told him to get lost, McCartan had no problem telling his INLA comrades and the IRA all he knew about Cahill, Foley, and all the other gang members. The IRA wrongly suspected that Cahill was involved in the distribution of heroin, which was tearing apart estates in large swathes of working-class Dublin. Several members of Cahill's own family were junkies but he never touched drugs, preferring to make his money the traditional way, by planning and executing elaborate robberies. Cahill regarded himself and his gang members as Ordinary Decent Criminals and stayed away from drugs despite the huge profits on offer.

After the intelligence-sharing meeting the IRA made contact with Cahill and told him they wanted to meet him and that it would be wise to show up. Cahill wasn't afraid of the Provos and he happily went along to meet them at a café in Crumlin village. He knew what they wanted and he mocked the two senior members present, joking that their lot wouldn't have the wherewithal to carry out such an audacious operation. The two volunteers congratulated Cahill on the success of the job but then got straight to the point and informed him that the movement expected half of the profits. Cahill had expected that the IRA would be irritated and jealous that he had managed to get away with such an impressive haul, but he couldn't believe the cheek of this demand. He angrily told them that if they wanted money they would have to pull off their own strokes because they wouldn't be getting a penny from him or his men. The IRA warned him that there would be consequences for his decision, but Cahill told them where to go and walked out of the meeting. He had no respect for the IRA and regarded them as second-rate compared to his band of merry men who were running the gardaí ragged and getting rich in the process, without having to shoot or bomb innocent people. But his somewhat belligerent attitude at this meeting foreshadowed a serious falling-out with the IRA that would have major repercussions for both Cahill and Foley.

In 1983 Ireland was in shock over the extent of the heroin problem that had come out of nowhere and hit Dublin hard. The main people responsible were Larry and Shamie Dunne, two friends and associates of Foley and Cahill, who were the first to import heroin into Ireland in the early 1980s. They sourced the drugs from underworld contacts in London and Manchester and had approached Cahill and asked him to be their partner. They raved about the amount of money they were making but Cahill turned them down. The Dunne family were all living in mansions and driving top-of-the-range cars within two years of getting into drugs. They relied on a network of young criminals, mainly drug addicts, to handle and distribute the heroin, while the Dunnes sat back and counted the profits. Drug dealers would literally walk into schoolyards and give teenagers free heroin for weeks until they became helplessly addicted and were forced to start paying for their fix. Within months of its arrival in Ireland, kids as young as twelve were walking around with the zombie-like look in their eyes that indicated heroin had taken hold of them. Dublin's north and south inner city were especially badly hit, with places like Dolphin's Barn becoming virtual no-go areas because of junkies who were robbing old women to feed their habit. Handbags were regularly snatched from cars stopped at traffic lights and used needles were found in kids' playgrounds with alarming regularity.

Crumlin was badly affected by heroin and Martin Foley and his friends watched neighbours become addicts in double-quick time. It took everyone by surprise, especially the government, which didn't know what to do to tackle the problem. Because the country was flat broke, there was no budget to try to arrest the spiralling crisis. Parents, politicians and gardaí were almost paralysed as the curse of heroin spread like wildfire.

Unbeknownst to Cahill some of his men who had taken part in the O'Connor's robbery had not fenced their jewels through Les Beavis, but had instead gone to the Dunnes and invested in shipments of drugs that they reckoned would make them far more than £40,000. Martin Foley wasn't one of them, though, and as a fitness freak he never touched drugs. He had many long conversations with Cahill and Shavo Hogan about the way their area was being destroyed in front of their very eyes. Foley was disgusted but he felt there was little he could do about it, so he concentrated on his day job as a robber. Gradually ordinary decent people started to plan the fight back against the blight of drugs that had reduced their kids to crumbling, skinny wretches who lived for their next fix. Many of these youngsters, who had little education and had never worked, would eventually die of overdoses.

Even though Cahill and Foley had no involvement in drugs, the Ordinary Decent Criminals, who relied on the support of the local community to thrive, were also blamed for the drugs scourge, which angered and frustrated them. In 1981 a group of worried parents from St Theresa's Gardens in Dublin 8 formed the Committee Against Drug Abuse. They met with the minister for health and demanded basic things like more treatment for addicts under eighteen, emergency detox beds and more specialist in-patient treatment units for addicts. They had limited success but their organisation acted as a template for others, and in 1983 parents' groups sprang up in many working-class areas, with the aim of turning the tide against drugs.

On 16 February 1984 the Concerned Parents Against Drugs (CPAD) organisation was formed at a meeting in the hall of the Christian Brothers' school in Crumlin. The group decided that the only way to win the war on drugs was to tackle the dealers head on.

The first thing the new movement did was to police the schoolyard of Scoil Iosagain primary school in Crumlin after rumours spread that heroin was being given out free to kids there. The local women patrolled the yard as the children went to and from school, while the men put together plans for the first big march, which was scheduled to take place three days after the group was formed.

They planned to march in large numbers on the homes of known drug dealers and warn them off pushing drugs on local youngsters. If the dealers refused and continued to sell heroin they would be evicted without notice, and by force if necessary. Dealers were hard men when faced with helpless junkies, but with hundreds of determined adults knocking on their doors they would have little choice but to flee.

The CPAD reasoned, probably naively, that if they got rid of the dealers there would be no drugs and no more youngsters would get addicted. It was the ultimate display of people power, with men patrolling the entrances to the flats complexes that had been taken over by addicts and pushers, setting up barricades and warning dealers and addicts to stay away.

One of the main figures behind the CPAD was John 'Whacker' Humphrey, a thirty-three-year-old married man who had moved to Crumlin only a few months previously and was appalled by what he saw on the streets. Whacker Humphrey was a colourful character who had convictions for armed robbery, assault and malicious damage, although these offences had taken place years before. Humphrey worked in his family's flower business and operated a successful stall at the gates to Mount Jerome Cemetery in Harold's Cross.

On Sunday 19 February hundreds of angry Crumlin residents marched on a freezing cold day to Clogher Road and Rutland Avenue. Among the crowd were small boys from Scoil Iosagain and the Parnell Road National School, as well as older boys from the secondary school on Clogher Road. They were accompanied by their parents and the message was clear: our kids are not going to be preyed

upon by drug dealers. The Crumlin residents were joined
by parents from St Theresa's Gardens and Dolphin's Barn,
just across the nearby Grand Canal. Men acted as stewards
for the march and carried walkie-talkies to communicate
with each other. A boy who was armed with a broom
pole had it removed by a steward and the stewards totally
rejected suggestions that they were vigilantes, preferring
the term community watchdogs. One told the *Irish Times*,
'We're definitely not vigilantes. We don't use violence and
we don't keep a blacklist and we are very careful about
accusations made against individuals.' The paper was told
that the previous Friday a pusher had been seen operating
on Parnell Road and gardaí were called to arrest him. The
day before the march the group said they found a youngster
in the act of pushing and that they handed him over to the
gardaí. 'We work with the guards and we work with the
approval of the teachers. It's the nine- and ten-year-olds
that are at risk in the schools now, and we're doing this out
of concern for them.'

The organisers said their group was having instant
positive results. None of the stewards would give their
names but one organiser maintained: 'The guards say they
haven't had a single call since our meeting last Thursday,
and the teachers say four years ago they had a massive bill
for vandalism. Since our Neighbourhood Watch campaign,
crime is way down, the pushers have moved on, break-ins
are fewer and the area is now quiet.' The Irish National
Teachers Organisation (INTO) praised the group, with
delegate Finian McGrath, who would later be elected as
an independent TD, saying he had nothing but admiration
for them. The movement caught the imagination of
communities around Dublin, and soon twenty-six areas

north and south of the Liffey were being 'policed' by
Concerned Parents Against Drugs.

Not everyone was in favour of CPAD, though. County
Councillor Myles Tierney said that the organisers were
vigilantes and were usually Sinn Féin members. 'If there is a
particular policing problem in the area, the proper response
is not the self-appointed vigilante group, but recourse to
the forces of the law,' he said. The CPAD maintained that
they were careful not to target the wrong people, but The
General disagreed. At the beginning of the first big march,
the protesters made their way to the homes of several
suspected drug dealers and chanted, jeered and shouted
abuse, ordering them to leave the area at once. The dealers
didn't have a clue what was going on. Most of them didn't
read newspapers so they had no idea that a new parents'
group had been set up three days previously to focus on
their illicit activities. Most of the bemused dealers opened
the door when a CPAD member knocked, but shut it as
soon as they saw the crowd outside, and rushed back to
relative safety.

The group also called to the home of Martin Foley's good
pal, Seamus 'Shavo' Hogan. Hogan was one of the Ordinary
Decent Criminals in that he preferred robbing banks with
a gun than selling smack to kids. Hogan was furious that
he was singled out and he had a blazing row with Whacker
Humphrey on the doorstep of his house on Balfe Road
East, in Crumlin. Things looked like they were going to get
heated but the CPAD withdrew before any violence broke
out. They weren't finished, though, and they made for the
home of The Viper's best friend, Thomas Gaffney. Thirty-
four-year-old Gaffney was a petty criminal who had served
time with Humphrey in Mountjoy, and the pair had never

got on. Gaffney was a member of The General's gang, and like Hogan, he was not a drug dealer, although some of his relatives were suspected of dealing. He had been arrested over the O'Connor's jewellery robbery but had not actually been involved, although he did hide some of the proceeds of the crime in Mount Jerome cemetery, where he worked as a gravedigger. Gaffney was well able to handle himself and he stormed out to confront the marchers. He admitted that three members of his family were addicts and that Ma Baker, the notorious heroin dealer, was a family friend, but that was the extent of his involvement in drugs. He warned Humphrey and the other Concerned Parents not to harass his family or there would be serious consequences. There was a tense stand-off, with abuse and threats exchanged between the two men, but they both backed down and the crowd departed to target others.

After the confrontation between Thomas Gaffney and Whacker Humphrey the march broke up and people went their separate ways, although the men continued to patrol the flats complexes to keep them free from drugs. Gaffney and Shavo Hogan were shocked by the events of the day and decided to meet in Crumlin village later that night for a few pints and to discuss what they were going to do. They couldn't sit back and be accused of dealing drugs when they were doing nothing of the sort. They weren't prepared to turn the other cheek and let the matter rest.

They were joined by Martin Foley and his new girlfriend, local girl Pauline Quinn. Foley fell for Pauline soon after he met her and they quickly became an item, although he still had an eye for the ladies. The couple tried to calm down Hogan and Gaffney, but when closing time came, Shavo was concerned that in order to get home he would have to pass through one of the Concerned Parents' cordons, which were by now extending to the main roads. Foley said that he, Pauline and Thomas Gaffney would travel with him in case he was stopped and questioned. The four headed off in two cars, but Foley had a feeling that this wouldn't be enough and decided they should stop at Sundrive Road Garda Station and ask for an escort. The cheeky criminal was sent on his way and told to fend for himself.

When the two-car convoy reached Rutland Avenue they encountered a checkpoint. One of the CPAD members ordered Foley to open his boot so that it could be inspected. Foley was furious and after he told the CPAD member to fuck off, an argument broke out. Punches were thrown by both sides and a passing patrol car spotted the melee and called for back-up to help break up the fight. Foley's group was taken off to Sundrive Road in a car for their own safety until the tension was defused. The Concerned Parents were ordered home but it was clear that confrontation between the group and the local criminal fraternity was going to be the norm. Foley rang The General to arrange a meeting the next morning. Something would urgently have to be done.

The following morning a group of Cahill's men, including Martin Foley, met at Shavo Hogan's house on Balfe Road East. The march on Hogan and Gaffney's homes by Humphrey and the CPAD led Cahill to believe that the IRA was directing the group from behind the scenes and it was targeting those who had information about the O'Connor's robbery, with the ultimate aim of extorting money from the gang.

In typical eccentric fashion The General proposed a whacky plan for his group of Ordinary Decent Criminals to get their own back on the anti-drugs organisation. He

This iconic photo of Martin Foley was taken during one of his many periods in custody. He was given the nickname 'The Viper' because the two tips of his moustache resembled snake fangs.

© *Sunday World*

Martin 'The General' Cahill was Martin Foley's friend and mentor until they had a very bitter falling out. The General specialised in robbing banks and factories and he planned his raids with meticulous care, like an army general.

© *Sunday World*

The General caught on CCTV, about to rob a bank.

© *Sunday World*

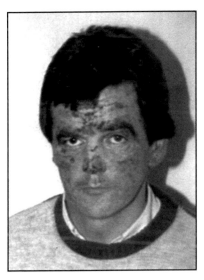

Seamus 'Shavo' Hogan infamously rubbed his face with his own excrement when he was arrested for questioning over a murder.

Paddy Shanahan approached Martin Foley with the idea to steal the Beit paintings from Russborough House. However, he was frozen out of the heist and was shot dead in 1994.

Paul 'Hippo' Ward was a key member of the Gilligan gang and was present when The Viper survived the 2006 assassination attempt.

© *Sunday World*

Eamon Daly started out as a member of The General's gang and eventually took over from John Gilligan as one of Ireland's biggest drug suppliers.

© *Sunday World*

'Factory' John Gilligan was the undisputed king of Irish drug dealing until he planned the murder of Veronica Guerin. His empire crumbled after a massive garda investigation into the assassination of the journalist.

© *Sunday World*

Gilligan (left) enjoying a sun holiday with his right hand men, Brian 'The Tosser' Meehan (back) and Peter 'Fatso' Mitchell (right).

© *Sunday World*

Brian 'The Tosser' Meehan was responsible for the botched murder attempt on Martin Foley in February 2006.

© *Sunday World*

Detective Superintendent Christy Managan (second from right) with his colleagues from the Garda Cold Case Unit. He was a thorn in Foley's side during his time in the Garda National Drugs Unit.

© *Sunday World*

Detective Inspector Gerry O'Carroll spent much of his career investigating Martin Foley and his criminal friends.

Detective Chief Superintendent Felix McKenna led one of the Tango Squad units that followed The Viper twenty-four hours a day. He later became head of the Criminal Assets Bureau.

Detective Superintendent Denis Donegan was in charge of policing in Crumlin and knew Martin Foley as well as any garda.
© *Evening Herald*

Detective Garda Gerry O'Connell was viciously assaulted by Martin Foley. The attack had a huge impact on the brave garda's life.
© *Sunday World*

proposed that they set up their own group to counter-balance the CPAD. After some debate it was decided that they should call themselves the Concerned Criminal Action Committee (CCAC) and march to the homes of the Concerned Parents activists. He called a march for three o'clock that afternoon and ordered his gang and a load of other young criminals who looked up to him to turn out in force and show their rivals that they were not to be messed with. By the appointed time a healthy crowd of sixty Concerned Criminals had gathered in Crumlin. They were a sight to behold, a motley crew of gougers, thieves and general troublemakers. The mob was led by Martin Foley and Shavo Hogan and had no pretence of any political aim except to stop CPAD annoying them and let them go back to robbing like before.

The crowd of intimidating thugs, egged on by Foley, who was loving being the leader of the pack, called to the doors of several Concerned Parents and shouted abuse at them, demanding that they stop harassing innocent criminals. The sight of sixty criminals would be enough to unnerve most people and the Concerned Parents were no different. They meekly denied any knowledge of anti-drugs activity and like the dealers who had been targeted the day before, they disappeared into the safety of their homes. John 'Whacker' Humphrey also received a special visit, and rocks and other missiles were thrown at his home, breaking several windows.

The Concerned Criminals retired to a local pub but later the same night some of them returned to Humphrey's home, forced their way in and destroyed it. Noel Sillery, who was a senior figure in CPAD and a member of Sinn Féin, got the same treatment.

War had been declared between the two groups and things quickly escalated further. Shortly after midnight CPAD activists Joe Flynn and Paddy Smyth were on patrol in the St Theresa's Gardens complex when they were confronted by two armed and masked men who came out of the shadows. The Concerned Parents turned on their heels but the criminals fired off five or six rounds, hitting twenty-nine-year-old Flynn in the legs. He collapsed to the ground and was rushed to hospital by ambulance. Luckily, his injuries were not serious. Gardaí knew that this was a major development because they had intelligence that there were in fact IRA members within CPAD and that there was no way they would tolerate such a reckless attack. Word soon spread that the two men responsible for the shooting of Joe Flynn were Martin Foley and Shavo Hogan.

The founding members of CPAD no doubt had good intentions and the movement was born out of frustration with a situation they felt they needed to gain control over. However, members of Sinn Féin and the IRA soon infiltrated the group and they were more than happy to resort to violence. Most of Sinn Féin's support has traditionally been from areas that are overwhelmingly working class, such as Dublin's north and south inner city, Crumlin, Drimnagh and Tallaght, so it was no surprise that party activists got involved. They were good workers on the ground and were happy to fight issues that other politicians didn't have the courage to face. But Sinn Féin was inextricably linked with the IRA, and when the Provos became involved, the Garda Special Branch was bound to follow, and CPAD came up against the gardaí almost from the day it was founded. The gardaí were right to be suspicious of the group, because later events would reveal that IRA men who were on the fringes of CPAD had in fact been using the marches to collect intelligence on The General and his men.

The Flynn shooting caused sensationalist headlines in the newspapers, which excitedly wrote about a war between drug dealers and vigilantes. The shooting did not put off the Concerned Parents as The General's gang had hoped, but rather made them more determined. On 21 February 1984 over 1,000 people gathered for a very tense and angry meeting in Lower Crumlin, where Whacker Humphrey addressed the crowd. He admitted that some people had been wrongly identified as drug dealers and he apologised for the errors, but he said that the shooting of Joe Flynn would not deter them from the fight against the dealers. Twenty-five people were openly accused of being drug dealers at the meeting. Many of these people were present and they stood up and defended themselves, denying that they were involved in the sale of narcotics. The crowd was furious over the media portrayals of the events of the previous few days. One speaker said that it took two sides to make a war, that the drug dealers were the only side with guns and that the Concerned Parents had used peaceful means to try to achieve their goals. At the end of the meeting the following statement was issued to the media:

> The people of St Theresa's Gardens would like to express their deepest shock and concern at the shooting and wounding of Mr Joseph Flynn early this morning. While we have no clear indication of the motive behind this shooting we have to assume that it was related to the recent Concerned Parents Against Drugs campaign. While Mr Flynn was not a leading figure in the drugs campaign, he was one of the many parents who gave

his active support to the campaign against drug pushers, a campaign that has had, and still has, 100 per cent support from the people of St Theresa's Gardens. The circumstances surrounding the shooting of Mr Flynn has led us to assume that he was selected at random by the perpetrators of this most foul deed. We should like to stress the point that when politicians and media personnel make statements and newspaper headlines link Concerned Parents with vigilantes, they are providing drug pushers and their terror gangs with a license to come into innocent communities and shoot at random. They must take their fair share of the blame for this shooting. The people of St. Theresa's Gardens remain united in their campaign against drug pushing. The shooting has not frightened us or lessened our determination. We sincerely hope that it will not frighten our community, who must now unite together against drug pushers.

The day after the large community meeting, members of Concerned Criminals congregated at Shavo Hogan's house. Foley and Hogan were unofficial spokesmen for the group and agreed to talk to a journalist with the *Irish Press* who had requested an interview. You could cut the tension in the locality with a knife and Foley moaned to the hack that the CPAD had started contacting the gardaí and telling them where individual criminals were going at night. He stressed that no members of his organisation were involved in drug dealing and that they were being wrongly and unfairly singled out by the mob. He admitted that the shooting of Joseph Flynn had been down to what he called rising tension and he said, 'We admit we are criminals, but we are not pushers and we can hardly move in the area at night without being reported to the cops by the Concerned Parents Against Drugs group. We have already protested to the CPAD and we are planning further action, including protest marches around the estate.' Foley was enjoying his high-profile job as a spokesman and he even agreed to go on the RTÉ current affairs show, *Today Tonight*, although he insisted on wearing a disguise. He maintained that the Concerned Criminals Action Committee was opposed to drug dealing and he complained again about Ordinary Decent Criminals being unfairly singled out for attention by CPAD. He warned the group that they would not be allowed to get in the way of criminals making livings in areas of crime that were unrelated to drug dealing.

After Foley's TV appearance and the massive media interest, both sides realised that they would have to organise some sort of truce. The unrelenting spotlight was taking its toll on both sides, and the strain of being constantly under the microscope was clearly showing. The criminals felt that they had the upper hand because they had put on a display of force that showed they were not going to be bullied or pushed around. The Concerned Parents were at a disadvantage because they had lost the high moral ground after they admitted that marchers had accused people who were innocent of any involvement in drugs.

A peace summit was organised and Foley was appointed to lead the criminals' delegation. Alongside him were his two best friends, Shavo Hogan and Thomas Gaffney. The leader of the CPAD delegation was convicted IRA member John Noonan. Noonan was a prominent figure in Sinn Féin and lived in nearby Tallaght. During three tense meetings, which were full of recrimination, it was agreed that they would try to keep conflict to a minimum and that the Concerned Parents would be more careful about who they fingered. If there were unfortunate incidents involving the two sides, Foley and Noonan would lead investigations into their own members' actions and try to resolve issues before they got out of control. Foley was very pleased with the resolution and he was praised by his fellow criminals for having done a good job as their lead envoy. His joy, however, would be short lived.

Provos, Kidnaps and Underpants

THOMAS GAFFNEY WAS A creature of habit. Every Sunday afternoon he enjoyed a few pints in the Park Inn pub in Harold's Cross, not far from Crumlin. On 11 March 1984 Gaffney was drinking as normal when he was briefly joined by The General, who had popped in to give Gaffney a message before leaving again. Shortly afterwards Martin Foley also came into the pub and chatted with his best mate for a while. Unbeknownst to the pals, there were four men in the pub who were closely observing them. The men had also been present the previous week and they stuck out among the regular clientele. Two of the four got up and left the pub, and when The Viper left a few minutes later, he spotted them in a red Hiace van parked outside the pub. Foley thought he saw that one of the men had a gun but he did nothing and jumped on his motorbike and rode off.

At around 6 p.m. Gaffney was preparing to go home for his dinner when the remaining two strangers in the pub stood up and approached him, one on each side, and led him out the door. The gravedigger knew he was in trouble and he turned and shouted to the barman to call the gardaí.

One of the men turned and laughed and shouted, 'We are the police,' before bundling Gaffney into the waiting Hiace. The helpless Gaffney was quickly overpowered, handcuffed, gagged and bound with heavy industrial tape and driven off. The four men were members of an IRA active service unit and they kidnapped Gaffney in broad daylight, making little or no attempt to disguise themselves. It was a remarkable display of arrogance.

By the time gardaí arrived the kidnappers were long gone and it later emerged that Gaffney had been transferred to another van to avoid detection and driven to a safe house in County Tipperary. Gardaí knew Gaffney well and they were keenly aware of the tension between the criminals and Concerned Parents Against Drugs. There was also the possibility that he was snatched by rival criminals who thought he had information about the O'Connor's jewellery heist the previous year. Several gangs, as well as the IRA, wanted to get their hands on the loot.

The gardaí launched a major investigation into the kidnapping. But while detectives at Crumlin Garda Station held a case conference to review the leads in the case, Foley, The General, Shavo Hogan and several other members of Cahill's gang also met to discuss the troubling events of the day. It didn't take a genius to work out that the IRA, under the guise of CPAD, was responsible for the abduction. Cahill was adamant that if the IRA wanted to go up against them, they would take them on with everything they had.

Foley and Shavo Hogan were dispatched to meet with John Noonan the following morning, as had been agreed at the peace summit a few weeks previously. They left Noonan in no doubt that Sinn Féin members and IRA volunteers would be targeted if Gaffney wasn't released immediately, unharmed. Noonan said he knew nothing about the kidnapping but that he would make inquiries. He added that if the IRA was responsible, they did not have permission from the organisation's general headquarters.

The Concerned Criminals Action Committee would under no circumstances give in to the intimidatory tactics of the IRA, so they decided to resume their campaign against the Concerned Parents in protest over the kidnapping of Gaffney. On 14 March a strong contingent of CCAC members turned out at a morning protest and, as usual, Foley was one of the most visible and vocal of the band of merry criminals. The march, led by Foley, headed towards St Theresa's Gardens in the south inner city, an estate that had seen some of the worst of the drugs carnage. The group called to the homes of several CPAD activists, shouting insults and demanding that Gaffney be freed. At one point a masked man fired shots in the air. The message from the Concerned Criminals was clear: we are here, and we're ready, willing and able to take on our rivals.

When the criminals arrived at the flats complex they were met by a large number of uniformed gardaí who had intelligence that the protesters were on their way. The entrance to the estate had been cordoned off and was patrolled by residents who quizzed people on the way into the flats about the nature of their business there. Martin Foley and Shavo Hogan emerged from the criminal mob and went to speak with representatives of Sinn Féin/IRA and members of the CPAD. Things became quite heated but, having made their point that things would escalate if their friend did not turn up safe and sound, the criminals eventually headed back to Crumlin.

At this stage the criminals believed that Gaffney was

dead. But Sinn Féin/IRA seemed to want to placate the
CCAC and Foley was told to go to a pub in Clondalkin
the following afternoon at 3 p.m. Foley went with some
back-up and, shortly after they arrived, three men walked
into the pub and seemed to be checking it out. The men did
the same at the bookie's shop attached to the pub. A few
minutes later Foley was told there was a phone call for him.
He was ordered to go to a pub in Tallaght, where he was
met by a senior Sinn Féin man, who claimed that Concerned
Parents Against Drugs had asked the IRA to take action
against Gaffney. He said that the IRA had resisted getting
involved with the CPAD but that a local unit had acted
independently and without permission. Foley was told that
he would receive more information the following day.

But the next day a known member of the IRA told The
Viper he was amazed that his Sinn Féin counterpart had
talked about Gaffney and he denied that any IRA unit –
sanctioned or unsanctioned – was involved in the abduction.

Foley and his associates were becoming hugely frustrated
with the contradictory information and they tried to get
Dominic 'Mad Dog' McGlinchey involved. They travelled
down to Limerick to meet with the INLA boss, who was
hiding out there. McGlinchey also made contact with
INLA members up north to see if they would back up the
criminals if they went to war with the IRA.

Foley offered a £5,000 reward, following a fundraising
effort with Gaffney's friends. Gaffney's brother, Peter,
made a public appeal for his return, saying, 'We hope he
is alive, for the sake of his wife and baby. But it's gone too
far. We'd rather hear the bad news now, if there is any.' He
also offered a hint of the frustration felt by Foley and Cahill
that could potentially turn violent: 'We are under a lot of

pressure and are trying to hold people back from any nasty or ill-judged action.'

Foley approached long-time *Sunday World* columnist Fr Brian D'Arcy to see if he would act as a mediator between the two sides, if the need arose. Fr D'Arcy pleaded for Gaffney's return, saying, 'Whoever has Tommy must realise it's a man's life. I've done too many funerals in my life. Nothing is to be gained by killing anybody, or making people suffer. If someone wants to contact me in a confidential way on where Tommy Gaffney is, I in turn can pass that information on to the family.' Fr D'Arcy had mediated in several similar disputes but this was the first time he had gone public, because he was so concerned that Gaffney had been executed by his IRA kidnappers.

In the early hours of 20 March, nine days after Tommy Gaffney's kidnap and with no word of whether he was alive or dead, gardaí made their move and lifted Foley and Shavo Hogan in connection with the shooting of Joe Flynn. The pair feigned shock and protested that they had nothing to do with the shooting and had in fact been playing good samaritans by visiting a sick relation of Hogan's when Flynn was shot. Spending long hours in custody was nothing new to the two hoods and they had no problem coping with their thirty-six hours at the station. They were released at 9 p.m. on the evening of 21 March. Foley went home to Cashel Avenue and had a restful evening with Pauline. Little did he know that his sleep would be interrupted that night and that he would find himself face to face with a snatch squad similar to the one that had kidnapped his mate ten days previously.

At around 6.45 a.m. the following morning, Martin Foley and his partner, Pauline Quinn, were asleep in Foley's house when there was a knock on the door. Foley's older brother, Dominic, got up, went downstairs and looked through the peephole of the front door. He saw what appeared to be a postman outside and, thinking he must have a package for his brother, he opened the door. Instead of delivering a parcel, the fake postman stuck a gun in Dominic's chest and forced his way into the house. Three masked men then rushed in and Dominic was forced into the kitchen, pushed violently to the ground and had his hands tied behind his back. The men said they were from the IRA and that they were there to deliver a message to The Viper. The intruders asked Dominic which room his brother was in and two members of the active service unit ran up the stairs to confront the sleeping criminal.

Foley was a light sleeper and had been woken by the commotion downstairs. He got up and went to the bedroom door, where he was confronted by a masked man carrying a sawn-off shotgun. Foley was a skilled fighter; he knew that the masked man wasn't there to make him breakfast, so he went for him. He grabbed the barrel of the gun and tried to pull it from his attacker. The two struggled and ended up doing several laps of the room while a shocked Pauline Quinn looked on in horror. The other three Provos realised something was up and rushed to help their colleague. The 'postman' went to the window to keep a lookout for the gardaí and told his pals to 'quieten the fucker'. The three men beat Foley with a baton and a shotgun, loosened his grip on the gun and pushed him onto the bed. A gun was pushed into Foley's face while Pauline, who was in floods of tears, cowered in the corner of the room. She was living a nightmare.

One of the men tried to handcuff Foley. The Viper knew he was about to be kidnapped, so he made a bid for freedom. He jumped off the bed and punched his assailant in an effort to push him through the bedroom window. The terrorists responded by giving Foley a bad hiding with the batons and they managed to subdue him on the bed, where he was eventually cuffed. This wasn't the end of Foley's fighting spirit, though. He managed to wriggle free and run out of the bedroom towards the stairs, with three of the IRA men in hot pursuit (the 'postman' kept guard downstairs). The four men brawled and ended up falling down the stairs, with Foley landing in a heap and the would-be kidnappers landing on top of him. The cuffed criminal was dragged into the kitchen and dumped on the floor, where two of the intruders sat on him to keep him still. They wrapped duct tape around his legs and over his eyes and mouth so that he couldn't move, see or talk. He was then wrapped in a pink blanket and bundled into a green Hiace van that was parked outside his front door. Two of the Provos got into the back of the van with Foley and sat on him while the other pair jumped into the front and sped away. As the van left Cashel Avenue, one of the kidnappers pushed a gun into Foley's face and told him, 'If you don't stay quiet I'll blow the fucking head off you. You'll get the same as Tommy if you don't stay quiet.'

What the gang didn't know was that as they escaped, a neighbour happened to be looking out his window at the commotion. He dialled 999 and alerted gardaí to the kidnapping. He gave a description of the green van and soon every officer in the city was on high alert. Squad cars rushed to the area, looking for the suspects' vehicle. As the van travelled down the Crumlin Road, at the junction of Kildare Road a passing squad car, driven by Garda Tony Tighe, spotted it. Sergeant Declan O'Brien, Tighe's colleague from Tallaght Garda Station, was also in the car. One of the men sitting on top of Foley shouted to the driver, 'The police are behind us, take it easy and don't panic.' At first they didn't know if they had been rumbled or not, and the driver made sure to obey the rules of the road so as not to draw attention from the cops. He stopped at a red light outside Sundrive Road Garda Station and the squad car did the same. When he drove on, the garda car followed. As the van cruised along at 30 m.p.h., the squad car was joined by another garda vehicle and the gang knew the game was up and they would have to make a decision – surrender or take on the gardaí.

The cops decided to make their move as the van made its way down the South Circular Road towards the Phoenix Park. A third garda car arrived on the scene from Con Colbert Road and the driver performed a U-turn in an attempt to block the van. The van driver drove onto the footpath and went around the squad car. The Provos had decided there would be no surrender. The OJ-Simpson-style slow pursuit now turned into a full-blown high-speed chase towards the Phoenix Park as armed gardaí from the Special Task Force (STF) and men from detective units across the city joined in. The kidnappers had a radio tuned to the gardaí's frequency and they heard the commands being issued and the plans being devised. They knew they were in trouble and that they would be lucky to get away in one piece. At this stage the van was heading up Conyngham Road and it took a sharp left into the main gate of the Phoenix Park, just a stone's throw from Garda Headquarters. One of the pursuing garda cars drove up the wrong side of the road so that it was directly alongside the speeding van. The IRA driver tried to ram the garda car off the road. When this didn't work, the side door of the van slid open and one of the masked men aimed a handgun at the garda car. He wasn't bluffing, and he fired several shots at Garda Tighe's vehicle. One of the rounds hit the windscreen wiper directly facing the brave officer. Foley later said in a statement: 'One of them started crying ... and another one said, "It's no use; they are all around us." One of them then broke the back window of the van and a few shots were fired. There was a lot of panic at this stage, and one of them said, "We'll hold this fella as hostage," meaning me.'

The kidnappers continued to fire at Garda Tighe and the officer had to swerve the car to avoid the bullets. They even fired rounds from a shotgun, despite knowing the damage that shotgun pellets cause when they disperse. The windscreen of Garda Tighe's car was shattered, leaving him very exposed to the gunfire. The Hiace van turned onto Wellington Road in the Phoenix Park, but gardaí had set up a roadblock about a mile up the road, knowing that if the kidnappers turned onto the road, their path would be blocked. This proved to be the case and the four IRA men were forced to stop and jump out of the van. They ran towards the steps that serve as a pedestrian entrance to the park from Conyngham Road. They initially tried to carry Foley as a hostage, but there was no way he was going to allow this to happen. In the end they realised that he would only slow them down, so they reluctantly left him, their main interest now being in escaping arrest.

A posse of heavily armed gardaí had flooded the park and Conyngham Road and they were determined to catch the IRA men. The gang saw gardaí approaching and they fired off a couple of rounds. They were the last shots they would get off, because detectives let loose with sub-machine guns, pistols and revolvers. Three of the gang were forced to dive for cover and they hid, crouched together, in a nearby wooded area. Three armed gardaí, Aidan Boyle, Paul Donohue and Kevin Lynch, spotted the men and shouted, 'Armed garda; come out with your hands up.' Realising that they were goosed, two of the gang surrendered and were immediately taken into custody by the relieved gardaí. The third man was more reluctant but when a shot was fired over his head he changed his mind and surrendered too. Amazingly, nobody was hurt in the incident. The fourth kidnapper was arrested just off Conyngham Road, by Detective Garda Anthony Fennessy. He went to put his hand in his pocket but thought better of it when Detective Garda Fennessy fired a shot over his head as a warning not to act the maggot.

A pistol and two shotguns were recovered by gardaí, as well as balaclavas, gloves, eight shotgun cartridges and two walkie-talkies. Martin Foley was rescued by Tony Tighe and put into the back of a garda car to recover. He was dressed in just his underpants and he had a fractured jaw and cuts and bruises from the beating, but he was otherwise unhurt and he was very relieved that his sworn enemies, the gardaí, had saved his bacon. He repeatedly thanked the officers involved for their hard work. The whole ordeal lasted less than half an hour.

The identities of the gang members were soon discovered. The driver had been twenty-three-year-old Sean Hick, a butcher from leafy Dun Laoghaire, who was a college graduate and had joined the IRA soon after he was awarded his degree. The kidnapper who had fired the shots was twenty-two-year-old Derek Dempsey from Ballyfermot. He was little more than a young thug who had been attracted to the glamour of the Republican movement just months previously. The third man was twenty-two-year-old university graduate, Liam O'Dwyer, who hailed from an affluent family in Castleknock, not far from where he was arrested. The leader of the unit was thirty-three-year-old bar manager and experienced terrorist James Dunne, from Finglas. The botched kidnap was an embarrassing blow to the credibility of both the IRA and the CPAD, and a great victory for gardaí.

Foley was taken to hospital, where he was treated for a few hours. He was then reunited with Pauline Quinn and he apologised to her for what she had been through, promising that everything would be fine from now on.

Later Foley happily picked out his four kidnappers from an identity parade. He was obviously fired up over the incident because he spat at and tried to attack one of the men, before being restrained by gardaí. The arrested Provos must have been terrified of Foley, considering he had nearly got the better of the four of them as they tried to abduct him. Over the next two days The Viper made three detailed statements to gardaí.

While Foley was eagerly recounting his ordeal to gardaí, the IRA and CPAD met to discuss their next move. They had been undermined by the botched kidnap, and with four volunteers in custody being quizzed by the Garda Special Branch there was no telling what could happen. They decided to cut their losses and free Thomas Gaffney. In the early hours of the morning of 23 March, Gaffney was released in an isolated part of rural Limerick. He was

dumped out of a van and told he was a free man. He had
to walk for over an hour and a half before he found help,
when he spotted a young factory worker at around 1.45 a.m.
The young man brought him to the nearby presbytery in
Abbeyfeale and woke Fr Joseph Kennedy and asked him to
contact the gardaí.

Gaffney was taken to the station at Newcastle West. He
told investigators that he had been blindfolded, put in a van
and driven for around three hours before being released.
Gaffney's wife, Margaret, was brought to Terenure Garda
Station and given the good news. Many of the missing man's
family and friends, as well as the gardaí, had feared that he
had been executed. Gardaí said that Gaffney had not been
injured and that he was greatly relieved, as was his wife.

During his time in captivity Gaffney had been repeatedly
interrogated about the Concerned Criminals group. The
activities of Martin Cahill were of particular interest to the
IRA, especially the O'Connor's jewellery robbery. He was
also asked about Martin Foley and the Joe Flynn shooting.
Before he was released he was told about the foiled kidnap
of Foley, and his abductors ordered him to tell gardaí that
the group that held him were 'concerned about the chronic
drug problem in Dublin'. Gardaí had no doubt that the two
kidnap incidents were linked and they believed that IRA
members who tried to kidnap Foley may have been involved
in interrogating Gaffney.

Following Gaffney's kidnap and release and the
attempted kidnap of Foley, both the Concerned Criminals
and Concerned Parents pulled back from the brink and an
uneasy peace settled on Crumlin. The IRA went off to lick
its wounds – and to regroup.

The *Irish Press* welcomed Gaffney's and Foley's

narrow escapes, but the paper said the kidnappings were symptomatic of emerging problems in society. An editorial in the paper entitled HAPPY RETURN read:

> It is a triumph for the gardaí, whose rescue of Martin Foley early on Thursday morning was the turning point that ensured the happy return of his friend, Mr Gaffney. But while the outcome is satisfactory, the kidnapping and its circumstances are disturbing. The full story has yet to emerge but it is clear that Mr Gaffney had become yet another victim of Dublin's dreadful drug problem. Lawlessness breeds – and we are now paying the price for allowing the heroin trade to grow unchecked in the inner city and working-class suburbs. Whoever was at fault, the fact remains that distraught parents were given little help from the forces of law and order in the fight to save their children from the pushers. So they are handling their own law enforcement. They have become Concerned Citizens. They reject the term vigilante – but could anyone blame them if they did embark on vigilante activities? The fault does not lie with the parents. Yet it was inevitable that once they began to fight the pushers, the drug trade would fight back. Inevitable that innocent people would get hurt. Unless the whole area of drug racketeering can be brought quickly – and effectively – under control of the gardaí there will be more cases such as that of Tommy Gaffney.

Nobody would have predicted in 1984, though, that one of the chief targets of the gardaí three decades later, in their pursuit of organised criminals and drug dealers, would be one Martin Foley.

On 23 March 1984 James Dunne from Farnham Drive, in Finglas; Derek Dempsey from Raheen Drive, in Ballyfermot;

Sean Hick of Glenageary Avenue, in Dun Laoghaire and
Liam Adams from Stockton Park, in Castleknock, appeared
before an emergency sitting of the Special Criminal Court,
charged with the attempted murder of Garda Tony Tighe.
They were also charged with the false imprisonment of
Martin Foley, of having guns with intent to endanger life
and of using them to prevent arrest on 22 March of that
year. They all pleaded not guilty to the charges. Patrick
MacEntee, senior counsel for the men, said he had been
instructed to apply for bail on their behalf but that he
understood that gardaí would be opposing the application.
They were all remanded in custody.

The following week Sean Hick made an application to the
court for bail. Foley's old nemesis, Detective Superintendent
Ned Ryan of Crumlin Garda Station, objected to bail on
the basis that he believed Hick would not attend the trial
if he was freed. Hick's father, John, told the court that he
believed his son would attend and that his son was a blunt
person who would not tell a lie. Hick's girlfriend said that
she had planned to marry Hick in August and said he was
a very honest person. She also believed Hick would turn
up to stand trial and she produced evidence of a building
society savings account with a balance of £12,000. Hick's
girlfriend said that she would be prepared to post bail for
her boyfriend. Judge Hamilton, however, said that the
charges were too serious for bail to be considered and he
remanded Hick in custody.

Following the charging of the IRA men, independent
TD Tony Gregory came out in defence of the Concerned
Parents Against Drugs group. They had been drastically
undermined by the kidnappings but Gregory was resolute
in his defence of the organisation. His comments followed

remarks from Minister for Justice Michael Noonan, who said that it would be tragic if a community, in an attempt to reject criminal elements, was to become beholden to terrorist organisations. Gregory dismissed this, saying he had no misgivings whatsoever about CPAD and that he admired the way they had stood up to 'the most serious intimidation imaginable'. Asked if the IRA could possibly infiltrate the group, he said, 'Any group is open to infiltration by all sorts of people with varying motivations, but certainly the groups I've been involved in are very conscious of that and they wouldn't allow that to happen. I've been very closely involved in the Concerned Parents movement on the north side of the city since it was set up and I am not aware of any paramilitary infiltration whatsoever.'

Four days after the four IRA volunteers were charged at the Special Criminal Court in connection with Foley's kidnap, The Viper's name was mentioned at a sitting of Dublin District Court. The criminal was being blamed for a row that led to gardaí producing their batons. The court heard that Foley had called gardaí 'pigs' and shouted other abuse at them in Rathfarnham Garda Station the previous January. After Foley started mouthing off a melee broke out, which led to two of Foley's friends being charged with assaulting a number of officers, breach of the peace and of being drunk and disorderly. James and Anne Kelly of Cushlawn Park, in Tallaght, were before the court, and their solicitor, Myles Shevlin, asked Garda David Gahon why Foley was not facing any charges, considering his outburst. He replied that it had been Mr Kelly who assaulted the officers, not Mr Foley. 'Why none against Foley?' asked Shevlin, to which the garda replied, 'He did not assault us and that was the size of it.' The court heard that Sergeant

John Byrne struck James Kelly with his baton in order to restrain him and that he also used it against Kelly's wife after she struck him with her handbag and fists. Myles Shevlin said it was Martin Foley who had initially been abusive to gardaí and that Kelly only intervened after his wife had been knocked to the ground by gardaí. He said that Martin Foley had turned up in court to give evidence on behalf of the defendants and to tell the judge that he had been to blame for the incident at the station. In any event Foley was not charged with anything and his intervention – holding his hands up to try to get the couple off – didn't work either. The Kellys were both hit with fines and bound to keep the peace.

Gardaí continued their investigation into the kidnaps of Foley and Gaffney as well as into the activities of the CPAD. They said publically that they believed the IRA had infiltrated the organisation, and on 28 March detectives moved to arrest a leading member of CPAD, Paul Humphries, in connection with the Gaffney abduction. At the same time Sinn Féin man and leader of the CPAD peace delegation, John Noonan, was lifted under the Offences Against the State Act. One hundred and fifty people turned up outside Crumlin Garda Station to protest against the arrests, and CPAD issued a statement unreservedly condemning the arrests, saying: 'We believe the continued harassment and now detention of members is a blatant misuse of garda powers.' Both men were later released without charge.

The trial of the four men for Foley's botched kidnap began at the Special Criminal Court on 4 July 1984 and senior counsel for the prosecution, Noel McDonald, said in his opening statement that guns blazed in the Phoenix Park as gardaí pursued the kidnappers. He said it was the State's contention that the four men were guilty of the charges put to them and that this would be proven beyond reasonable doubt.

The first witness called to give evidence was Martin Foley. After his three statements to gardaí and the identity parade, gardaí knew that The Viper was crystal clear on the circumstances of his kidnapping and rescue. Gardaí had had Foley under round-the-clock surveillance since the foiled kidnap because his eyewitness testimony would virtually guarantee a conviction against the four accused. However, when he was asked in court to recount the events of the morning of 22 March, he said he had very little recollection of what had happened. 'I was half asleep and I can't remember what I did. I don't know if I was standing up or still in bed. I remember some noises in the bedroom. What I remember after that was sitting in a patrol car in dense fog with, I think, a lot of police around me. I was on a tarmac road in dense fog and there were fields and trees and a lot of uniformed gardaí around.'

It was obvious that something had happened during the previous three months that had caused Foley to change his mind about cooperating with the gardaí in trying to put his kidnappers behind bars. When asked if he remembered making statements to gardaí, he said, 'I don't remember. I remember one of the gardaí telling me that I had been kidnapped or something.' When it was put to him that he had in fact signed a detailed statement after the incident, he said, 'I was in court when it was read out and it is completely untrue,' as though that was the first he had heard of it.

An application was made to treat Foley as a hostile witness and when this was granted he was questioned about picking out two of the men in an identity parade. He told

the disbelieving court, 'I picked out, I think, three men.
I had seen their pictures on the wall of Terenure police
station.' He said he had never seen the men before in his life
and that he had been 'spoofing' when he had a discussion
with two gardaí about the trial a week before it had opened.

Detective Garda Pat Culhane tried to counter Foley's
bout of amnesia by giving evidence about the signed
statement he had taken from the forgetful felon. The
statement was read out to him in full immediately after
Foley had given it and he said, 'That is what happened,'
after the detective had finished.

Detective Sergeant Gerry O'Carroll also gave evidence
about attending the identity parade with Foley the day after
the abduction and of how Foley had fingered two of the
men. Dr Charles O'Malley spoke of examining Foley on
the morning he was rescued and said Foley had cuts and
bruises and that he had complained that he was repeatedly
hit across the head with a baton and a pistol. The doctor
said Foley had complained of double vision and had been
semi-conscious for about five or ten minutes. Paul Carney,
who was representing Dempsey and Dunne, asked if being
semi-conscious could result in short term amnesia and
said that this might explain the differences between Foley's
testimony and his statements.

It later emerged that before the trial Foley had met
with senior members of the INLA and was told that his
kidnapping had led to tensions between the INLA and the
IRA and that he was to withdraw his evidence. The INLA
men told Foley that he would be asked in the box if he
was a drug pusher and that this would cause a row with
the IRA, so he should keep his mouth shut. Foley replied
by saying that the Provos had been trying to kill him and

that he was going to get his own back on them. But he later received a message from the IRA, warning that if he said anything during the trial they would pay him another visit and that this time they wouldn't just abduct him. He obviously heeded the message.

Foley's recanting of his evidence was a blow to investigators, but there is an old garda adage that you should never trust a gouger, so it wasn't that big a shock to the detectives. Anyway, there was still a good deal of evidence against the accused. Martin Foley's brother, Dominic, was called to give evidence because he had witnessed the kidnapping. He said he had seen two men, one armed with a small handgun, kidnap his brother and that he heard Martin screaming after he was hit with a gun. He said that to his knowledge his brother was 'not big on the drug scene' and that he did not know if any of Martin Foley's friends were involved in drug dealing. During the second week of the trial Garda Tony Tighe took the witness box. He described how a balaclava-wearing gunman leaned from the green Hiace van during the high-speed pursuit and fired five or six shots at him from a handgun. He said the first shot shattered the rubber and chrome surround of the patrol car windscreen and that the gunman then retreated into the van. Thirty yards on the garda heard a very loud noise, like a blast. 'The back window of the van shattered onto the roadway and something hit the patrol car. It was like shrapnel of some description. The van turned towards the Wellington Monument and stopped at the forty steps. I stopped about twenty yards behind it. Four or five men jumped out and ran down the embankment. I jumped from the patrol car and a man came running towards me. He was wearing a vest and underpants and had handcuffs on. I now know he was

Martin Foley.' He then told how he pursued the kidnappers to the side of the embankment at the bottom of the forty steps, where they opened fire again. 'One of them was holding a sawn-off shotgun. I ran for cover. As I ran, I saw our own plainclothes men in cars arrive. I lay down on the grass. A number of shots were being fired between the gunmen and our plainclothes men.' Garda Tighe said at this stage he feared for the safety of the kidnapped man who had been placed in the back of the patrol car. He ran back to the car and threw his handcuff keys to another officer to open Foley's cuffs so that he would be safer. He described how plainclothes officers helped him rescue Foley, who was then placed in a van and brought to Kilmainham Garda Station. Garda Tighe removed the duct tape from Foley's mouth and noticed that he had facial injuries, which he described as being black and blue.

The case took a bizarre twist on 17 July when James Dunne and Derek Dempsey both dismissed their legal teams. Paul Carney, who is now a highly regarded judge, was sacked as Dunne's senior counsel, and junior counsel Patrick Gageby and their solicitor, Ann Rowland, were also let go. Mr Gageby said that following instructions from his client, counsel felt they should withdraw from the trial. Dunne later said that they had taken the step after consultations with Paul Carney because they had concerns about two witnesses leaving the jurisdiction. The court had earlier agreed to release two garda witnesses from the trial to allow them to go abroad on holidays. The lead Judge, Mr Justice Thomas Doyle, told the two accused that they had been defended capably and it was very unwise to discard their legal help. Dunne replied: 'We have listened for two weeks to a lot of lies and it has got to the stage where we are no longer going to participate.' Dempsey said that he and Dunne wanted to reserve the right to cross-examine witnesses. On 18 July Detective Garda Bernard Sheerin of Ronanstown Garda Station told the trial that he had interviewed James Dunne, who was a father of five and had no criminal record, the day after the failed kidnap. Dunne told Sheerin that he would plead guilty to the offence if he was given bail. Sheerin said he advised Dunne to have the matter sorted out before he went to court and that the suspect replied: 'If I knew I would get bail I would plead guilty to it, but I know I won't get bail. Anyway, I don't trust ya.' Dunne said he would look at the book of evidence before deciding on how to plead. Detective Garda Ridge from Kilmainham Garda Station said he interviewed Dunne at Kevin Street Garda Station on the day of the botched kidnap attempt and asked him if the operation had gone wrong. Dunne replied: 'I suppose you could say it did. You could say a faux pas was made.' He told the detective that he didn't agree with shooting at gardaí and said that he hadn't fired any shots.

Detective Garda Michael Gormley of the Central Detective Unit gave evidence that he saw Liam O'Dwyer at Terenure Garda Station on the day he was arrested and that O'Dwyer's nose was swollen and grazed and that one of his hands was also grazed. He asked O'Dwyer what had happened to him and was told: 'I got this in a tussle with your lads in the Phoenix Park this morning.' Dr Percival Patton said that he had examined O'Dwyer and Dunne at the Bridewell and Kevin Street Garda Stations on the morning of their arrest and that both had signs of injuries, which he believed could have come from either blows received from a baton or a fall on a hard surface. O'Dwyer claimed during the trial that his hair had been pulled, a gun was stuck into his back and he was kicked while wearing handcuffs. Several gardaí strenuously denied that they had assaulted any of the accused while they were in custody.

Detective Sergeant Patrick Ennis of the Garda Ballistics Section said that he carried out tests on an Italian .22 revolver found in the Phoenix Park after the arrests and also that he examined the garda car that had been shot at. He said there were marks on the squad car that could have been caused by shotgun pellets. There was also a mark on the bonnet and a bullet hole in the panel on the driver's side that could have been caused by a bullet. He produced the Italian revolver and said that tests had shown that two shots had been fired from it. It was also heard that particles of firearms residue were found on James Dunne's clothing and hands and that similar residue had also been detected on the clothing of Dempsey and Hick.

Dunne and Derek Dempsey, who were now defending themselves, having dismissed their legal teams, put it to Detective Sergeant Tim Hickey from the Garda Technical Bureau that he had threatened to show photographs of Dempsey to a witness who was about to attend a witness parade. DS Hickey denied this. Dempsey asked another garda witness: 'Did you say to me that I should have shot Martin Foley dead because it would be one less drug pusher on the streets of Dublin?' The garda denied having said anything of the sort.

On 25 July 1984, after a three-week trial that captivated the public, the verdict was announced. James Dunne, Sean Hick, Liam O'Dwyer and Derek Dempsey were all found guilty of false imprisonment, of shooting at Garda Tony Tighe, of the possession of firearms with intent to endanger life and of resisting arrest. The three-judge court said there had been evidence identifying each of the accused and linking them to the crime. Dempsey had been seen removing a balaclava and putting it in his pocket while putting a handgun into another pocket. There was evidence that Hick had driven the van in which Foley had been abducted, and Dunne had been identified as the front seat passenger. Just before O'Dwyer was captured he had crouched down and hidden two guns. Physical evidence had also linked the four men to the crime. However, they were all cleared of attempted murder. When this verdict was announced the friends and supporters of the Provos who were gathered in court began to whoop and cheer, which led to the presiding judge, Mr Justice Doyle, to warn that he would clear the court if there were any more outbursts. In giving the reason for the not guilty verdict on the attempted murder charge, the judges said, 'There is room for some doubt, even if slight, that the shot or shots discharged by the defendant were fired from the open side-door of their moving Hiace van with the necessary intent to murder Garda Tighe in his pursuant garda patrol car.'

After the verdicts were delivered, several of the convicted IRA men said the crime was committed as part of an effort to crack down on drug dealing in Dublin. James Dunne, the leader of the active service unit, said, 'What we did was honourable and just.' Derek Dempsey read from a prepared statement: 'We would not be in the dock were it not for the appalling heroin problem in the city.' He said that drug dealers were destroying young people's lives and that they were allowed to operate with near impunity. Seamus Sorahan, senior counsel for Liam O'Dwyer, said his client 'felt he was doing something to frighten those who traffic in hard drugs and cause tragedy, degradation, wrecked lives and even in some cases, death'. Sean Hick said the kidnapping was not carried out for a selfish motive or for personal gain.

Judge Doyle refused to allow questions from Seamus Sorahan about whether Martin Foley was known to gardaí as a prominent hard-drug trafficker. Detective Inspector Cornelius Keane said the abduction of Foley was in the style of a vigilante operation and was connected to drugs.

The following morning when handing down sentence, Judge Doyle said that the excuses given to justify the robbery as some sort of public service act against drug dealers were not convincing. 'Even if this had been proven, it could provide no excuse or justification for a violent usurpation of the powers and duties of the forces of law and order. Any such activity must be severely dealt with by the court.' Derek Dempsey, who the court heard had previous convictions for robbery, assault and car theft, received a nine-year jail sentence. Sean Hick, who had a B.Comm degree from UCD and James Dunne, whose wife was expecting their sixth child, were both handed seven-year terms. Liam O'Dwyer, a former UCD student who was studying commerce in Rathmines College, was jailed for five years.

As the men were led out to begin their sentences Derek Dempsey raised a clenched fist in the air and shouted, 'Up the Provos,' while supporters in the large public gallery stood and cheered loudly.

A week after the trial ended, Martin Foley and Pauline Quinn got married. Foley felt bad about the ordeal Pauline had been through and he popped the question soon after he was released from hospital. They went to sunny Northern Ireland on honeymoon.

The Art of Robbery

MARTIN FOLEY AND MARTIN Cahill had come a long way in a few short years. They had carried out the biggest robbery in the history of the State, had been thorns in the side of gardaí and had frustrated several high-profile criminal trials. They were delighted with their progress and they planned to move on to bigger and better things. The only problem was that the pair had become very well known after the O'Connor's jewellery heist, the Dr Donovan bomb, the Concerned Criminals group and Foley's kidnap and subsequent bout of amnesia. It is one thing to be well known to the gardaí, but when the general public becomes familiar with you, trouble inevitably follows. Then politicians get involved and more pressure is put on gardaí to crack down on you.

Martin Cahill was very frustrated with the attention he was getting from the boys in blue, but instead of keeping his head down and getting on with things while waiting for the heat to die down, he decided to break his silence and give his first ever interview to *Irish Times* journalist Padraig Yates. It was a fascinating interview. The reporter commented that the smiley, chubby-faced Cahill looked nothing like what one expected a criminal mastermind to look like. Cahill told him: 'The gardaí told you I was mean, didn't they? They think I should be going around in a flashy car, spending loads of money, with women on my arm. I'm not like that. I'm quiet. I don't drink; I don't smoke or gamble. It's not what they expect. I did own a big car once, a Mercedes, but it was second hand. If you own a Mini and it's brand new, it's still a Mini. If you own a Mercedes and it's clapped out, it's still a Mercedes. People still talk about that Mercedes.'

Cahill said that he had been living modestly in a Corporation house with his wife and kids but that he was forced to move out because he feared that gardaí were going to kill him. He said he granted the interview to put this fear on the record. Cahill, who was named only as The General in the piece, said: 'Harassment doesn't mean anything to me. It's water off a duck's back. The only time the cops worry me is when I can't see them, and I haven't seen them for the past three weeks. For about nine months now the guards have been spreading rumours about my involvement in drugs. A lot of people are against drugs and this is the thing to jump on the bandwagon with. Drugs, I hate them. They have ruined members of my own family. I have no need for drugs, no need to look for money. I was asked to go into drugs the last time I came out of prison, but everyone involved was knackered. They would sit around all day talking about drugs and money, but they had no money. I said, "If you want money, let's talk about a robbery," and they'd say, "Yeah, that's right, let's do a robbery," and then they started talking about robbing drugstores and I knew I was wasting my time. Never trust a drug fella; they're like a helpless thing, not a human being at all.'

It wasn't only drug dealers that irked The General. He was also disdainful of the IRA. 'Fifty per cent of the Provos in Portlaoise incriminate themselves or allow themselves to be verballed by the cops. They think they're big until they're pulled and the guards just steam into them. The people who control them don't train them properly. They know there are more if they lose a few on a job. They can't even go and rob for themselves any longer. They have to rob ordinary criminals who have done the work and taken the chances. There's nothing lower than someone who robs a robber.'

The General admitted that he had pulled off armed robberies and that his favourite partners for robberies were 'people interested in their families, working class guys, who've no other chance of setting up their own business or getting anywhere. I help them out.' He also admitted his trade was becoming ever more difficult because of garda surveillance. 'The police have asked people to set up robberies. When I get information on a robbery I have to check out the source before going any further.' He said that he had to abandon planned robberies because of the gardaí and that officers had tried to plant guns and drugs on him.

Cahill refused to discuss the details of specific crimes, but he vehemently denied that he was responsible for the bomb attack on Dr Donovan. He also, surprisingly, said he supported the Concerned Parents movement, despite being the brains behind the criminals' retaliation group. He said the lives of criminals were being made more difficult by the Concerned Parents but that they were entitled to protect their communities.

The gardaí were delighted to hear that they were getting to The General and it made them all the more determined to keep up the pressure. Ned Ryan told Garda Headquarters that this was the only way to disrupt the gang and he pleaded for the resources to make the surveillance permanent, otherwise the gang would soon be back to their old ways.

By the end of 1985 the gardaí had drawn up their Most Wanted list of organised criminals operating in the Dublin Metropolitan Area. They realised that if they wanted to stop the criminal masterminds, they would have to collate intelligence centrally and make it available to the different branches of the force, such as ordinary uniformed gardaí, district detectives and detectives from specialised units. It was vital that each group shared their intelligence and that any links between different gangs were noted. Basically, any information that might give the gardaí the upper hand needed to be shared across the force.

Twenty serious criminals from the south inner city out as far as Tallaght were included on a hierarchical list. The General's name, predictably, was at the top of the list. Not far behind him, in fifth place, was Martin Foley. Garda intelligence was that there were around two dozen members of the Cahill/Foley gang. Around the same time as the gardaí were putting together their intelligence dossier, Martin Foley was approached about another daring robbery that would cement the gang's place on the Most Wanted list.

In the summer of 1985 Paddy Shanahan, a university-educated former auctioneer from Kildare, was released from prison in England and travelled home. He was an art expert and an accomplished villain who had known Foley and Cahill since the early 1970s, when he had carried out several armed robberies with them. Shanahan was regarded as an upper-class, Walter Mitty type who liked the danger and intrigue of crime. The good thing about Shanahan was that although he was a prolific criminal in his day, and had robbed mailbags from the same train in Kildare each week for nearly ten years without being caught, he had no criminal convictions in Ireland and was not known to gardaí. However, he hadn't been so lucky in England, and in May 1981 he and two London-based accomplices were each jailed for four years after carrying out an armed robbery on the home of a well-known seventy-two-year-old antiques dealer, Sam Firman. Firman had suffered a heart attack during the robbery and had almost died.

While Shanahan was in prison he researched valuable works of art in Irish stately homes with a view to carrying out a robbery after he was released, to help get him back on his feet. He quickly identified Sir Alfred Beit as a vulnerable target. Beit had a valuable collection of paintings at his home, Russborough House, in County Wicklow. Russborough House is an imposing Palladian mansion set in stunning parkland, and the aristocrat was justifiably proud of his home and his magnificent art pieces. Sir Alfred was a financier and came from a wealthy South African diamond-mining family. He was also a former Conservative MP and had come to live in Ireland in 1952.

Beit's private collection was legendary in the art world. Most of the paintings were by the Dutch Masters, with Vermeer's *Lady Writing a Letter* alone reckoned to be worth anything up to £20 million. It was the only Vermeer in the world in private hands, except for one owned by Queen Elizabeth II. It was estimated that the entire collection could be worth in excess of £40 million on the black market, and Shanahan knew that to rob the paintings would be the job of a lifetime. He contacted Martin Foley and asked if he and The General would be interested in teaming up with him.

Shanahan wasn't the first criminal to think about robbing the Beit collection. On 26 April 1974 an IRA gang led by Rose Dugdale, the daughter of a wealthy English stockbroker, broke into the country house and made off with nineteen paintings, worth £8 million. Beit and his family and staff were held at gunpoint and the gang was in and out of the premises in just seven minutes. A ransom of £500,000 was demanded following the raid, along with the transfer of political prisoners from English to Northern Irish jails. Eleven days after the robbery, thirty-three-year-old Dugdale was arrested in a cottage in County Cork, with three of the stolen paintings. The remaining sixteen works of art were found in a hired car. At her trial the heiress pleaded 'proudly and incorruptibly guilty' to receiving the stolen paintings. Four other charges in relation to the crime were dismissed as part of this plea bargain.

Sir Alfred and his family and staff were unhurt during the incident but he subsequently decided to donate the art collection to the Irish State. It would be known as the Beit Collection and, as part of the deal, Russborough House would be opened to the public so that everyone could enjoy the priceless works. The house was opened in 1978 and each year thousands of visitors flocked to it and happily paid the £1 entrance fee.

Shanahan made a number of trips to Russborough House, casing it out for security, and he satisfied himself that the Dugdale robbery had not led to much modernisation of the security systems. He approached Martin Foley and Shavo Hogan with his idea in early 1986. The two listened with interest and said the heist sounded like a great idea on the face of it but that they would have to discuss it with their boss. The General was equally enthusiastic and loved the idea of robbing from the State, whose agents were putting him under such pressure. He did not trust Shanahan, however, and devised his own plan to hit the Wicklow mansion, while at the same time letting Shanahan believe that he was central to the proposed robbery.

Russborough House was opened to the public after Easter Sunday each year, and every Sunday for two months, Cahill, Foley and Shavo Hogan paid their £1 and visited, making detailed notes on the layout of the house and its meagre security systems. They posed as art aficionados and were often accompanied by Shanahan, who pointed out the most valuable paintings to them. The gang knew they would have to act quickly, because four of the masterpieces in the collection were due to be transferred to the National Gallery. The Vermeer, two works by Metsu, *A Man Writing a Letter* and *A Woman Reading a Letter*, as well as *Portrait of Dona Antonia Zarate* by Goya, would not be at Russborough House for much longer. The combined conservative valuation of these four paintings was £27 million. It was a bonus that the paintings were insured, so there would probably be a ransom available for their safe return, which would mean cash for the mob.

Paddy Shanahan was dispatched to England, ostensibly to make discreet inquiries about potential purchasers for the paintings, as well as to seek out an alarm expert to bypass the mansion's security system. However, this was merely a ruse to get rid of him while the real planning got under way.

Cahill put together a team of men to help pull off the heist, reckoning that a dozen able criminals would be needed. Martin Foley and Shavo Hogan, who had originally come to Cahill with the idea, were the key men in the operation. Most of the others chosen had been involved in previous heists with the gang. The General decided that the Dublin Mountains was the ideal place to store the paintings after the robbery: the mountains were close to Russborough and offered thousands of hiding places. The General had buried loot there before and he was convinced that nobody would find the paintings. He dug a bunker in the middle of a dense forest and revealed the location to just a couple of key gang members. The bunker was about twelve feet from the road and was six feet deep and five feet wide. It was lined with concrete blocks and plastic sheeting to keep the rain out, and it had an air vent to allow the canvases to breathe. The bunker was accessed through a manhole cover and the spot was camouflaged with moss and other vegetation so that it blended in with the landscape and did not arouse the suspicion of passers-by.

During one reconnaissance trip to Russborough House, in a van belonging to a legitimate security company, Cahill and Foley saw Paddy Shanahan and his UK alarm expert on the grounds, so they decided that the robbery would have to be carried out at the earliest opportunity. They chose 21 May 1986 as D-Day, and on 17 May two four-wheel-drive vehicles were stolen to be used in the robbery.

The gang met shortly after midnight on 21 May. Sir Beit and his wife had travelled to London and would not be home. The administrator of Russborough House, Lieutenant Colonel Michael O'Shea, the Beit chauffeur, Tom Brosnan, and their families would be in the house.

The gang decided to approach the house from the rear. The two stolen jeeps, containing the rest of the gang members, were parked along the boundary of the estate.

Cahill, Foley and Hogan slowly walked towards the house, in almost pitch darkness. To guide the jeeps up to the house the trio stuck long sticks in the ground, fifty yards apart, with white plastic bags tied to the tops of them. The men then cut a pane of glass out of a French window and forced it open. Cahill crept into the building and deliberately walked in front of an alarm sensor, which was linked to the local garda station, in Blessington. The alarm went off and he tampered with the sensor so that it would not be activated a second time once the system had been re-set.

The three criminals then retreated into the shadows and watched Colonel O'Shea go out to check that everything was okay. O'Shea didn't notice the damage to the French window and when the gardaí arrived he informed them that things seemed to be in order. Satisfied, the gardaí left, while O'Shea went back to bed, no doubt relieved that it had been a false alarm.

Then the gang struck. They parked the jeeps outside the house and the twelve-strong team breezed in undetected and stole eighteen paintings. They were in and out in one minute less than the IRA had managed twelve years previously. Seven less-valuable paintings were thrown away but the four that were destined for the National Gallery were kept, as were seven other beautiful works of art. The gang split up and headed for home while Cahill hid the haul in the specially-constructed bunker. On his way home he was stopped by gardaí at 3.15 a.m. but was sent on his way because gardaí had no reason to detain him.

It wasn't until 9 a.m. the following morning that the burglary was detected. The robbery was a major embarrassment for the government and the gardaí, who seemed to be having rings run round them. Sir Alfred Beit was devastated by the robbery and said in an interview that he believed the IRA was probably responsible. 'I cannot think other than one of these sort of revolutionary movements are behind the thefts and they are seeking a ransom, which they won't get. It's not me who has been robbed this time, it is the Irish people, since the collection is now in trust for the State,' he said.

While Sir Beit was inconsolable, Foley, Cahill and Hogan were cock-a-hoop. They had again managed to pull off a once-in-a-lifetime robbery and they were now the undisputed kings of Irish organised crime.

The jubilation didn't last, however. Although they didn't know it at the time, the Beit paintings would bring the gang nothing but bad luck. Shavo Hogan later said of the robbery: 'Robbing the paintings was the easy bit. Everybody thought they were going to be millionaires, but after that night everything went downhill. There was a curse on those paintings.'

Paddy Shanahan, who was furious that he had been shafted and cut out of the robbery, pointed out the first problem. He told the theives it would be next to impossible to get rid of the art works because the ones they had chosen were so famous that it would be instantly obvious to an art expert that they were stolen. The gang would have been better advised to swipe lesser-known paintings that would be easier to fence, and Shanahan could have told them this had he not been squeezed out. There was also a host of valuable antiques in the house that would have been much easier to sell on, but the robbers had ignored these.

Martin Foley was still on good terms with Shanahan, as he had put the blame on Cahill for freezing Shanahan out. So The Viper was appointed as the liaison with the antiques expert. He was told to smooth things over and get Shanahan back on side to introduce them to potential buyers. But Shanahan eventually told them they would have to get rid of the art works by themselves, because there was too much heat attached to them. It was a massive blow to the gang, but they didn't give up, convinced that they could still make a profit.

The robbery had caused a huge storm in the art world and police forces with dedicated art-theft units throughout the world were in touch with gardaí, offering to try to set up meetings with the gang, posing as potential buyers. Cahill was aware of this and he warned his fellow criminals to keep their heads down and leave the problem of offloading the paintings to him, in case undercover gardaí tried to trick them.

Art historian Dr James White, a former director of the National Gallery, offered a reward of £50,000 for information leading to the return of the paintings, but the gang wasn't about to hand over £40 million worth of paintings for a measly fifty grand. Instead Cahill approached his friend Noel Lynch, whom he had met in prison. Lynch had a security company that specialised in the 'recovery' of stolen goods, debt collection and in securing the movement of large amounts of cash. The convicted armed robber was asked to act as a middleman between Cahill and anyone who was interested in buying the paintings or who was offering a reward for them. Noel Lynch approached Dr White and said he was a private investigator and could help him recover the paintings. He said he had information that the gang responsible for the robbery had been offered huge sums of money to sell the paintings. Dr White became suspicious and wisely refused to have any dealings with Lynch.

Gardaí planned an elaborate sting codenamed Operation Moonshine and consulted with Interpol, the FBI and Scotland Yard, before launching it in July 1986. English policemen posing as wealthy art buyers contacted a fence from Drogheda who had been making attempts to sell the paintings in the UK. The fence fell for it and contacted Cahill and asked him to show the potential buyers some of the paintings. But The General smelled a rat and he failed to show up for the appointment. After that the operation petered out.

In January 1987 gardaí flew to Virginia to meet with the FBI and plan another sting, involving undercover federal officers, but this came to nothing. That July a criminal from the UK, who was based in Amsterdam, offered to buy the paintings for £1 million. He travelled to Dublin with the money but he was under constant garda surveillance, after they learned of the plot from Interpol. Again, Cahill got cold feet and sent the criminal away without doing a deal.

Cahill decided it would be wise to leave the paintings in storage for a period, until the heat died down.

In late summer 1987 a potential buyer emerged but there were months of negotiations and trust-building before the gang was prepared to do a deal. On 27 September 1987 Cahill and Foley, along with Eamon Daly and Shavo Hogan, brought an 'art dealer' to Killakee Wood in the Dublin Mountains for a viewing. The criminals didn't realise that the art dealer was an undercover Interpol agent and that a posse of gardaí was waiting to move in and arrest them. In a lucky twist of fate for the gang, the garda radio system broke down, and the gangsters, who were suspicious of the dealer's increasingly nervous disposition, stopped their car on the way to the hiding place, deposited the agent on the

road and fled the area. Gardaí later found the undercover
Interpol man abandoned on the road. They had been within
minutes of catching four of the country's most serious
criminals.

At this stage the gardaí were angry, embarrassed and
frustrated. The Interpol operation had caused a split within
the gardaí because only a select group had known about it,
which caused serious resentment internally.

When Cahill learned of the narrow escape he used it to
taunt the officers, who were still paying him far too much
attention for his liking. The mob hadn't done much serious
business in the previous year because of the garda heat,
although they had managed to carry out some small-time
robberies for pocket money. Now Cahill, Foley and Shavo
Hogan began to think they were untouchable and they
started to plan major robberies again.

A week after the botched sting operation, Foley teamed
up with Eamon Daly, Cahill's brother, John, and a skilled
armed robber by the name of 'Factory' John Gilligan. The
plan was to carry out an armed robbery on Portlaoise post
office. When they hit, on 3 October 1987, the job went
like clockwork and they escaped with £100,000 in cash,
cheques and registered letters. It was a welcome return to
form for the gang and although gardaí strongly suspected
the gang, there was little they could do to prove that they
were responsible.

Foley and John Gilligan teamed up again soon afterwards
and robbed a large consignment of cattle drench from the
Raheen Co-op, near Abbeyleix in County Laois. Next the
new partners made off with a truckload of Aran jumpers,
stolen from a factory in Falcarragh in Donegal. Gilligan
made his escape in the truck but somehow forgot Foley,

who was left to make his own way back to Dublin.

This persistent taunting of the gardaí was getting to the authorities and the situation was further exacerbated in late 1987 when Martin Cahill broke into the office of the Director of Public Prosecutions and stole 145 extremely sensitive criminal files. The files related to pending trials involving members of Cahill's gang and his family, as well as to cases of murder, armed robbery and drugs offences. The cheeky criminals later used the stolen files as bargaining chips when they were stopped and questioned by gardaí or were facing serious charges.

Other serious crimes were taking place, leading to newspaper headlines and public outrage. The government was left red-faced and crime became a major electoral issue. Out of control INLA man Dessie O'Hare kidnapped Dublin dentist John O'Grady in November 1987 and went on the run, evading gardaí for nearly four weeks. O'Hare even chopped off the dentist's little fingers and left them in a church in County Carlow. The kidnapper was eventually captured after a shoot-out.

The O'Hare saga was not long ended when French police intercepted a ship called the *Eskund*, containing a massive haul of arms destined for the IRA. The Libyan leader Colonel Gadaffi had given them as a gift to the terror group and the shocked government declared a national emergency, with 8,000 troops being deployed along with the gardaí to search 50,000 properties across the country. Embarrassingly, Operation Mallard resulted in just two empty underground arms bunkers being discovered.

The gardaí were under more pressure than ever to get to grips with crime and to put away the likes of Martin Cahill and Martin Foley. Detective Superintendent Ned Ryan and his officers had been arguing for years for more resources to take on the pair of brazen criminals, but their pleas had fallen on deaf ears. However, in late 1987 Eamonn Doherty was appointed the new garda commissioner and given strict orders to enforce the law and stop criminals and subversives running amok. Doherty immediately called a meeting of his senior managers at Garda Headquarters and reviewed the intelligence files on all of Dublin's most serious criminals. Commissioner Doherty didn't need to be told that Martin Cahill and the likes of Martin Foley, Eamon Daly and Shavo Hogan were causing his force the most headaches on the ground. He asked the question: 'What are we going to do about this man Cahill?' Detective Chief Superintendent John Murphy, the head of the city's Central Detective Unit, which incorporated the Serious Crime, Fraud and Drug Squads, was the first officer to answer. Over the next few minutes he proposed a tactic that would put The General and The Viper under unprecedented pressure. The plan would change the criminals' lives and drive them both close to breaking point.

You've Been Tangoed

DETECTIVE CHIEF SUPERINTENDENT JOHN Murphy's plan was simple but effective. It was arguably brilliant, and arguably a waste of money. He told Commissioner Doherty that if he and his elite detectives were given unlimited resources they could put the Cahill gang out of business within six months. He proposed an in-your-face surveillance operation designed to harass and antagonise the gang members as much as possible. A similar tactic had been successfully used by the London Metropolitan Police in tackling the infamous Kray twins in the late sixties. At worst, the highly-visible garda presence would reassure the general public and leave people in no doubt that the authorities were taking action against the gangsters.

Doherty agreed to the formation of a large squad of gardaí to overtly watch designated targets twenty-four hours a day, seven days a week. The majority of the squad would be made up of experienced Central Detective Unit (CDU) detectives who already reported to Murphy, but he was also given permission to recruit fifteen young, ambitious, hard-nosed uniformed officers. Some of them had been gardaí for no more than a year, but they all had good reputations.

On 7 December 1987 ninety gardaí met at Harcourt Square in Dublin and were addressed by Chief Superintendent Murphy, who was in charge of the unit. Also present was Murphy's deputy, Detective Superintendent Noel Conroy (who would later be appointed garda commissioner). The two senior officers briefed the assembled gardaí about the new Special Surveillance Unit (SSU) as it was to be officially known. The squad was divided into four teams, each commanded by an experienced CDU detective sergeant. The four detective sergeants were Felix McKenna (who would later head up the Criminal Assets Bureau), Noel Keane, Denis Donegan and Martin Callinan (the current garda commissioner).

Seven primary surveillance targets were identified: Martin Foley, Martin Cahill, Shavo Hogan, Eamon Daly, Christy Dutton, Noel Lynch and Cahill's brother-in-law, John Foy. Tabs could also be kept on other criminals if and when it was necessary. The object of the surveillance was to stick like glue to the assigned target, to try to prevent the seven targets from meeting, and to cut the seven main men off from other criminals, who probably wouldn't want to be seen around the targets when gardaí were observing them. Basically, gardaí were trying to isolate the gang from other criminals and make it impossible for them to operate.

The squad were given criminal profiles of each of the targets, as well as a list of their likes, dislikes, habits and quirks. Detective Superintendent Ned Ryan, who knew Cahill and his cohorts best, told the new unit: 'They'll put everything up to you and you must be prepared to give as good as you get. They cannot see that you are afraid of them.'

Each of the seven main targets was given a number. Martin Cahill was Target One, or Tango One; Foley was Target Seven, or Tango Seven. Thus the Special Surveillance Unit became commonly known as Tango Squad, a term that has gone down in garda history. The Tango Squad underwent an intensive three-week training course in the use of firearms and driving techniques and were put through the mill to test each garda's mental strength and resolve. By the end of the training there were just over seventy men and women remaining in the squad.

Tango Squad was scheduled to begin operations on 1 January 1988. The seven targets probably had sore heads on New Year's Day after the festivities of the previous night. They must have thought they were still drunk when they looked out their front windows to see gardaí standing casually outside their gardens, waving and grinning at the criminals like they were old friends. Each unit had around six officers attached to it and they had the permanent use of three official cars for the purpose of tailing their target.

Eamon Daly probably didn't know it, but the first sign that his world was turning on its head had come the night before when he was stopped by gardaí close to the Rathmines Inn. He was asked to get out of his car to be breathalysed and after he was given the all clear and sent on his way, he found that all four of his tyres had been slashed. The General traditionally ordered a spate of tyre slashings in middle-class areas whenever a member of his gang had been in trouble with the law. Now the gardaí were sending a message that they could play the criminals at their own game.

On the morning of New Year's Day, Martin Cahill went out to his car with his wife and children and was greeted by jeering gardaí, shouting at him from one of their unmarked cars. Cahill was bemused and he told them to 'Fuck off away from me.' The guards responded by telling him he had better get used to the attention. Cahill drove away angrily, followed closely by the gardaí. Frustrated, the criminal slammed on his brakes, causing the unmarked car to rear-end him. The gardaí laughed as The General complained of whiplash and was brought off to hospital.

There were similar scenes at the homes of the other six targets. Shavo Hogan later recalled: 'The first week it started we thought, *This is great craic*, but it became a nightmare, beeping horns and shining torches into the house at night. It really fucked up everything. You could not go out for a drink without a cop sitting beside you.'

Often the seven targets would be stopped and searched by the Tango Squad only to be stopped again a few hundred yards down the road. They couldn't go anywhere without being followed. Visitors to the targets' homes were stopped and questioned and it soon began to wear down the criminals – all of them except for Cahill, that is, who let on that he didn't mind at all.

Martin Foley found the attention particularly gruelling and would lose his temper at the drop of a hat, which provoked furious laughter from his surveillance squad, causing him to become even angrier.

In the first month of the round-the-clock surveillance the gang did little or no 'work'. The media had a field day with the surveillance and the public couldn't get enough stories about criminals trying to go about their business while being tailed by the gardaí and shouted at. Whenever Foley saw a TV camera or a journalist he spat and snarled and threatened, his days as the media liaison for the

Concerned Criminals far behind him. Martin Cahill took a different tack, however. On 10 February Cahill was stopped on the street by Brendan O'Brien of RTÉ's *Today Tonight* programme. He had just collected his £92-a-week dole payment. The journalist put it to Cahill that he was the crime boss known as The General. Instead of getting angry Cahill gave an impromptu interview.

He told O'Brien, 'There must be another Martin Cahill somewhere else.'

O'Brien said, 'I'm sure there is another Martin Cahill. Well who do you think The General is?'

'I don't know; some army officer, maybe.'

He told O'Brien he didn't know he was being followed by gardaí because 'I never see them; I never see them. Seriously, I don't see them at all.' The RTÉ man said that the gardaí had circulated notices saying Cahill was wanted for a series of robberies in rural Ireland and asked him if he knew why they had done that. 'I suppose they're trying to blacken me for some reason. Ah, I know why they're blackenin' me; it's Ned Ryan,' he said, referring to the Garda Detective Superintendent he despised so much.

When asked about the Beit robbery, Cahill said he was working as a private detective for his friend Noel Lynch and that 'I am on standby with Martin Foley and Eamon Daly for a job to get them [stolen paintings] back.'

It wasn't just Cahill who was paid a visit by the *Today Tonight* reporter. Christy Dutton was cornered coming out of a bookies' on Meath Street when O'Brien confronted him. 'I know nothing about any crimes, right,' he shouted before attacking O'Brien and the cameraman, who he pushed to the ground. Shavo Hogan and Eamon Daly were also filmed as they came out of court, but they wisely said nothing.

Cahill might have thought the interview was harmless but it caused a national outcry and focused even more attention on the gang. Cahill was the subject of a Dáil debate, and Progressive Democrats leader, Dessie O'Malley, asked the obvious question: why did Cahill still have a council house when he also owned a house worth £80,000 in an upmarket South Dublin estate? 'I am not entirely clear as to the reason for this, except perhaps either property is not big enough for him to hang his collection of paintings. Perhaps he needs two houses so he can gaze at his collection of seventeenth century Dutch masters,' mused O'Malley. Cahill's dole payments were suspended pending an investigation into how he could afford a private house when he had no declared income.

Cahill also got an ear bashing from Martin Foley after Foley was contacted by the Department of Social Welfare, asking why he was working as a private investigator when he was claiming the dole. Foley told the Department that he didn't know who The General was and that he planned to sue him for defamation over the comments.

Noel Lynch and Christy Dutton were also fuming over Cahill's playing to the cameras and they thought that it would only make a difficult situation worse.

The pressure was taking its toll on Foley. On 19 February he and Shavo Hogan were driving from their native Crumlin into Dublin city centre, tailed by the three Tango cars. One of the unmarked vehicles went ahead of Foley as he drove down Lower Bridge Street. The driver slammed on his brakes and Foley rammed into the back of him. A furious Foley got out of his car and started shouting and cursing at the gardaí in the middle of the road. The Viper then claimed that he wasn't feeling well and demanded that an ambulance be called. Foley and Hogan were taken to St James's Hospital in surgical collars, followed by the two gardaí.

The Viper was lying in a bed waiting to see a doctor when Detective Garda Gerry O'Connell visited to make sure that Foley was okay, not that he was in any doubt that the whole charade was a crude attempt by the two criminals to get compensation from the State. Foley took grave offence to the visit and, despite his injuries, jumped out of bed and punched the young officer square in the jaw. He knocked the officer out and broke his jaw in three places with a cheap sucker punch. Detective Garda O'Connell slumped to the ground and his colleagues and medical staff rushed to help him. The badly injured officer was treated and Foley was taken into custody as soon as the doctors established that there was nothing wrong with him.

After he was released from Kevin Street Garda Station, The Viper went to collect his car, but it broke down almost as soon as he started it. Someone had poured a large bag of sugar into the petrol tank. As Foley cursed his misfortune, Tango Squad members, obviously furious that their colleague had been viciously assaulted, looked on and smiled.

The following day Foley appeared before a special sitting of Dublin District Court, where he was charged with dangerous driving arising out of the car accident that had put him in hospital. He was also charged with assaulting Detective Garda O'Connell. He was remanded in custody for three days or until he came up with £1,000 bail money.

On St Patrick's Day 1988 Foley was again in trouble with the law, when he was charged with assaulting Detective Garda Conor O'Reilly at Foley's home, of being in possession of a crossbow and arrows with the intention to cause grievous bodily harm and of being in breach of the peace.

When the trial got underway in June, evidence was heard that Foley had been under garda surveillance for the previous six months. Detective Gardaí Conor O'Reilly and Seán Hogan gave evidence of following Foley home in the early hours of 17 March. Foley's wife, Pauline, was driving the car and Foley was sitting in the front passenger seat. The Foleys left the Rathmines Inn at 11.45 p.m., drove to Swan Grove in Rathmines and went into Martin Cahill's house, where a St Patrick's Day party was in full swing. At 3.30 a.m. Foley and his wife emerged from the party with Eamon Daly and his wife. Pauline Foley drove to Meadowbanks, in Terenure, to drop the Dalys off and then headed home. At Lower Kimmage Road Pauline Foley slammed on the brakes and her husband jumped out of the car and ran towards the following patrol car, armed with an iron bar. He threatened to kill the two detectives and then hopped back into the car. When they arrived at Cashel Avenue, Foley threw stones and milk bottles at the gardaí, who had continued to tail them. He called the officers 'scum' and shouted, 'Next time I have a mask on I'll rip your head off.' Foley threatened the wives of the two detectives and told Conor O'Reilly that someday he would find his wife dead because Foley would 'slit her throat'. The clearly demented criminal then ran into his house and came out armed with a crossbow. He put an arrow in it and raised it to fire. At this point O'Reilly pulled out his official garda revolver and pointed it at Foley, shouting: 'Armed garda, drop your weapon.' The Viper ran back into his house when he saw the gun.

Martin Foley gave evidence that he had become hysterical after three garda cars and a motorcyclist had pulled in front of the car his wife was driving on six different occasions, repeatedly forcing them to stop. He claimed they had tried to drive to Terenure Garda Station to make a complaint but that the cars had blocked their way. When the Foleys got home there were more gardaí parked in their driveway. Martin said he asked them to stop harassing him and his wife but that they ignored him. He said he then went berserk and went into the house and got the crossbow, which he said was not loaded. He claimed that he only wanted to get rid of the gardaí. The Viper said he usually had a very good relationship with the detectives who were following him and that they sometimes asked him not to go jogging in the morning because they could not keep up with him. He said that the gardaí would go along with him when he went out for a jog or to walk his dog. Pauline Foley also took to the witness box and repeated the claim that three garda cars and a motorbike garda had all followed her car from the moment they left The General's house. At one point, she claimed, there were garda cars hemming her in on both her right and left sides while the garda on the motorbike slammed on his brakes in front of her. She said that other garda cars obstructed her for five or ten minutes.

Foley's defence solicitor, Garret Sheehan, said that his client's account of what happened was the only reasonable explanation of events and that the gardaí had deliberately provoked Martin Foley into committing the offence. Detective Sergeant Felix McKenna, who was the head of the Tango Squad unit involved, said only one car had followed Foley from Meadowbank to Cashel Avenue and he suggested that Foley had become agitated because of the amount of drink he had taken.

Judge Brian Kirby convicted the thirty-six-year-old of

assault and breach of the peace saying, 'A crossbow is a lethal weapon.' But the judge said there was 50/50 doubt about whether the crossbow was loaded, so he dismissed the charge of possession of the weapon with intent to cause grievous bodily harm.

Garret Sheehan said he would like to hear Judge Kirby's opinion of Pauline Foley's claims about the behaviour of the gardaí on the journey home from Martin Cahill's house and he claimed that if what she said was true it would place her husband's behaviour in context and should be treated as a mitigating factor when it came to sentencing. He added that Foley was an unemployed tyre fitter and that his wife was pregnant with their second child. Judge Kirby said that a lot of extraneous matters had been brought up by both sides and that the evidence seemed to have been put together over a long period of time and it had been suggested to him that it had been taken from newspaper reports going back over two or three months. He said that every day on television you could see police forces in other jurisdictions using machine guns to deal with people who threw stones and bottles at them. 'Fortunately, this cool, calm, well-trained detective did not use force. In my view he very calmly and bravely dealt with it.' Judge Kirby said that common sense had prevailed and that Foley had put down the crossbow and gone back into his house. He added that there was conflict in Foley's evidence about garda harassment and he did not accept that there were three or four garda cars around Foley's house or that gardaí had played 'Ring Around the Rosie' on the Lower Kimmage Road, as Foley and his wife had alleged. The judge also said that the breaches of the peace charge was aggravated by some of the threatening and offensive language used by

Foley and he accepted that the garda evidence in relation to this was true. He also said the fact that Foley had admitted to having been at 'a good long session' at a pub and then at a boozy house party in Martin Cahill's house probably contributed to what happened.

Detective Sergeant Felix McKenna said that Foley had thirty-one previous criminal convictions, committed mainly before 1979. The convictions were mostly for road traffic offences but included seven prison sentences between 1970 and 1979 for receiving stolen property, obstruction, possession of house-breaking implements, assault on a garda and possession of an offensive weapon.

Judge Kirby sentenced Foley to six months in prison for the assault charge but said he would suspend it because he had no convictions since 1979 and had not been in prison so far in the 1980s.

One would expect that after clashing with the gardaí during two very serious incidents over the previous few months, Foley would have counted his blessings, realised he was lucky not to be in jail and calmed down a bit. But that wasn't his style. Shortly after the trial he turned up outside the base of Tango Squad at Harcourt Square in central Dublin and demanded to meet a detective with whom he had a major gripe. The garda came down to meet Foley and the furious criminal challenged him to a 'straightener' on the street. The garda laughed at Foley and told him to go on his way or he would be arrested.

Foley's claims in court that he had a cordial relationship with the Tango Squad were rubbish; he despised them and was aggressive and argumentative with them at every possible turn. When out walking his rottweiler dogs, which he bred, he would regularly snarl that he was more than happy to let them loose on the detectives to see who would win the fight. The fearless gardaí gave as good as they got, and told Foley that if he let the dogs off their leads they would have no option but to shoot them.

Although Foley was a hard man he also had a soft side: he loved his dogs and was devoted to his wife and two young daughters. On one occasion, while Foley was walking one of his dogs in Poddle Park, a detective walked up to him and admired the animal. He asked Foley if he bred the dog himself. Foley didn't realise he was being set up for a fall, and when he said that he did, the detective, deadpan, replied: 'Oh, I thought so all right; he looks the spit of you.' The Viper, realising he had been had, told the plainclothes man where to go in no uncertain terms, while the rest of the Tango Squad unit laughed at him.

The gardaí regularly played another trick on Foley, and he invariably fell for it. The Tango targets started to dress identically in anoraks and balaclavas and would emerge together from Cahill's house and scatter in different directions to try to throw off the waiting gardaí. The police would randomly shout out 'Daly' or 'Hogan' to try to get the hood to look around, but the criminals were too cute and rarely responded. Except for Foley, that is, who could never resist looking around when his name was called. The Tango members got a good laugh out of how he always fell for it.

The Viper was given a break from the intensive surveillance in July 1988, when he was jailed for six months. He was convicted of assaulting a garda detective in Ballyfermot on 21 January 1988 and of a breach of the peace on the same day. He was also convicted of another assault on the same detective and breach of the peace after another incident outside his home on 24 January. He was given two concurrent six-month sentences for the assaults and was bound over on good behaviour for three years on the breach of the peace charges, with a bond of £1,000. He was warned that he would face an immediate one-month prison sentence when he was released from serving the six-month sentence if he intimidated the garda or his family.

The Cahill gang was increasingly unhappy with how they were being treated and the members decided they would make life as difficult as possible for Tango Squad. They thought the best tactic would be to intimidate the mostly young gardaí who had been so doggedly pursuing them and hope that they would back off if they were scared. The gang began using counter-surveillance techniques, following the officers to their homes. When a garda stopped them, they asked how the officer's wife was and used her name. They would casually drop the name of an officer's child and say they saw them in the yard of their school that morning, making sure to mention the name of the school.

Martin Cahill took a sick pleasure from this approach and would often drive to the home of the Tango Squad member who was following him and flash his headlamps into the garda's front room. Cahill's message was clear: 'I know where you live and I am a dangerous man.' Ned Ryan had warned the squad to expect such behaviour from their targets. He had gone through similar experiences with Cahill and told the young cops that they had to stand their ground and not give an inch. It was sometimes hard, though. One detective, who always sat right beside his target when he went into a pub, was told in graphic detail what happens when a bullet is shot through a man's head.

Cahill organised for young thugs who looked up to him and his gang to steal cars, go joyriding in them and then smash into garda cars to put them off the road. He organised for dozens of cars in middle-class estates to have their tyres slashed each night, in an effort to turn public opinion against the operation. The following day the criminals would often find that their own car tyres had been slashed in retaliation.

Cahill even managed to have the greens dug up at the garda golf club in Stackstown, so that the gardaí couldn't enjoy a relaxing eighteen holes in their spare time.

Five gardaí were openly threatened by the gang. Many of the Tango Squad members grew beards, changed their hairstyles and routinely slept with their official firearm under their pillows. An informant claimed Cahill had taken out a contract on Ned Ryan because he blamed him for the surveillance operation. Detective Sergeant Gerry O'Carroll, armed with a gun, moved into the Ryan household for two months to make sure his boss wasn't targeted. Ryan refused to be intimidated and he used the death threats to make the young gardaí even more determined to nail Cahill and company.

A week after Martin Foley was arrested and charged over the assault of Detective Garda O'Connell, two other Tango targets were also nabbed. Shavo Hogan and John Foy were arrested as they were about to carry out an armed robbery in Walkinstown. A uniformed garda chased Hogan, and as the robber tried to make his escape, he turned to open fire on the garda. But his gun jammed and seconds later a garda van bumped into him to stop his escape and he was arrested. In the back of the squad car Hogan tried to strangle an officer with a walkie-talkie strap and he broke another member's nose when he punched him in the face.

Hogan was jailed for eight years. He also pleaded guilty to two other charges of assaulting Detective Sergeant Noel White during a Tango Squad search of his house, in Walkinstown. John Foy was jailed for seven years over the same incident.

In March 1988 Eamon Daly was arrested with three other men during an attempted robbery of the Atlantic Homecare DIY store in Stillorgan, South Dublin. He was charged with attempted robbery and possession of a firearm and was remanded in custody until his trial date. He received a twelve-year jail sentence and a further five years for another armed robbery.

The day after Daly's arrest, Martin Foley went to Martin Cahill's home in Cowper Downs, in Rathmines, and joined The General on top of his pigeon loft. Cahill often sat on top of the loft and shouted abuse at the detectives watching him, singing songs to them and offering them cash.

While the two hoods sat on the loft, a video camera was recording them from Cahill's back window. Cahill suddenly began shouting abuse in the direction of an elderly neighbour's home, accusing the retired businessman of cooperating with the gardaí. Cahill jumped down off the loft and shouted sexual obscenities about his neighbour's invalid wife. Foley, obviously well briefed by his partner in crime, then started throwing stones at Cahill, shouting: 'We will get you Cahill; we will burn you out.' He did this in a country accent, pretending to be a garda. Cahill turned and shouted back at The Viper, 'Guard, get off me wall.'

The Tango Squad members looked on with open mouths, thinking the pair had finally lost their marbles. Bizarrely, the criminals were trying to make it look like Cahill was being assaulted by his detail and they were attempting to record the 'stoning' as evidence.

Cahill tried every tactic in the book to frustrate his detail and cause as much trouble as possible. He burnt down three houses in his own estate and taunted the gardaí about how hot it was as he watched the fire brigades arrive to put out the infernos. When one detective called him a 'dirt bird', Cahill went to a nearby bin, took out a mouldy sandwich and started eating it in front of the disgusted officer. Cahill told his gang that it took days for the putrid taste to leave his mouth. On another occasion a detective was in a tree overlooking Cahill's house when The General sneaked up behind him and shouted 'Boo!', startling the garda into falling out of the tree with a bang. Cahill retreated into his house laughing.

Cahill had become a household name. After he was arrested following the slashing of tyres on 197 cars in Rathmines, a posse of photographers was waiting to snap him when he was released from the Bridewell. The *Irish Independent* printed a photograph on the front page of Cahill walking up the street, followed by Tango Squad's Detective Sergeant Denis Donegan. The caption read, 'The hooded Martin Cahill leaving the Bridewell in Dublin yesterday … but the law wasn't far behind.'

The General again made the front pages of all the newspapers when he dressed in Mickey Mouse shorts and T-shirt for his and the public's amusement.

But Cahill was becoming isolated from his gang members, who were avoiding him because he was so unpredictable and erratic. The gang was dissipating and Cahill was losing his power. Christy Dutton and Noel Lynch told Cahill that they were leaving the gang and going their separate ways because they could no longer handle the relentless scrutiny. Martin Foley, Eamon Daly, Shavo Hogan and John Foy were all in jail. And in June 1988 Cahill himself was sentenced to three months on Spike Island prison for failing to pay a fine levied on him after he admitting threatening his neighbours.

At this point the decision was taken to disband the Tango Squad. The attitude of garda management was that they had done what they had set out to do by curtailing the gang's activities and they had secured a number of heavy sentences for some of the key players.

The effectiveness of the Tango Squad has been the subject of much debate within the force since it was scrapped. Some argue that it was successful, but that it did not put the gang totally out of business as had been John Murphy's aim. It had failed to bring any worthwhile charges against Martin Cahill, who essentially sentenced himself to the three months he served for not paying a fine he could easily have afforded. Nevertheless the gardaí had shown that they were able to deal with the dual threats of subversives and organised crime and that they would not sit back while the likes of Foley and Cahill ran riot, robbing all around them.

The General didn't go away, though. In May 1989, a senior social welfare official, Brian Purcell, who was due to testify against Cahill in a bid to have his dole payments stopped, was abducted and shot in both legs. Purcell was seriously injured and while recovering in hospital he received a get well card with the message: 'The General prognosis is good.' There was no doubt that Cahill was behind the atrocity. Purcell recovered from his injuries and is now secretary general at the Department of Justice.

Foley served four months of his six-month sentence, in the high-security Portlaoise Prison. He spent most of his time working out, lifting weights and running around the exercise yard. He still had to face trial for assaulting Detective Garda O'Connell and he wasn't looking forward to it one bit. Foley knew he would most likely be jailed for longer than six months for the savage and unprovoked attack. His trial was due to get under way in October 1989 and he had no option but to plead guilty and accept his medicine. Anyway, most of his close friends from the gang were already serving long stretches for armed robberies, so he would have plenty of company inside.

But at the last minute Foley decided that he didn't want to go back to prison and be parted from Pauline and his two girls. He upped sticks and fled to England with his family, where he stayed with relations of his wife. He failed to turn up for the trial but was still in touch with his friends and neighbours in Crumlin, so gardaí knew where he was. They applied to have him extradited after he didn't show up in court, but it took nearly six months for the paperwork to come through. Foley was finally brought back to Ireland in March 1990 and was remanded in custody. Two months later he appeared before the Special Criminal Court, where he pleaded guilty to assaulting Detective Garda Gerry O'Connell, causing actual bodily harm on 19 February 1988.

Detective Sergeant John O'Mahony told the court that

Detective Garda O'Connell was knocked unconscious by Foley's savage punch to his left cheek and that his cheekbone was shattered. He said the brave garda was out of work for over a year and was still receiving medical care as a result of the assault. Dr Brendan O'Reilly, who treated the detective at St James's Hospital, said the force necessary to cause such an injury was 'quite massive'.

Adrian Hardiman, Foley's senior counsel, said his client had been under twenty-four-hour garda surveillance for six months. 'It came to the point where most of his acquaintances and family would have nothing more to do with him. He became virtually a banned person.' Hardiman added that Foley was prone to panic attacks and was treated with tranquilisers.

DS O'Mahony told the judge that Foley had thirty-three previous convictions, eleven of which were for crimes of violence. Foley was jailed for two years and forfeited the £1,000 he had lodged as bail money.

Martin Foley's brutal assault on Gerry O'Connell had massive consequences for the courageous young garda and his family. O'Connell had been diagnosed with multiple sclerosis in 1985. He showed few signs of the illness – the occasional tingle in his arms or legs was the only symptom he experienced. His condition never interfered with his work and colleagues of the young detective said he was one of the best and most dedicated members of the Tango Squad, who lived for his job and loved being a garda.

O'Connell had been marked for greatness in the force from an early age and was made a plainclothes detective just two years after graduating from Templemore, which is almost unheard of. The detective, who was from Pinewood in Glasnevin, prided himself on his ability to relate to

criminals and talk to them as ordinary people, despite the
fact that they often had little or no respect for the forces of
law and order.

After Foley assaulted him, Gerry O'Connell's health
went rapidly downhill. Just days after being released from
hospital he started to show more serious symptoms of MS.
The force of the blow with which Foley had struck him
had caused a massive head injury, and his brain had been
badly affected by the trauma. Although Detective Garda
O'Connell briefly returned to work, it was obvious that the
assault had caused his MS to deteriorate very quickly, and
he eventually required twenty-four hour care.

Garda O'Connell sadly lost his battle for life in May
1993, five years after being assaulted by Martin Foley. He
was just thirty-five years old.

Foley had been charged with assaulting the brave garda,
not killing him, and it is unfair on Foley to say that he was
responsible for the onset of Detective Garda O'Connell's
multiple sclerosis. Nevertheless, it is no coincidence that
he became very seriously ill so soon after the trauma to his
brain caused by Foley's unprovoked and angry punch.

The shocking assault by The Viper on Gerry O'Connell
is still a cause of great anger and bitterness to the garda's
colleagues, nearly twenty-years after he passed away. One
of his former Tango Squad colleagues said, 'It would be
hard to meet a more dedicated garda than Gerry. He lived
for his family and his job and was absolutely crazy about
being a guard and trying to make society better by taking on
the likes of Martin Foley and other criminals. He was such
a decent and honest person and what happened to him was
a real tragedy. He simply wasn't well enough to work again
after the attack and you can only imagine how hard that was

for a man who was in love with his job. But he showed great courage and bravery during his illness, which was typical of the man. No matter what Martin Foley does in life, he will never be able to make up for what he did in that hospital that day. Gerry was only doing his job and he was viciously assaulted for absolutely no reason. I hope that Foley regrets what he did but many of us will never be able to forgive him for his actions that day. He will never be able to make amends and we will never get Gerry back. He is still missed by so many people.'

After he was jailed for the assault, Foley shared a cell with Shavo Hogan in Portlaoise and the two became inseparable. Meanwhile Martin Cahill had formed suspicions that Hogan was a garda informer. His evidence was fairly flimsy. He suspected that Hogan had provided the gardaí with information that led to John Foy being arrested while on his way to pick up guns for another armed robbery. Cahill had been the target of the garda operation but he left the scene just minutes before the cops struck. Cahill had also accused Hogan of planting a pistol that was later seized during a search of his home.

Cahill put the word out that Hogan had been ratting and he ordered that he be targeted in Portlaoise and taught a lesson. Hogan meanwhile vehemently denied that he had ever given information to gardaí. He was segregated from the rest of the prison population in September 1990 for his own protection. Martin Foley stood by his mate and told the other gang members that Hogan wasn't a tout and that Cahill had become paranoid. This caused tensions and created divisions within the mob.

On the morning of 8 October 1990 Hogan was exercising alone in the yard at the back of the E1 landing when he was set upon by three men, including fellow gang member Harry Melia. The attackers used the leg of a table, which had been fashioned into a crude knife, to slice off the tips of both Hogan's ears. It was an old gangland ritual reserved for people who are suspected of being informants. The object is to make the victim resemble a rat. Hogan needed forty stitches and later successfully sued the State for compensation.

Foley was furious with Cahill over the attack and both sides issued threats. Foley reminded The General that Hogan was one of the few people who knew where the Beit paintings were stashed and that slicing off the tips of his ears would only encourage him to talk to gardaí, if indeed he was an informer, and Foley still did not believe he was. Cahill sent a message that Hogan was not to be touched again, but the damage had been done. The relationship between Foley and Cahill broke down for good.

Old resentments bubbled to the surface. The Viper felt that Cahill's behaviour had exacerbated the garda surveillance and brought too much heat on the rest of the gang. He was also annoyed that none of the gang made a penny from the Beit robbery because of Cahill's ill-judged insistence on cutting Paddy Shanahan out of the job. Foley had never been comfortable with The General's treatment of Shanahan, especially as the job had been Shanahan's idea in the first place.

Martin Cahill then started spreading rumours that maybe it hadn't been Seamus Hogan talking to the authorities, but Foley. This caused yet more bad feeling and recriminations and the old friends became confirmed enemies.

Cahill gave an interview to British magazine *GQ* in 1991, in which he discussed his falling out with Foley. He said that Foley had tried to set him up to be arrested and that the assault of Detective Garda O'Connell had been set up by the gardaí and Foley. Cahill claimed that Foley came to him and said they had to come up with a plan to do something about the injured garda so that he would be unable to give evidence in The Viper's assault case. Cahill claimed that Foley was trying to lure him into a trap that would get him locked up and he told Foley that he wanted nothing to do with it.

Foley also broke his silence about the bust-up in 2001, saying: 'I walked away from Martin in 1991 because he went off the rails. It was nothing to do with money or informing. But the reason me and Martin parted friendship, I will carry that secret to the grave. I don't want to dig up old sores. I walked away because I wasn't happy with something that he done and somebody else went and got involved. No matter what has been claimed, Martin never accused me of being an informant or a rat. I wouldn't be friends with his brothers if I was a rat.'

Whatever happened between the pair, they never worked together again.

The trial of the three men charged with assaulting Shavo Hogan was due to get underway in May 1991. Harry Melia, Christopher Shannon and Martin Ryan were all facing stiff sentences if they were convicted. The court was told that two army battalions and helicopters would be needed to provide security because eighteen serious criminals had been subpoenaed to give testimony for the defence. These included the 'Border Fox' Dessie O'Hare, Eamon Daly and Larry Dunne. The barrister for the State said that the witness list was designed to cause mayhem and was an abuse of the process of the court because none of the 'witnesses' had actually witnessed the assault. However, on the day the evidence was due to get underway the State entered a nolle prosequi and withdrew the charges on the grounds that Hogan refused to testify against the men – hardly the actions of an informant.

Foley and Hogan had come to believe that armed robberies were for mugs. They decided that when they were released from prison they would do what Cahill had never permitted; they were going to move into the drug trade.

The New Guard

AFTER HIS RELEASE FROM prison in 1992, Foley kept his head down. He spent a lot of time at home with Pauline and his two girls, making up for lost time after his prison stretch. He had missed his family and he vowed that he would never be sent down again.

Foley and Hogan were still involved in robberies and general criminality but it wasn't until the end of 1994 that the pair got their act together and began buying small quantities of cannabis, which they turned around, making modest profits. They brought a young protégé of Foley's, Clive 'Wigsy' Bolger, into the partnership and he acted as the salesman, selling the drugs to young associates. The trio were initially supplied by Eamon Daly, Foley's old friend and neighbour from Cashel Avenue. Daly was in turn sourcing his drugs from Foley's old occasional partner in crime, 'Factory' John Gilligan. However, Foley's gang soon established its own contacts in the UK and were supplied from there. Gilligan and Daly knew this but turned a blind eye because the gang was so small and wasn't likely to step on bigger players' toes.

Foley, Hogan and Bolger did what all smart criminals did and stayed away from the actual product, leaving young mules to handle the drugs and take all the risks for little reward. The principle of staying at an arm's length from the drugs you owned was established in the 1980s by Ireland's first major importers of drugs, the Dunne family. Larry Dunne had masterminded the importation of massive amounts of heroin, but would never so much as look at the stuff, never mind touch it. The foot soldiers who handled the gear always joked that 'Larry doesn't carry' because their boss knew that if gardaí seized one of his shipments they wouldn't be able to physically link it to him because he would never have come into contact with it. This made it next to impossible for officers to prosecute him, even though they knew he was the beneficial owner.

With a ready supply of good product available through the UK supplier, the Three Amigos distributed drugs around Crumlin and Drimnagh, on a small scale at first, but they had grand designs and were determined to get bigger. Foley and Hogan sold only cannabis and ecstasy, and Foley made it clear that he would not consider selling heroin. He had been shocked and disgusted by what the drug had done to local kids in the 1980s and he didn't want to be associated with it. He probably felt that cannabis and ecstasy were recreational drugs and were not addictive, unlike heroin. If people wanted to smoke a bit of pot or pop a pill at the weekend, he was happy to help them out. He wasn't feeding the habits of junkies or getting kids hooked on heroin, so he was doing nobody any harm.

By the time The Viper decided to dip his toe into the drug trade, John Gilligan had graduated from robbing factories to become the undisputed king of the Irish drugs market.

Gilligan was born in Ballyfermot, in Dublin, in March 1952 and got involved in crime in his early teens. He received his first conviction in July 1967, after he was nabbed stealing chickens from a farmer in Rathfarnham. He was charged with larceny and given the benefit of the Probation Act. Gilligan went to work with his father, John Snr, as a seaman with the B&I Line. He spent a decade working there, and he and his father and several other workers devised a scam where they would let hundreds of passengers onto the ferries but would register only half of them, pocketing the extra cash for themselves. Gilligan eventually left the company in the early 1980s and was rated as very good in his employment record, having completed thirty-six voyages. B&I must have been understanding employers because they stood by him when he was sent to prison for the first time, in 1976, to serve six months for theft.

Gilligan met his wife, Geraldine, when he was still a teenager and the couple had a son and a daughter by 1975 and had moved to a new estate in Corduff, in Blanchardstown, West Dublin. Gilligan decided that he would concentrate on robberies as a way of making ends meet and his main partners were John 'The Colonel' Cunningham, who was also involved in Martin Cahill's mob, and George 'The Penguin' Mitchell. These two criminals were instrumental in Gilligan's rise to the upper echelons of the drugs trade. Gilligan specialised in robbing containers that had just come off the ships in Dublin Port. He made good money selling consignments of toilet rolls and tracksuits in the working-class estates of West Dublin.

In 1977 Gilligan was jailed three times. He received an eighteen-month sentence for handling stolen property, three months for armed robbery and a year for a robbery at a bookmaker's store. When he was freed after serving less than a year for the three offences, he began to associate with truck drivers in various pubs in Ballyfermot. The truck drivers tipped him off when they were due to carry a valuable load and in return he paid them for the information. Becoming more ambitious, he moved on to large warehouses in industrial estates across West Dublin. He was so prolific that West Dublin became known as Gilligan's turf and other robbers avoided the area. He learned how to short-circuit alarms and even knocked holes in brick walls to break into factories.

Gilligan came up with the ingenious idea of robbing cars and setting them alight against the walls of factories. The fire brigade would eventually come and put out the blaze, but the intensity of the inferno would have weakened the walls of the factory, so when Gilligan arrived a couple of nights later, the wall would crumble when he drove a car into it.

Gilligan was a one-man crime wave in the early 1980s and security and alarm companies were so concerned that they had to develop more complex systems in an effort to thwart him. Before going to rob a factory or warehouse Gilligan carried out detailed surveillance and he knew the movements of security staff and the response times of the gardaí.

At the end of 1985, when gardaí were drawing up the list of the biggest criminals in Dublin, Martin Cahill and John Gilligan were Nos. 1 and 2 respectively. Intelligence reports described him as the most prolific burglar in Ireland and he was suspected of carrying out a robbery every week. Such was Gilligan's notoriety that when he was charged with robbing a builders' providers in Enniscorthy, County

Wexford, the Director of Public Prosecutions (DPP) decided that he should face trial before the non-jury Special Criminal Court, which normally dealt only with terrorists and the most serious criminals.

In November 1990 Gilligan was acquitted of burglary but convicted of receiving stolen goods and he was sentenced to four years in Portlaoise Prison. The judge said, 'He has been involved in serious crime for many years and it appears probable he has never had lawful employment.' He was half right.

When Gilligan was released from Portlaoise in September 1993, after serving an extra six months for assaulting a prison officer, he vowed that he was finished with prison life for good. Gilligan decided to become a drugs smuggler because it carried less risk and greater rewards. In Portlaoise Gilligan had befriended young Crumlin criminals Brian 'The Tosser' Meehan and Paul 'Hippo' Ward. He took the pair under his wing, thinking that they would be great enforcers when he started his new venture.

Around the same time, Gilligan's old associate John 'The Coach' Traynor was also looking to get into the drugs business and he had made useful international contacts while serving a jail sentence in the UK. The two men teamed up. Traynor had connections in the INLA and a long-standing relationship with Martin Cahill and Martin Foley. He used this relationship with Cahill to secure a £150,000 cash loan to start himself and Gilligan in business.

The new partners imported their first batch of cannabis in early December 1993, through Dublin Port. They had bought the drugs in Amsterdam through Simon Rahman, an associate of Traynor's. The consignment arrived at the port hidden in various legal products with legitimate paperwork, so the authorities never suspected a thing.

Gilligan and Traynor distributed the cannabis through Meehan and Ward, as well as through Peter 'Fatso' Mitchell. They paid Gilligan and Traynor up front and then sold the drugs on the street. The two Johns used the money from Meehan and Ward to fund further shipments. Within weeks regular shipments, each containing 100 kg of hash, were coming in on trucks through Dublin Port. By the summer of 1994, Gilligan and Traynor had imported over 1,000 kg of hash. They were paying £1,200 per kg and selling it to Meehan and the other dealers for around £2,000 per kg. They in turn sold it on the streets for an average of £2,300 per kg. In little more than six months Gilligan and Traynor made a profit of around £800,000, while Ward, Meehan and Mitchell split around £300,000. Former soldier, Charlie Bowden, was brought into the business and acted as a deliveryman, delivering large quantities of drugs to regular customers each week and returning with the cash owed to the mob.

The business continued to expand at an exponential rate. In August 1994 alone, Rahman organised the shipment of 900 kg of cannabis into the country, and the gang shared a profit of around £900,000. Gardaí estimated that John Gilligan's gang turned over just under £40 million in their first two years of business.

Martin Cahill, who by this stage was more unpredictable than ever due to the fact that he was refusing to take his medication for chronic diabetes, had heard about Traynor and Gilligan's meteoric rise to unimaginable riches and he came looking for his money back. He reckoned that he was owed £500,000 – £350,000 more than he had lent the pair to get started – as he felt that they would not be in business at all were it not for him. He also demanded a percentage of the men's future income. This went down like a lead balloon with Gilligan. Traynor made excuse after excuse to his old boss, saying that the rumours about them making a fortune were not true and that all their money was invested in product. Cahill was having none of it, though. He knew that Traynor was a conman and that he would try to talk his way out of the debt if he could.

Gilligan was determined not to pay a penny to Cahill and he decided to take him out rather than pay up. The INLA was willing to do the deed, as they had also been having troubles with Cahill. In July 1994 one of Cahill's relations was evicted from a Dublin Corporation flat she had been illegally living in for over a year. An INLA man was supposed to move into the flat but Cahill objected and said he wouldn't allow it. When the INLA ignored him and moved their man in, Cahill responded by burning the flat to the ground, causing huge tensions between the two parties.

The IRA had no objection to Cahill being taken out either. They blamed him for helping a UVF murder squad to organise an attack on a Sinn Féin fundraising event in the Widow Scallan's pub on Pearse Street, in Dublin's south inner city, in May 1994. An IRA man was shot dead as the hit squad tried to enter the pub with an 18 lb bomb. The squad fled before they could set off the bomb and a massacre was averted. Subsequently Gilligan and Traynor spread rumours that Cahill was responsible for tipping off the UVF about the fundraiser. The Provos requested a meeting with Cahill to discuss the incident, but he told them where to go, enflaming the situation.

The IRA also harboured resentment over the fact that they didn't receive a penny from the O'Connor's robbery, and they were furious that Cahill had sold some of the Beit paintings to the UVF, in a deal brokered by John Traynor.

Both Gilligan and Traynor had strong INLA connections from their stays in Portlaoise Prison and they held a series of meetings with senior figures in the organisation to discuss getting rid of Cahill.

On the afternoon of 18 August 1994 Martin 'The General' Cahill was sitting in his car on the corner of Oxford Road and Charleston Road, in Ranelagh. A gunman approached Cahill and fired five rounds from a .357 Magnum revolver at the criminal, from close range. Ireland's most notorious criminal died instantly, aged forty-five. There were few tears for Tango One's death as his increasingly erratic behaviour had made him too much of a liability. Nevertheless a host of criminals, including Martin Foley, turned up at his funeral to pay their respects. The INLA claimed responsibility for the murder in the hours after the shooting, but the IRA, using a recognised code word, also contacted Dublin newsrooms saying that they had murdered Cahill. The Provos gave information about the location of the getaway motorbike in order to add credibility to their claims. Bizarrely, following the IRA claim, the INLA again got in touch with journalists, recanted their earlier statement and denied any involvement. They even threatened to murder anyone who said that they had taken out Cahill and they confirmed that the Provos had been responsible.

The IRA propaganda magazine, *An Phoblacht*, ran the following statement following the murder:

> It was Cahill's involvement with, and assistance to, pro-British death squads which forced us to act. Cahill's gang was involved closely with the Portadown UVF gang which,

apart from countless sectarian murders in the twenty-six
counties, was responsible for the gun and bomb attack
on the Widow Scallan's pub. The IRA reserve the right to
execute those who finance or otherwise assist Loyalist
killer gangs. We have compiled a detailed file on the
involvement of other Dublin criminals with Loyalist death
squads. We call on those people to desist immediately
from such activity and to come forward to us within
fourteen days to clear their names.

It has never been fully determined who was responsible
for Martin Cahill's murder. Whoever it was, they have not
been caught, but in the years since, gardaí have received
intelligence that the INLA arranged for the IRA to take the
blame, or credit, for the murder and that each organisation
received £30,000 from the Gilligan gang and further
monthly payments as a form of protection money, to be
allowed to continue in business. The INLA, which was led
by the psychopathic Declan 'Whacker' Duffy, was given
drugs in exchange for high-powered weapons and his men
operated in tandem with the Gilligan mob.

It has been claimed that Martin Foley was abducted
by the IRA a month after Cahill's murder and questioned
about the likely whereabouts of The General's money. Foley
didn't want the same fate as Cahill to befall him, so he put
up less resistance than he had in the 1984 kidnap attempt.
He pleaded ignorance and was released unharmed.

This was the environment in which Martin 'The Viper'
Foley, Seamus 'Shavo' Hogan and Clive 'Wigsy' Bolger were
running their new business. Everyone was making money
with the blessing of Gilligan and his crew. Foley and his
cohorts seemed to be on to a winner because they had a
relationship with 'Factory' John going back twenty odd
years and they got on well.

Two months after Martin Cahill's execution, another one of the old guard met an untimely end. Paddy Shanahan, the UCD-educated middle-class villain who came up with the idea of robbing the Beit paintings but was shafted by Cahill, had gone legit, becoming a successful builder and property developer. Shanahan was shot dead as he walked into Speares gym in Crumlin. As with Martin Cahill's murder, there appeared to be no clear-cut reason why the forty-year-old was murdered. It has been speculated that John Gilligan ordered his murder because he suspected that Shanahan was informing gardaí about the criminals, from whom he was trying to distance himself. One of Gilligan's cronies, Eugene 'Dutchie' Holland, a known hitman, was arrested for questioning about the murder but was released without charge. Intriguingly, Shavo Hogan was also detained for questioning, but he was also released without any charges being brought. Infamously, while he was in custody for that crime, Hogan smeared his own excrement on his face in a bid to put detectives off questioning him. Nobody has ever been brought to justice for Shanahan's murder.

1995 was a steady year for the newly formed Foley/Hogan/Bolger drugs gang. They were sourcing their own drugs from the UK, with the knowledge and blessing of John Gilligan, and although they were buying just a couple of kilos of cannabis at a time and selling it on for a small profit, they were learning their trade and building their business. However, things very nearly came to a premature end when Foley found himself staring down the barrel of a gun towards the end of the year.

On the evening of 5 December 1995 Foley was visiting

a young woman at a flat in the Fatima Mansions complex, in Rialto, which had been the scene of several Concerned Parents Against Drugs marches in the 1980s. Despite being a married man, Foley was very close to the young woman and he called to her home several evenings a week to socialise with her. After spending a number of hours in the flat, he emerged at around 10.30 p.m. and was about to get into his car when a gunman stepped out of the shadows and opened fire with a .38 handgun, from just a few feet away. The Viper was hit in the arm and the stomach before he even knew what was going on. He fell to the ground but, realising he was in grave danger, he desperately moved from side to side and managed to avoid another shot fired from point-blank range.

The frustrated gunman fled the scene and locals dialled 999. When gardaí arrived at the scene Foley looked to be in a bad way. He thought he was going to die and told uniformed officers that the IRA had been responsible. He had good reason to believe this considering the number of run-ins he'd had with the IRA over the years.

Foley was rushed to nearby St James's Hospital, where doctors described his condition as satisfactory after they treated his chest and abdominal wounds. A hospital spokeswoman said his injuries were not minor but neither were they life threatening. Armed gardaí watched Foley for several days while he was in hospital, in case whoever shot him came back to finish the job.

Once Foley realised that he was going to be okay, he immediately changed his attitude and stopped cooperating with the gardaí. He wouldn't even tell them his name, not that it was a mystery to them. A garda spokesman said it was unclear whether the gunman meant to kill or merely to injury Foley, but certainly more than two shots had been fired at him. Newspapers wrote that gardaí were treating the incident as drugs related and that Foley might have been shot because of his burgeoning drug business. Minister for Justice Nora Owen said she was very concerned about the Foley shooting and that most incidents like this occurred as a result of thieves falling out.

Three other people had died as a result of gangland hits in the two months before Foley was targeted and there was predictable public outrage that criminals were settling scores with guns and killing each other. Two of the shooting victims, Eddie McCabe and Catherine Brennan, had been killed together in a car in Tallaght, and Shavo Hogan was later arrested for questioning about the double hit.

Gun murders were becoming worryingly common, but the amount of money being made by the Gilligan gang from drugs made assassinations inevitable; life became cheap. There were seven gangland murders in 1995, and after Foley's shooting the *Evening Herald* front-page headline, CITY ON THE BRINK OF MOB WAR, perfectly summed up the situation. However, as gardaí investigated the shooting, it became obvious to them that a professional hitman had not been responsible and that the shooter had shot wildly and then run away in panic instead of coldly finishing the job like an experienced gunman would.

Investigators soon determined that Foley was in fact shot because of his close friendship with the woman from Fatima Mansions. His reputation as a ladies' man had come back to haunt him. There was no mob or Provo involvement at all.

Detectives speculated that Foley knew the identity of the man who had tried to kill him and they appealed for a man on a bicycle who was in the area at the time of the shooting to come forward. A man who was known to Foley's lady friend was the only person arrested in relation to the shooting, but Foley refused to make a statement and the man was never charged. Gardaí categorised the shooting as a crime of passion. What Pauline Foley made of it all was anyone's guess.

Within weeks The Viper, who was forty-four years old at this stage, was back on his feet, despite serious injuries to his spleen, which had to be removed. He would live to fight another day and to stare down the barrel of another gun. He did find out the identity of the shooter and along with Clive Bolger he carried out surveillance on the man's known haunts, hoping to exact retribution. However, word filtered back from the IRA that the gunman was not to be touched.

More Lives Than a Cat

MARTIN FOLEY HAS A terrible reputation in the underworld for gossiping and talking about people behind their backs. His frequent bouts of verbal diarrhoea have often got him in trouble over the years.

Although John Gilligan was happy enough to supply drugs to Foley and Shavo Hogan he didn't trust the pair, because rumours regularly circulated that they were garda informants. Gilligan's partner in crime, John 'The Coach' Traynor had a particular dislike for Foley. The two criminals never got on, although they had regularly met and socialised during the height of the Cahill gang's power. Traynor seldom wasted an opportunity to spin a story against The Viper to Gilligan. And unbeknownst to everyone Traynor was also frequently in touch with a number of journalists, including the *Sunday Independent*'s Veronica Guerin. He planted stories about Foley and other criminals to distract the journalists' attention from the ever-expanding empire he and Gilligan were building.

Traynor's annoyance at Foley and, by extension, Hogan, was exacerbated by the fact that the pair kept plaguing him for a share of the money from the sale of some of the Beit paintings to the UVF, which had been brokered by The Coach a few years previously. Traynor claimed to know nothing about any deal. He said the only person who might have had information about it was Martin Cahill, who was of course dead.

Traynor feared that the two frustrated criminals might try to shoot him, so he went on the offensive. Untrue rumours had been spreading that the Gilligan gang had been dealing heroin, which would not have gone down well with the IRA. Traynor told Gilligan that his sources believed Foley had instigated the rumours. Gilligan was furious because the last thing he needed was to have the Provos on his back over some made-up allegation. Things went from bad to worse in early January 2006 when Brian Meehan was called to a meeting with the IRA and bluntly asked about the rumour that the gang had graduated to selling smack. Meehan said that this was totally untrue and that he didn't know where the rumour had come from.

The IRA, like Traynor, had no love for The Viper and they told Meehan that Foley had given them the information. They made it clear that although they could turn a blind eye to the sale of cannabis, heroin would be an entirely different matter. Meehan had heard the stories about the IRA and the Concerned Parents in the 1980s and he had no doubt that the Provos were serious. He was released and reported straight back to Gilligan and Traynor. They discussed what could be done about Foley and unanimously agreed that they should kill him.

The job was assigned to Brian Meehan and he began to plan the hit, plotting what the best course of action would be. Gilligan and Traynor weren't interested in the specifics, as long as there was a successful conclusion. Meehan didn't tell anyone about his mission, and on 29 January he phoned Charlie Bowden, who, as well as looking after the gang's customers, was now the gang's arms man. His job was to hide caches of guns that came in with drugs shipments from Amsterdam and to keep them in tip-top condition in case they were needed at short notice. Bowden had been an army sharpshooter and keeping firearms oiled and tuned was second nature to him. He kept dozens of guns available at short notice to the mob and favoured graveyards as hiding places. Meehan told Bowden to meet him in the car park of Bridget Burke's pub, in Tallaght, and when he arrived Meehan was waiting for him, along with Paul Ward. Meehan said he wanted to test out an Ingram machine pistol that had recently arrived from the Netherlands, so the trio travelled up to the Jewish cemetery on the Oldcourt Road, where the gun had been hidden. Bowden took the Ingram out from behind a gravestone and also produced a .45 automatic pistol. They were serious firearms, used by special forces units throughout the world, and could inflict frightening damage on a target. Gangsters around the world also liked to use the Ingram because it was such a lethal weapon.

Meehan asked Bowden to give him a crash course in how to use the machine pistol. He had decided that he was going to take out Martin Foley himself but he needed to be able to use the gun competently so that he didn't make any mistakes. Bowden fitted the gun with a silencer and attached a full magazine of bullets. He then tied a plastic bag to a tree to use as a makeshift target, in a field at the back of the graveyard. Meehan emptied the whole magazine into the plastic bag and repeated the process two or three times until he was happy with how the gun felt and fired.

He did the same with the .45 pistol, and by the time they left he was happy that he was familiar enough with the guns and that they would not let him down. Bowden took the two guns and stored them in a lockup he had rented near Walkinstown and awaited the order to deliver them to his boss.

He didn't have to wait long. On 1 February Meehan phoned Bowden and told him to bring the guns to Hippo Ward's house, in Walkinstown. He said that he had arranged to meet Foley at 7 p.m. to discuss a drugs shipment and that he and Ward intended to kill him. Bowden was used to taking orders without question from his days in the army, so he turned up to the house at the appointed time and gave Meehan and Ward the guns.

Meehan had arranged to meet Foley at a pub in Crumlin, and at 6.55 p.m. The Viper reversed his grey Mazda 323 out of his driveway on Cashel Avenue and headed towards the turn for Captain's Road. Meehan and Ward were waiting for Foley in a stolen Honda Civic at the corner of Cashel Avenue. They saw Foley driving towards the Captain's Road turn and, dressed in balaclavas, they jumped out and ran towards Foley's slow-moving car. Foley spotted them as they were getting out of the Civic and he threw his car into reverse and sped backwards, putting as much distance as he could between him and the shooters. The two criminals opened fire with the Ingram machine pistol and the .45 pistol, riddling Foley's car with bullets. The Viper jumped out of his Mazda and ran for cover, miraculously only having been hit in the finger. He hopped over the wall of a neighbour's front garden. Meehan gave chase and continued to shoot, but he couldn't hit the moving target. Ward gave up and ran back to the stolen car so he would be ready to whisk Meehan away to safety once he had finished the job.

Foley, adrenalin pumping, ran through the back door of a house and turned the kitchen light off so the darkness would give him cover. A shocked couple and their thirteen-year-old daughter didn't know what to do when The Viper burst into their kitchen shouting, 'Call the police; they're after me.' The horrified family made towards the front door, trying to get as far away from Foley as possible. But when they opened the door they were met by Meehan, who was still brandishing the machine pistol. 'Where's the fucker? Get out of the way!' he demanded and pushed past the terrified family.

Ward had followed Meehan in the getaway car and was parked outside the innocent family's home. The traumatised woman was screaming that someone was being murdered in her home and Ward told her to 'Shut the fuck up; there's no-one going near youse.' Foley had run up the stairs by this point. Meehan opened fire from the bottom of the stairs and hit The Viper in the back. Foley ran for his life and several bullets whizzed past him before he got through a bedroom door at the top of the stairs. The bullet hadn't slowed Foley down and he ran through the back bedroom and threw himself straight through the window. He landed on the roof of the house extension, jumped down into the garden and hopped over the wall into the next-door neighbour's property. Meehan climbed out onto the extension roof and opened fire on his fleeing target, missing again.

Foley ran through several more gardens and then burst through the back door of another house and locked it behind him. He ran straight to the front door and locked that as well in case Meehan or Ward tried to get in that way. The homeowner was frozen to the spot with fear, and her two young kids looked on, horrified, as the bleeding Foley pleaded with her to call the gardaí. The woman didn't dare move, so Foley dialled 999 and said he would need the gardaí and an ambulance. With that, The Viper collapsed.

The hapless Meehan knew the game was up and he jumped down off the extension roof, walked out the side gate and got into the waiting getaway car. He was furious as they headed to Ward's house, on Walkinstown Avenue, where Charlie Bowden was waiting for them to return. The former soldier had a police scanner and he had heard details of the attempted murder over the radio. When they arrived back the garage door was open and they drove inside and parked up. Meehan claimed that the gun had jammed, otherwise Foley would be dead. He said he hit his target in the back from close range and he hoped Foley might yet bleed to death.

Gardaí flocked to Cashel Avenue and they were joined by dozens of curious onlookers who couldn't believe what had just taken place. Foley's Mazda had collided with a parked Suzuki as he reversed. Five bullet holes could be seen in the windscreen, making it clear that Foley had a lucky escape – his second in under two months.

Foley was rushed to St James's Hospital and remained there for three weeks with a garda protection detail outside, costing the taxpayer £500 a day. The top of his finger had to be amputated, but apart from that Foley made a good recovery and didn't suffer any long-term damage. It really was a miraculous escape. Any other person might not have survived – Foley's fitness and determination had saved his life.

In 2003 Foley gave a rare interview and spoke about escaping the two hitmen. He explained:

I was reversing out of the house and I noticed a white Honda Civic move out slightly with no lights on. I saw two masked men, one behind the steering wheel, one behind the passenger seat. The passenger got out and opened up with a sub-machine gun. It would have only been seven weeks after I had been shot previously. My immediate priority was to get out of the car – reverse, drop and get out of the car. I had read a lot of books about survival, well, techniques to avoid being assassinated. I had the door unlocked in the car; I kept it open. It would be a bad mistake for anybody to stay in the car, because if the car is put out of action, you're still stuck in the car. I jumped over a nearby back wall, into a house and up the stairs. The back door had been open. I could hear crackling. I later learned that one of the guns had jammed. As I was going up the stairs, I was shot in the back. I had the entry of a .45 bullet in the back and the exit in the stomach, through the lung and so on. I kept going – you're inclined to run a little bit fast when somebody is firing at you. I jumped feet first through a window. I rolled down and jumped off. He was still firing out the back window.

Foley said that throughout the ordeal he was confident that he wasn't about to meet his maker. 'I knew I was going to survive. Sure, he was a fucking eejit anyway. He was after firing fifty fucking rounds and he still couldn't get me. It didn't make a difference. Sorry, it was forty-three rounds, to be precise. It was an Ingram machine gun. That holds fifty rounds to the double magazine, so I have been told. I don't use the firearms.'

Foley initially had no idea who had tried to murder him and could not think of any reason why he would be targeted. He put together a list of possible suspects but did not think for a second that Brian Meehan had been responsible. Meehan even brazenly called to see the injured criminal in hospital. Foley later recalled that his visitor seemed very nervous, but he naively put this down to Meehan's concern for his well-being, and the fact that Brian Meehan was known to be a cocaine user.

It wasn't until three months after he was shot that it dawned on The Viper that Brian Meehan had been the trigger man. Foley had reluctantly agreed to undergo a few sessions of hypnosis to see if he could remember any other details of the attempt on his life. During his first session with an alternative therapist in a Dublin health clinic, Foley was hypnotised and was brought through the night in February, minute by minute. When he got to the point where his would-be assassin shouted 'Where's the fucker?' Foley jumping up with a start. The therapist realised that Foley had remembered something significant and told him to calm down and explain what he had recalled. The criminal made his excuses and left, saying he had more important things to do than carry on with such quackery.

However, hypnosis had a huge effect on The Viper and had brought back something that he had long ago forgotten. He told friends that when he was in his relaxed state and he heard the words 'Where's the fucker?' he recalled carrying out a factory robbery with Brian Meehan nearly a decade before and that Meehan had spoken the exact same words about a security guard who happened upon the robbery and fled to try to raise the alarm. He had matched the voices and was in no doubt that Meehan had been responsible for his attempted murder, obviously at John Gilligan's behest. The only problem was that the Gilligan gang was untouchable. They were the kings of Ireland's gangland and couldn't be messed with, so powerful were they. Foley had no choice but to make peace with Gilligan and his organisation. He essentially had to accept the fact that they had tried to murder him, and move on.

John Traynor had struck up a working relationship with *Sunday Independent* investigative journalist Veronica Guerin and he had become one of her main underworld sources. Guerin, a married mother of one, had started out as a freelance journalist in the early 1990s and moved to the *Sunday Independent* in 1994, quickly making a name for herself. She was fascinated with Ireland's burgeoning drugs scene and in the summer of 1994 she approached John Traynor, who was impressed with her gumption and spoke to her regularly. Traynor thought he could use the journalist by planting stories about his enemies and he felt it would be a great advantage to have a high-profile journalist 'on side'.

Traynor gave Guerin some juicy scoops, including one about The General's relationship with his wife's sister, and his wife's acceptance of the situation. She also ran articles speculating about who had shot The General, and kept tabs on many criminals active in Dublin at the time.

Guerin was obviously getting up somebody's nose, because in October 1994 a bullet was fired through the front window of her home in an attempt to get her to back off from writing about serious criminals. It had the opposite effect, though, and on 29 January 1995 she revealed that Gerry 'The Monk' Hutch had availed of the government's tax amnesty to declare some of the proceeds of the spectacularly daring £2.8 million robbery of the Brinks Allied cash holding centre in North Dublin. The following evening there was a knock at her front door and, when Veronica answered, a man wearing a motorcycle helmet and carrying a gun bundled her into her hallway. He knocked her to the ground and pointed the gun at her head, but then lowered it to her leg and shot her in the thigh. The bullet narrowly missed a major artery and she was rushed to hospital.

Even being shot failed to put Guerin off writing about the murky figures of Irish gangland. Gardaí initially suspected that The Monk was behind the shooting because of the article about his tax affairs. Hutch was furious that he had been linked to the crime. He was impressed by Guerin when she personally delivered letters to his home, demanding to know if he was behind the shooting and he gave her an exclusive interview. She believed his denials and he was soon ruled out of the equation.

Gardaí then believed that Veronica's source, John Traynor, was responsible for the shooting. They were convinced he had it carried out to stop rumours that he was talking to Guerin and had purposely tried to embarrass the Cahill family with the story about The General's complicated love life, which of course he had. Traynor was arrested for questioning about the shooting but there was nothing to link him to it and he was released without charge.

Guerin told friends that she didn't trust John Traynor and that he could easily have set her up to be shot, or even have pulled the trigger himself. However, she continued to talk to The Coach.

By the summer of 1995 Guerin had heard the rumours about John Gilligan becoming the new Mr Big of Irish organised crime. She was determined to shine a light on Gilligan and his activities and she asked Traynor to organise a meeting for her. Traynor refused and he warned her off, saying Gilligan was extremely dangerous. The *Sunday World* was the first newspaper to write about Gilligan, in August 1995, and John Traynor was the source for the story. The paper ran Gilligan's picture, but pixelated it for legal reasons and did not name him. Nevertheless, Gilligan went ballistic over the story, and Traynor warned the *Sunday World* reporter to back off and be careful, because the criminal had the potential to go after journalists and their families.

On 7 September Veronica Guerin wrote a letter to John Gilligan and posted it to his £5-million luxury mansion, equestrian centre and stud called Jessbrook, located close to Enfield in County Meath. She asked Gilligan if he would be prepared to grant her an interview. Unsurprisingly, she heard nothing back from him. This rejection didn't deter Guerin, though, and on the morning of 14 September she drove to Jessbrook and asked the receptionist if Mr Gilligan was there. The receptionist directed her to the private mansion. When Guerin reached a security gate she pressed an intercom button and could see CCTV cameras overhead. She was buzzed in without being asked to identify herself and she expected to be met at the house.

Inside, Gilligan was studying the journalist on the CCTV and was shocked at the cheek she was showing in confronting him at his own home. Veronica knocked on the door and Gilligan, still in his dressing gown, opened the door and snarled at her in greeting. The journalist explained who she was and said she wanted to talk to him about the source of his wealth and about how he could afford the equestrian centre. Gilligan lost the plot and shouted that he would shoot her and her family if she wrote anything about him in the *Sunday Independent*. He then physically attacked her, pushed her back towards her car and told her, in very colourful language, to leave his property.

Guerin sped away from Jessbrook, aching after being assaulted by Gilligan. She called one of her garda sources, Deputy Commissioner Pat Byrne, and told him about the assault. He immediately ordered an investigation, while Guerin went to the doctor and was diagnosed with shock and extensive bruising.

Gilligan went to meet John Traynor and said that he was going to sort out Guerin once and for all. The following morning Guerin went to see a barrister about the assault. While she was in the barrister's office Gilligan called her mobile phone and threatened, 'If you do one thing on me, or write about me, I am going to kidnap your son and ride him. I am going to shoot you. Do you understand what I am saying? I am going to kidnap your fucking son and ride him, and I am going to fucking shoot you. I will kill you.'

Guerin made a statement to the gardaí about the assault and the phone threats and the following week she ran a story about the assault. When she rang Gilligan looking for a quote, he again threatened to murder her.

Gilligan was quizzed in November 1995 about the assault allegations and he totally denied them. He was later charged with the assault and got Traynor to offer Guerin money to drop the charges, but she was having none of it; she wanted to see Gilligan answer for what he had put her through.

'Factory' John was facing a possible six-month prison sentence, something that would have serious consequences for his drugs business, which was making him hundreds of thousands of pounds a week at this stage. He also did not want to swap the high life of mansions and fast cars for prison. He became obsessed with his impending court case and with Veronica Guerin and he wouldn't listen when Traynor advised him to back off and forgot about it.

Threatening to murder Veronica Guerin only secured more garda attention for Gilligan, and a special operation, codenamed Pineapple, set about building up intelligence on the gang. Gardaí spent the first few months of 2006 monitoring Gilligan, Traynor, Meehan and Ward. They even called in Interpol and gradually built up a picture of just how much drugs the gang had been importing.

In March 2006 Gilligan received a summons to appear at Kilcock District Court on 14 May to face trial for the assault of Guerin. Traynor secretly told gardaí that 'Factory' John was losing control and had been ranting to all and sundry about Guerin. On 14 May the journalist attended Kilcock District Court with her husband, Graham, and prepared to give evidence against Gilligan. In a show of power, Gilligan arrived in a convoy of jeeps and cars, accompanied by his wife, Geraldine. In the end the case was adjourned until 25 June because of a technicality.

As the new court date approached Gilligan began to bring his gang in on a plot to murder Guerin. Nobody voiced any objections. The gang had got so big and so arrogant that they didn't realise that shooting a journalist from the country's biggest newspaper would bring the wrath of the entire State down on them.

Brian Meehan told Charlie Bowden that there was a serious problem between Gilligan and Guerin that needed to be sorted. If the boss got sent down, the supply of drugs would end, because Gilligan was the one with all the contacts. Meehan asked Bowden for a .357 Magnum revolver that had arrived with a drugs shipment the previous

January. He told Bowden they needed the firearm to murder Veronica Guerin. Meehan said he wanted to do the job himself but that Gilligan wouldn't let him because of the way he had botched the Foley hit. Gilligan instead brought in the feared hitman Eugene 'Dutchie' Holland because of his proven track record.

Guerin had naively told John Traynor that she was due in Naas District Court on a speeding charge the day after the assault case against John Gilligan was due to be heard again. Traynor dutifully told Gilligan and it was decided that she would be murdered after she left Naas.

On 25 June Veronica faced Gilligan again in Kilcock District Court. This time he was less threatening, obviously knowing what lay in store for the unfortunate journalist. The case was again adjourned, this time until 9 July. On his way out of court Gilligan said to a garda detective, 'She's a fucking stupid bitch. This case will never get off the ground.'

That evening Brian Meehan collected a stolen motorbike that was to be used for the assassination. He then met with Bowden, who had the Magnum ready, cleaned and loaded. He subsequently gave the gun to Dutchie Holland. On the morning of 26 June Meehan phoned Paul Ward and told him he had to 'bring the kids to school'. This was their code to confirm that the murder plot was going ahead. Ward turned on his garda-frequency radio scanner and waited. Meehan and Dutchie Holland would go back to Ward's after the murder and Ward would dispose of the gun and the motorbike.

At 12.54 p.m. Veronica Guerin was driving towards Dublin, having appeared at Naas District Court, when the stolen motorbike, ridden by Meehan, wove through the traffic on the Naas dual carriageway towards her car. Veronica stopped at a red light and the motorbike pulled up alongside her at Newland's Cross. Dutchie Holland put one foot on the road to balance himself, aimed the Magnum at the reporter and fired two shots. He fired a further four shots through the shattered window, but Veronica Guerin was already dead.

The murder of Veronica Guerin caused national outrage and led to the establishment of the Criminal Assets Bureau (CAB), which was empowered to seize the assets of criminals if they could not legitimately explain their means. Additionally, a dedicated unit was also set up to deal exclusively with the country's increasing drugs problem. The Garda National Drugs Unit (GNDU) led a massive crackdown against drug crime, which fell by 50 per cent in the year following the Guerin murder. A special garda taskforce, under Assistant Commissioner Tony Hickey, was set up to bring Guerin's killers to justice. Most of the main players in the murder received considerable sentences. Brian Meehan was jailed for life, John Gilligan was acquitted of the murder but jailed for twenty years on drugs charges. Paul 'Hippo' Ward was jailed for the murder, although this conviction was overturned on appeal. Dutchie Holland was never charged with the assassination but he died in a British prison in 2009. John Traynor fled Ireland in the aftermath of the murder. He was arrested in Amsterdam in 2010 and extradited to the UK to serve a seven-year sentence for handling stolen bank bonds. Martin Foley was delighted with the spectacular downfall of the Gilligan gang. He did not fancy the prospect of having to be nice to a gang of mobsters that had tried to shoot him dead. As usual Foley had the last laugh.

Most of the convictions for Veronica Guerin's murder were secured on the back of evidence given by Charlie Bowden, who became a so-called supergrass and turned on the gang in exchange for a new life in the Witness Protection Programme. Bowden's evidence was of real interest to Martin 'The Viper' Foley, who was quick to turn it to his own advantage, sensing there was money to be made.

Trying to Get Blood Out of a Supergrass

IN JULY 1999 THE 'supergrass' State witness Charlie Bowden appeared before the Special Criminal Court, where he lifted the lid on the activities of John Gilligan and other senior figures within Gilligan's organisation. While Bowden was giving evidence against Brian Meehan, who was on trial for Veronica Guerin's murder, he also repeated his claims about Meehan's involvement in the 1996 botched assassination attempt on Martin Foley.

Bowden told the captivated public gallery that Foley had told the IRA and the INLA, or the 'politicals' as he referred to them, that the Gilligan gang was selling heroin and cocaine. The IRA grilled Meehan about this, and he had to tell the Provos that it was a lie. Bowden claimed that Meehan was apoplectic with rage after Foley had ratted and he organised to have The Viper killed.

Bowden told of how he met Meehan and Paul 'Hippo' Ward and went with them to the Jewish graveyard in Tallaght, where he retrieved the two guns and taught Meehan how to shoot them. Bowden said that Meehan believed it was necessary to take out Foley because he had put their whole business in jeopardy by opening his mouth. Shooting him would 'keep the politicals off their back'. He went into great detail about tying the plastic bag to the tree and about how Meehan test-fired the sub-machine gun.

It was put to Bowden that with his background as a soldier and because he was an expert with firearms, he was the gang member with the most experience of using guns. He agreed that this was a fair point but added, 'There was a fair amount of experience in using guns in that gang.' Bowden denied suggestions under cross-examination that he had actually been the one who shot Foley and Veronica Guerin in his capacity as a gunman for John Gilligan. The weapon that had been used in the attempted hit on Foley had been seized by gardaí and it was produced in court. He identified the sub-machine gun and demonstrated how he had shown Meehan how to fire it. He said Meehan had handled the weapon and fired it in front of him.

Bowden said he had been at Paul Ward's house on the day Martin Foley had been shot and had listened to a radio scanner that could pick up the garda frequency. He was listening for any unusual messages or activity when Meehan and Paul Ward came in and changed their clothes before going to carry out the hit. He said one of his other jobs had been to 'get the gaff ready for Brian and Hippo to come back'.

Charlie Bowden came across as a believable witness and his testimony was key in securing the murder conviction against Meehan later that month. Meehan was sentenced to life in prison for the murder of the brave journalist.

When Martin Foley heard Charlie Bowden singing like a canary in court, he was shocked that he also revealed all about the plot to kill him. He decided to use it to his advantage, though. Instead of losing the head and vowing violent revenge, Foley, who was a notorious skinflint, decided to take a civil case against Bowden for damages and hit him where it really hurts – in his pocket. Charlie Bowden had been sentenced to six years for drugs and firearms offences, arising out of his involvement with the Gilligan gang, and was housed in a protective wing at Arbour Hill prison in Dublin.

A few months later Martin Foley's civil case for damages against Charlie Bowden over his role in his attempted murder was heard in the High Court before Mr Justice Dermot Kinlen. Charlie Bowden did not attend the court case and Foley's senior counsel, Ronnie Robbins, said Bowden had been advised that the case was proceeding. Because Foley's claim was uncontested, the purpose of the hearing was to assess the amount of damages The Viper should receive. Foley was described in court as a forty-five-year-old unemployed van driver. He claimed that because of Bowden's admissions during the trial of Brian Meehan that Bowden was complicit in organising the murder attempt on him and that this made him liable for compensation.

Opening the case Mr Robbins recounted the events of the night of 1 February 1996 and spoke of how Foley desperately reversed his car down the road to escape the two hitmen and then threw himself across the front passenger seat as bullets whizzed by his head. He said his client only escaped after running through a house, jumping out the back window, and scrambling through a series of back gardens. He said that one bullet struck the top of Foley's right ring finger, part of which later had to be amputated. As well as the injury to his finger, a bullet entered Foley's back and exited through his abdomen, damaging his lung. He said

Foley was in St James's Hospital for about three weeks and that it was months before the pain began to ease. Physically Foley had made a good recovery, but his main scars were mental in nature and he now suffered from post-traumatic stress disorder and was afraid to leave his house. The court heard that when he did venture outside, he became nervous and upset and was prone to panic attacks. If he heard a car or motorbike passing he became agitated and always made sure he got home before darkness fell. He had to be hyper vigilant and was constantly watching his back. This had led to problems in his marriage, which had, however, been largely resolved. The barrister said Foley had gone to a GP and a psychiatrist and had learned relaxation techniques to try to improve his condition. He also suffered from nightmares and flashbacks. He had made a few appointments with a counsellor but had not kept them.

With money to be made Foley was happy to chat about his ordeal, and when he took the witness stand he confirmed what his barrister said about his fear of venturing outside and the fact that he suffered recurring nightmares and flashbacks. He said he had matrimonial problems after the shooting and that he frequently lost his temper with his wife and was aggressive and screamed a lot. He told the court that he felt ashamed about the way he had been carrying on but that things had started to improve between Pauline and him. He also said he was relieved because most of the people who had been involved in the plot to shoot him were now behind bars. He said that the two would-be assassins who had tried to take him out were armed with a machine gun and a handgun but that he was not familiar with such weapons, having only seen similar ones on television.

Pauline Foley also confirmed that after the shooting she

and her husband had a lot of problems. They had been rowing a lot but they were getting over their problems, she said. She feared that there might be another attack and always made sure that she locked all the windows and doors of their house.

Dr Peter Fahy, a consultant psychiatrist, said he had met and assessed Foley earlier in the year and that the shooting had been the main thing on the criminal's mind. The doctor said Foley was suffering from post-traumatic stress disorder and had significant depression. If he had treatment and psychotherapy the doctor reckoned Foley would be doing well to be clear of his condition in twelve months. Mr Justice Kinlen asked what would be the position if somebody else were to 'take a shot' at Foley. Dr Fahy answered that this would have a 'serious exacerbating effect and would seriously raise his anxiety levels'.

General practitioner Dr Charles O'Malley said a bullet from the first time Foley was shot remained in his body because it was considered that it would be more dangerous to remove it, and the best course of action was to leave it be.

In his judgement Mr Justice Kinlen said it was clear that certain people were determined to kill Foley and that several attempts had been made on his life. He complimented gardaí and said it was a great tribute to them that those responsible for Foley's shooting were safely behind bars. He said that in his day there had only been one or two murders each year but now there were three or four judges dealing with murder and rape cases at any one time. He said that Dublin in 1996 was comparable to New York and Chicago of the 1930s, when the mafia ran things and murder and other serious crimes were rife. He said that people in Dublin could no longer go about their lawful business, because others were making assassination attempts and innocent members of the public could be caught in the crossfire.

Mr Justice Kinlen said that it was difficult to assess damages because the main injury suffered by Foley had been his nervous condition, which was totally understandable given the nature of what had happened to him. He ruled that Foley was entitled to the sum of £120,000 (€193,000) for his injuries and trauma, which was a major victory for The Viper. However, the chances of getting any money out of Charlie Bowden were slim. Even if he did get paid, the Criminal Assets Bureau (CAB) would be waiting in the background to relieve him of the big cheque.

If Foley had doubts about Bowden's ability or willingness to pay up he didn't show it when he left court. He smiled and waved to friends and associates as he left, but as soon as he saw a photographer he pulled his jacket over his head so he could not be snapped.

In October 2003 the increasingly desperate 'victim' was back in court chasing his €193,000. Interesting evidence emerged about Bowden's agreement with the State that led to him entering the Witness Protection Programme. In the hearing before the Master of the High Court, Edmund Honohan, it was disclosed that Bowden had been paid by the State the equivalent of the income he was earning before he got involved in crime. The exact financial arrangements were not disclosed because the agreement between the two parties was legally privileged, but the State did confirm that Bowden was not paid for giving evidence in the various trials concerning the murder of Veronica Guerin. A senior garda officer gave evidence to Foley's senior counsel, Rossa Fanning, that an agreement had been made 'some ime ago' through the Witness Protection Programme that Bowden would receive 'protection of his life and economic circumstances equating with his former life, unconnected with any possible criminal earnings'. For security reasons the garda's identity was not disclosed.

It was also revealed that the financial arrangement between the two parties was now over and that Bowden was off the State's pay bill and living at an undisclosed location, presumably with a new identity. The senior officer said he had been aware of the proceedings that Foley had taken against Bowden and that Bowden had gone to him seeking legal advice about the proceedings. When asked if Bowden was concerned about the case, the garda replied that he was. The officer was also asked if the judgement against Bowden secured by Foley had been part of Bowden's 'wish list' when they were negotiating about him going into witness protection. He replied that the question of his legal costs or bills had not formed any part of the discussion. The garda said it was policy that legal fees were not paid for anybody considering giving evidence for the State.

Foley's legal counsel said after the case that they would consider the evidence before deciding whether to seek further orders against Bowden.

That was the end of the matter, though, and Foley resigned himself to the fact that Bowden would never well his coffers. When he was released from Arbour Hill, Bowden was given a new identity under the Witness Protection Programme and relocated abroad.

❖   ❖   ❖

Being the Boss Is Not Easy

WITH JOHN GILLIGAN'S GANG smashed by the gardaí following the murder of Veronica Guerin, Foley's gang recognised there was a gap in the market and they needed a new Irish supplier, who could supply product quickly. They had done well out of selling cannabis on a small scale and had found their feet and learned the tools of the drugs trade. They were now ready to expand and Foley looked to his old friend Eamon Daly and asked him for help and if he would supply them.

In the months after the collapse of the Gilligan gang, Eamon Daly had grown into a big fish in the Irish pond. He was importing drugs from Amsterdam, sourced from escaped kidnapper John 'The Colonel' Cunningham. Cunningham had been one of The General's main associates. He had badly burned his right hand while torching the van that was used in the record breaking £2-million raid on O'Connor's jewellery factory, in 1983, leaving him permanently scarred. Cunningham came to public prominence when he was jailed for seventeen years in 1986 for one of the country's highest-profile kidnaps.

In April 1986 Guinness heiress Jennifer Guinness was snatched from her home in Howth, County Dublin by a gang led by Cunningham.

The gang demanded a ransom of £2.5 million, and for five days gardaí combed the country, searching empty barns and houses for the hostage. Officers eventually tracked the gang down to a house on Waterloo Road in Dublin 4. After a brief exchange of gunfire and lengthy negotiations, led by Detective Inspector Bill Sommers, the kidnappers surrendered.

In 1996 Cunningham walked out of Shelton Abbey open prison, after almost completing his sentence, and fled to Amsterdam. It is thought that John Gilligan arranged a false passport for him and set him up with contacts in Amsterdam. Cunningham quickly became a major player in the drugs importation business.

When Gilligan's mob was brought down, Cunningham realised that this presented him with a golden opportunity. The demand for drugs in Ireland had never been higher and Cunningham, through his Dublin point man Eamon Daly, was more than happy to be the main supplier. Because Daly had been friendly with Foley and Hogan for decades, he was willing to provide them with good quality cannabis at wholesale prices. So the gang expanded and began to buy and sell more cannabis than ever before, finally making some 'proper' money.

By the middle of 1998 gardaí classed the Foley gang as a medium-sized operation, dealing mainly in Crumlin and Tallaght. Foley and Hogan were the brains behind the gang, and Clive Bolger was in charge of looking after the actual product and making the sales. Bolger was an essential cog in the wheel and Foley saw a bit of himself in the youngster and set about mentoring him and schooling him in the criminal trade.

Clive 'Wigsy' Bolger was born in Dublin in 1970 and, despite being nearly twenty years younger than Foley, the pair struck up a close friendship from the time they met. Bolger was heavily involved in bodybuilding and had an impressive physique, much like The Viper. He got his nickname after he lost his hair and started wearing a wig. The wig didn't last long, but the nickname persisted.

Bolger was involved in the second-hand car business and was the epitome of the dodgy dealer. His gradual drift into a life of crime shocked and appalled his family, who were the height of respectability and owned a supermarket and car dealership in Crumlin. The dealership went belly up, partly because of Bolger's unscrupulous practices, which involved fraudulently taking out car loans and selling clapped-out motors to unsuspecting customers.

In January 1999 Bolger appeared before Dublin Circuit Criminal Court and pleaded guilty to two counts of fraud dating back to 1994, with three other similar offences taken into account. The case centred on Bolger's use of false car registration plates and VAT numbers to defraud AIB of more than £60,000.

Detective Sergeant Dennis O'Sullivan told the court that Bolger had conspired with Patrick Gallagher and Patrick Shovlin, who were the owners of Blakes restaurant in Santry, North Dublin. Bolger used his car dealership to receive £52,000 in car loans on behalf of the two businessmen, who were in financial difficulty. The scheme was only rumbled because the registration numbers chosen by Bolger were higher than the number of cars that had been sold in Dublin that year.

Gallagher and Shovlin paid back the money to AIB. Detective Sergeant O'Sullivan said that he and other gardaí had pleaded with Bolger to stay away from crime but the warnings had gone unheeded and Bolger was now associating with 'very serious criminals'. This was a reference to Martin Foley.

Judge Kieran O'Connor told Bolger that he was at a crossroads and he could either be an honest car dealer like his father, or slip into a life of crime that would inevitably lead to long prison sentences. He sentenced Bolger to three years in prison, which he suspended on condition that Bolger entered into a bond to keep the peace for three years, repaid £12,000 to AIB and carried out one hundred hours of community service.

But Bolger couldn't help but get involved in criminality. He later said in an interview: 'When we lost the business my family was left with nothing. It was devastating. I got involved in crime to make money. I did everything from fraud to robbery. It was around that time that I started hanging around with Martin [Foley]. To me he was this big impressive gang boss and we made a lot of money together. Martin and I had a great credit card scam, which lasted a few years. No one got hurt except the banks.'

Bolger bragged about how he managed to get away with scamming car finance companies: 'It was a great scam. People who were stuck for cash would come to me and I would ring up the finance companies and tell them that I was selling a car. I made up false registration and chassis numbers, and because I was a known car dealer, I would get the car no problem. I would take a percentage for myself and give the rest to the client who then paid it back. I suppose I stroked about £1 million out of car finance companies in a two-year period. When I pleaded guilty, the judge actually complimented me on it. I got a suspended sentence, a £12,000 fine and one hundred hours' community service.'

Bolger was an opportunistic criminal who took advantage of favourable circumstances to rob and swindle innocent people. In October 1998 he was prosecuted for the theft of furniture and fittings from an apartment he had rented in Rathmines in May 1996. Evidence was heard that he had stripped bare the apartment and that he set up a bank account under a false name to deceive the apartment owner. The court heard that Bolger set up a bank account under the name Francis Bolger when he took a twelve-month lease on the apartment in January 1996. Bolger said that he had left the apartment in May 1996 and returned to live in the family home in Naas and that he thought two other men, Gordon and Kenneth Smyth, were paying the rent. The owner contacted gardaí after the apartment was stripped of every valuable, including all its furniture and fixtures and fittings. Bolger was investigated and charged after it was discovered that the furniture was sold to an unknowing dealer.

Bolger denied any wrongdoing and said that the prosecution was trying to twist statements he made to the gardaí about his involvement in the apartment. 'Lots of people use their maiden name or another Christian name when setting up a bank account. I did nothing wrong.'

The expansion of Foley's drugs operation was not without its hitches. The INLA, run by the murderous Declan 'Whacker' Duffy, had begun to put the squeeze on the gang, demanding protection money for them to be allowed to continue to deal drugs. Foley had enjoyed a good relationship with the INLA, but the new INLA leadership had no interest in achieving a united Ireland, preferring to make money by trading on the organisation's reputation for violence. Foley refused to do business with them. Whacker Duffy is said to have subsequently sent a hit team to Crumlin to shoot The Viper, but they could not find him. It has been claimed that after this incident Foley began to pay cash to the IRA each week, after they agreed to keep the INLA away from him and his business. This tactic worked and Duffy and his thugs backed off.

On another occasion a list of thirty-six criminals and drug dealers who were targeted to be shot was sent to a Dublin newspaper. Foley and Hogan were near the top of the list. A vigilante group with Republican links is believed to have been behind the threats, and Foley and Hogan were given security advice from gardaí.

In July 1998 Shavo Hogan was the target of a drive-by shooting in Crumlin. He was walking down the street when shots were fired from the front passenger seat of a moving car, narrowly missing him. He was not so lucky on 30 August of the same year, when the forty-five-year-old was shot as he walked home from the pub with his wife, Lilly. The couple were walking down Moeran Road in Walkinstown when a gunman shot Hogan in the back with a sawn-off shotgun. He was rushed to St James's Hospital and treated for pellet wounds.

In addition to using Eamon Daly as a supplier, Foley's gang began doing business with Chris Casserly. Casserly was in his mid thirties and had never been convicted of a serious crime, but he was nonetheless a major player and had been one of Gilligan's biggest customers. Casserly was among the most-wanted crime figures and had managed to evade a series of garda operations aimed at bringing him down.

On 3 March 1999 Shavo Hogan went to collect a shipment of 28 kg of cannabis that had been sourced through Casserly, who by now was also being supplied by John Cunningham. The Dutch police and members of the Garda National Drugs Unit (GNDU) knew about the shipment and it had been placed under surveillance. When Hogan arrived for the handover of the drugs from Dean McCarney, one of Casserly's cronies, gardaí, led by Detective Inspector Brian Sutton and Detective Sergeant Christy Mangan, swooped to arrest the pair of unwitting criminals. When the pair saw the undercover officers ahead at a checkpoint, they tried to ram the officers with their car and were arrested at gunpoint. They were both charged with the possession of drugs with intent to supply.

This was a huge blow to Foley's gang because Hogan was such an important figure and it would be difficult to run the business without him. Hogan was dreading going back to prison, with the 'rat' knife attack he suffered in Portlaoise never far from his mind. Dean McCarney could not face the prospect of a long stint behind bars and he committed suicide after pleading guilty to the charges.

Since the establishment of the GNDU in the summer of 1996, several snitches had provided information that the Foley gang was involved in regular, large drugs transactions, so Foley, Hogan and Bolger were routinely monitored by the Garda National Surveillance Unit. On 5 July 1999 it looked like the hard work of the GNDU was about to bear fruit when they received intelligence that Foley and Bolger were going to receive a large shipment of cannabis that was due to arrive into Dublin Port on a lorry from the Netherlands. The criminals were scheduled to collect the shipment off the evening ferry the following day and hand over payment for the drugs at the same time.

An undercover garda team was dispatched to keep tabs on Foley and Bolger and at around 5.30 p.m. they observed Bolger park his car at a hotel in central Dublin and get into a waiting car driven by Martin Foley. They drove towards East Wall, close to the port and two other men followed them in a high-powered Saab. The driver of the Saab was a twenty-four-year-old neighbour of Foley's called Keith Hastings. The two cars drove around the local area using anti-surveillance methods to ensure that they were not being followed. Eventually the two vehicles pulled into the car park of a large petrol station where a tractor unit was waiting for them. Hastings and his pal went to speak to the driver and returned a couple of minutes later, telling Foley and Bolger that he was looking for £5,000. This was not part of the deal and Foley and Bolger jumped out of their car and got into the tractor unit to see why he was demanding money. Hastings and his pal got back into the Saab and kept a look out.

Little did the criminals know that their every move was being watched by discreet plainclothes gardaí. The undercover officers then made their move and burst into the back of the tractor unit, while other gardaí arrested the men in the Saab.

When Foley saw the gardaí he instantly thought they had been set up and he tried to dump a plastic bag he was holding. He sat on a second plastic bag and when he was made to stand up, it was clear that both bags contained cash. Between the two bags ST£52,000 was recovered, and a further IR£34,500 was later found in Bolger's car. But there were no drugs.

Gardaí later discovered that the money was being paid upfront and the drugs were due to arrive afterwards. The two men were arrested but because they did not have any drugs, there was no evidence to charge them with trafficking. The money was seized, though, because gardaí regarded it as being the proceeds of crime. A friend of Foley later claimed that the sterling belonged to him and that it was being used to import cars to be sold at a garage. Gardaí didn't believe this and the money was handed over to the Criminal Assets Bureau. Foley and Bolger would probably not have been arrested at all were it not for the driver demanding the £5,000. It turned out that he was due to be paid by a business partner of the criminals in Northern Ireland, and the pair were in the middle of spelling this out to him when they were lifted by the detectives.

That was not the end of the matter, however. Fourteen years later, in 2010, Clive Bolger applied to the High Court to have the IR£34,500 returned to him. Gardaí objected and said it was the proceeds of crime and that they believed the cash was being used to buy drugs. A judge agreed and the money was forfeited to the State and Bolger was forced to take the financial hit. Detective Sergeant Christy Mangan and Detective Inspector Brian Sutton were again involved in leading this operation and they were becoming serious thorns in the sides of the criminals.

Meanwhile the gang's run of bad luck continued. In August 1999 a former housemate and friend of Foley's, Brigid O'Hanlon, was convicted in a British court of trying to import over £1.6 million worth of drugs into Ireland. The forty-two-year-old widow once shared a house in Firhouse, South Dublin with Bolger, and Foley moved in with the pair during a brief separation from his wife. Gardaí suspected that O'Hanlon was acting as a courier for the gang and she was stopped in a car at Harwich on the English coast by customs officers. A search of her car uncovered 180 kg of cannabis, with a street value of £1.18 million, and 10 kg of ecstasy pills.

While O'Hanlon was being held on remand in a British jail, officers from the GNDU went to try to convince her to give them information about the activities of Foley and Bolger. She said the two men had threatened to hurt her child if she didn't act as a drugs mule for them. She told the officers that Foley and Bolger were very careful operators who went to great lengths to make sure that they were not caught. She said the pair were unbelievably suspicious of everyone and that they did not even trust each other. She revealed that both the men had made a fortune from drugs and that they had the money well hidden. However, O'Hanlon refused to go on the record and give any concrete information and she was eventually jailed for twelve years.

Emboldened by winning his compensation case against Charlie Bowden, The Viper became more litigious. On 19 September 1999 the *Sunday World* newspaper ran an exposé on Foley and the seizure of £8 million worth of drugs by French police. The paper said that the seized shipment of cocaine, ecstasy and cannabis had been sourced in Amsterdam by Foley's gang and a mob based in the border area. The drugs had been shipped from Amsterdam to Calais and were en route to Dublin Port via Dover and Holyhead. GNDU detectives were involved in the operation with their French counterparts and the newspaper said that the seizure illustrated how members of Martin Cahill's old gang had taken advantage of John Gilligan's downfall to claim a slice of the drug-importation pie. It reported that several former Cahill associates had become big players and now dominated the drugs scene in South Dublin.

The article was one of several in the *Sunday World* lifting the lid on organised crime in Ireland following the murder of Veronica Guerin. There was a huge appetite among the general public for naming and shaming drug-dealing criminals, and the *Sunday World* led the way in exposing their activities. Several other newspapers followed suit.

Foley knew that when criminals were put under the media spotlight, the gardaí invariably came under pressure to crack down harder than ever. Foley's solicitor wrote to the *Sunday World* on 19 October 1999 to complain that the article had 'in sensationalist fashion, [purported] to give a factual account of drug dealing activities alleged to have been carried out by our client. As you are aware these allegations are false and without foundation. The effect of the allegations is to portray our client as a sinister criminal figure, which is not only grossly defamatory of him, but exposes him to risk, a risk that the very article itself had identified. The purpose of this letter is to call upon you to publically admit that these allegations are false and without foundation and to publish an apology, in terms agreed with us, to our client. You should note however that such apology, should you chose to publish same, can only be treated as mitigating the damages to which our client is entitled.'

The *Sunday World* stuck to its guns and did not apologise to Foley or reply to his solicitor's letter, much to the annoyance of Foley's solicitor. The solicitor sent another letter on 2 November 1999, stating: 'We are disappointed not to have heard from you, in the meantime we would be obliged if you would indicate whether you propose to reply to correspondence or whether in the alternative it will be necessary to commence proceedings.'

The threat of legal action did not discourage the newspaper from focusing on Foley and on 7 November it ran an article about Foley and Bolger getting parts as extras in a semi-animated Jim Henson film entitled *Rat*. The two criminals were spotted on the set of the film, which starred Pete Postlethwaite and Frank Kelly, who played Father Jack in *Father Ted*. The article revealed that Foley and Bolger had been hired as extras, as had many of the residents of Cashel Avenue in Crumlin. Filming took place on Cashel Avenue for a week and the pair of criminals were reportedly paid £56 a day.

The article said that The Viper's appearance on the film set was ironic considering that he had been dumped as a member of the Cahill gang over suspicions that he was ratting to gardaí. This angered Foley further, and on 10 November his solicitor fired off yet another letter to the newspaper, saying: 'We are disappointed that rather than the courtesy of a reply dealing with our client's complaint in the matter, we note that you chose to publish further false defamatory matter of our client in your edition on the 7th November. We trust your failure to reply is an oversight and we look forward to hearing from you. When replying you might also note our client's concern of yours of the 7th November.'

The *Sunday World* did not engage with Martin Foley or his solicitor and waited for Foley to file a defamation suit in the High Court, as was his entitlement. Despite his solicitor's warnings nothing more ever came of the legal threat and the *Sunday World* continued to report on The Viper's criminal activities.

The gardaí were also paying a lot of attention to Chris Casserly's operation and, with the help of Dutch police, they made serious dents in his profits. Dutch police and the GNDU launched Operation Clover. They tapped the phones of John 'The Colonel' Cunningham and started listening to conversations involving Casserly, Martin Foley and Clive Bolger. This way they gathered concrete information – from the horse's mouth – about drugs shipments.

On 13 December 1999 Foley's neighbour and drug runner, Keith Hastings, went to collect 30,000 ecstasy tablets that had been sourced through Chris Casserly. Hastings picked them up from a truck driver in Northern Ireland and was kept under surveillance for the entire journey. After the pick-up was completed the Garda National Drugs Unit moved in and pounced on Hastings as he was driving through Ashbourne, County Meath. He was arrested and later jailed for seven years.

Just days after the Ashbourne seizure, Dutch police heard Clive Bolger talking on the phone with John Cunningham, arranging for another shipment of ecstasy to replace the one that had been seized.

There was a fresh blow to the gang in late January 2000 when intelligence gathered by the Dutch police led to the arrest of thirty-eight-year-old Campbell Lunn from County Down. RUC officers arrested Lunn when they found him to be transporting 200,000 ecstasy tablets and a firearm. The haul was to be split between Chris Casserly and the Foley/Bolger operation. Lunn pleaded guilty and was jailed for six years.

Again, a replacement haul was organised through John Cunningham. Casserly paid truck driver Gary McNulty to collect the drugs from Cunningham on 9 February, in the Netherlands. The night before the drugs were due to be transported to Ireland, undercover GNDU detectives observed Foley and Bolger meeting with Chris Casserly in the Leinster Pub on Harold's Cross Road. It is believed that the trio were discussing their plans to divide the drugs. But it was not to be.

McNulty had just crossed the border into Belgium when Belgian police made their move and arrested him. The Dutch were happy to let other police forces make arrests because if they were constantly detaining drugs couriers the criminals would soon smell a rat and work out that the information was coming from the Dutch. With police in Belgium, France and Ireland making the actual arrests, there was nothing linking the intelligence to the Netherlands, and Foley and Casserly didn't put two and two together.

Foley, Bolger and Casserly were furious that their three shipments had been seized and they suspected that someone was talking out of school. They believed that Detective Inspector Brian Sutton and Detective Sergeant Christy Mangan had cultivated an informant from within the gang. Foley and Bolger blamed Casserly's side for the leaks, and vice versa. Accusations went back and forth and Foley and Bolger's relationship with Casserly fell apart. The two sides split up and went their separate ways.

Foley was determined that the split with Casserly would not put him out of the drugs business, though, and he paid £90,000 sterling to a dealer from Northern Ireland for a new shipment from Cunningham.

However, Cunningham's operation was about to fall apart in spectacular fashion. The Dutch police were preparing to swoop and use their months of painstaking intelligence gathering to put him out of business for good. In March 2000 Cunningham was arrested at a house near Schipol Airport, in possession of a fully loaded pistol. Because he had been under constant surveillance, police knew where to look, and several warehouses and houses used by the mob boss were searched. Nearly £8 million worth of cannabis and ecstasy was seized, as well as a sizeable cache of machine guns and other firearms. Some of the items were hidden in a swimming pool at an apartment used by Cunningham and his wife. When Foley learned of John Cunningham's arrest, he recalled the £90,000 that he had paid to the drug dealer in Northern Ireland to source a batch of drugs from Cunningham. The drugs were already in transit and had been bought 'on account', to be paid for later. Foley told Cunningham's representatives that the money had been stolen from the cab of a truck driver in Paris when the driver went into a service station to get a sandwich. In reality The Viper thought that with Cunningham facing a long jail sentence, he would not miss the money. He was conning his supplier. But Foley didn't realise that Cunningham was in business with well-known Dublin criminal Christy Kinahan and he was not only stealing from Cunningham, but also Kinahan. The con would have serious consequences for Foley down the line.

John Cunningham was put on trial in April 2001 and the evidence garnered from the high-tech surveillance operation proved that he was the main figure in the gang. He had been careful about how he operated. In telephone conversations with his criminal associates, he spoke in code. 'Wallpaper' was code for money, 'computers' was cocaine, 'jokes' referred to weapons and 'nuts' was a code for ecstasy. When he was specifying the quantity of drugs involved in a transaction he used house numbers, and mobile phone numbers were given in SOUTHRIDGE code, which Dutch military experts cracked. S was one, O was two, U was three and so on, up to E, which was code for ten.

Cunningham had been filmed meeting a truck driver who was heading to Ireland, at a motorway stop in Antwerp, Belgium. Cunningham handed him an assault rifle and a semi-automatic handgun to take with him. Cunningham was later recorded on the phone describing how the driver was worried because the handgun was too bulky to fit in his pocket. The driver was arrested before he even left Belgium.

On another occasion, Cunningham sought to set up a new supply route because too many of his shipments were being intercepted. He met an Englishman in Blackpool and was given a diamond ring worth €7,500 as a gift. The ring had been stolen in a robbery in Manchester, and Cunningham later gave it to his wife as a Christmas present. The police recorded Mary Cunningham, oblivious to the origin of the ring, bragging to her friends in Ireland about her swanky Christmas gift.

The court heard how one shipment organised by Cunningham in December 1998 was hidden in pallets of pitta bread. It was only discovered when a forklift operator accidentally opened one of the pallets at a warehouse in Castleblayney, County Monaghan.

Police believed that from his Amsterdam base, Cunningham shipped as much as £20 million worth of drugs into Ireland in just a few years. He was buying ecstasy tablets for £1 from his supplier, and was making a 700 per cent profit after all his expenses were paid.

Cunningham was jailed for nine years, and as part of the sentence it was agreed that when he had served his time in the Netherlands he would be extradited back to Ireland to serve the remainder of his term for the Guinness kidnap.

John Cunningham was replaced by Christy Kinahan, the so-called 'Dapper Don'. He was a criminal from Dublin's south inner city who was a close friend and business partner of Cunningham's. So in the end it was business as usual and the supply of drugs into Ireland wasn't hit. However, circumstances would soon dictate that Foley couldn't deal drugs for a while, while one of his business partners would be put permanently out of the game.

The Re-emergence of Old Enemies

IRELAND AT THE TURN of the millennium was a prosperous country with a thriving economy, which meant that many ordinary people had plenty of disposable income for the first time in their lives. This inevitably led to a huge rise in drug use, and criminal gangs were making a fortune supplying cocaine and other designer drugs to the new upwardly-mobile young Irish. Martin Foley and his gang were no different.

Most gardaí were of the opinion that Foley and his gang were paying the IRA protection money. However, the terror group had split after the Good Friday Agreement, so even though you were paying one IRA leader to keep the organisation off your back, there was probably another senior member who would try to have you shot because he was totally opposed to drugs. It was a very confusing situation for the average drug dealer. The Provos had all but abandoned their political aims and they became involved in crime, with different factions competing with each other. Historically the IRA despised Foley, going back as far as the 1984 kidnap, and there were elements within the organisation who still did, and always would, loathe The Viper and his best friend and business partner, Shavo Hogan.

On 18 April 2000 two men were observed by gardaí, acting suspiciously on a motorbike close to the Cherry Tree pub in Walkinstown. Officers knew that Shavo Hogan was drinking in the pub. When gardaí approached the motorbike it sped off, but the passenger fell off after a few yards and an object also fell out of the man's pocket. The object turned out to be a fully loaded .38 Taurus revolver. The thirty-year-old suspect was from the south inner city and was a self-confessed Republican activist. He was a close friend of the hitman who had twice tried to shoot Hogan in 1998. The Provo was arrested and taken into custody.

The next morning the twenty-two-year-old driver of the bike was also lifted. He lived close to Hogan, in Walkinstown, and admitted that he had been following Hogan's movements and the movements of vehicles belonging to him and his family. This man was a member of Sinn Féin and when his home was searched, written details of vehicles used by Hogan and Martin Foley were found, as well as a hit list of known drug dealers. Hogan and Foley's names were close to the top of the list.

For some reason the DPP directed that no charges should be brought over the incident. The man who had the gun later murdered innocent father Joseph Rafferty, and he used the protection of the IRA to evade justice. Despite the reluctance of the DPP to prosecute, detectives were concerned about the sinister list of targets and they visited Foley and Hogan and warned them to watch their backs in case the Provos came for them. It was a wise warning.

On 12 September 2000 Foley was the subject of yet

another assassination bid. He left his home at around 8 p.m. to drive to the swimming pool at Terenure College, an upmarket private school. The pool was open to the public and Foley swam there most days to keep up his impressive levels of fitness. As he drove down Cashel Avenue he saw a blue Toyota Corolla with three occupants, which looked very much like an unmarked garda car. Foley stopped his car to allow the Corolla pass on the narrow street. The passengers hid their faces from him, but Foley thought nothing of it and he continued to Terenure. When he checked his mirror he noticed that the Corolla wasn't following him. He spent half an hour doing lengths of the pool and after showering and getting dressed, he walked past the receptionist and exited the main building at around 9 p.m. He looked left and right to make sure the coast was clear. As he had told the court in the Charlie Bowden compensation case, he was very wary after the 1996 murder bid and he took no chances, especially at night.

Foley walked quickly towards his car and pressed the remote unlock button to open the boot, into which he threw his sports bag. As he approached the boot he saw a man from the corner of his eye. The man was wearing a baseball cap and he had his jacket zipped up as far as possible, to cover his face. As Foley turned around, he realised that the man was running towards him and that he was armed with a semi-automatic handgun. The Viper made a run for the safety of the swimming pool building, but the would-be assassin opened fire from a distance of less than ten feet. Luckily for Foley the man was a poor shot. The only bullet that struck him hit his right ankle, shattering it, and then travelled up his leg and exited through his kneecap.

Foley fell to the ground in agony, his kneecap smashed.

His life must have flashed before his eyes when he looked up and saw the shadow of the gunman extending his arm to shoot his victim in the head. Foley wasn't going to give up without a fight, though, and he rolled to the left, the bullet missing his head by millimetres. He managed to get up off the ground and, defying terrible pain, he lurched towards his car, adrenaline spurring him on. As the gunman opened fire again, Foley took cover behind his car, managing to dodge the bullets as round after round made contact with the vehicle. One round grazed him on the side of his head, but miraculously caused only a cut, which left him bleeding badly but still very much alive. When the shooting stopped for a moment, Foley realised that the gunman must have run out of bullets. As the shooter reloaded, Foley staggered towards the building and managed to get inside before his assailant got a chance to fire off another volley.

The would-be assassin couldn't believe his misfortune and he retreated to a waiting motorbike and escaped into the night. He probably struggled to believe how he had missed when Foley was a sitting duck, lying on the ground.

Foley, knowing he was safe now that the gunman had fled, collapsed again, having survived a third attempt on his life, not counting the IRA kidnap. A receptionist in the swimming pool lobby saw Foley and immediately dialled 999. Gardaí were on the scene within minutes. As soon as Foley saw the officers, he started ranting at them, obviously in shock but still sharp enough to realise that he had had a lucky escape. 'This is getting fucking ridiculous. I don't know what I'm going to do about it,' he told them.

The pool was busy at the time and several members of the public witnessed the shooting, unable to believe that the blight of gangland was now encroaching on leafy Terenure.

One witness said that when Foley was being brought to the ambulance he asked about the whereabouts of his mobile phone, and, although blood was pouring down his face, he was conscious and didn't seem to be seriously injured.

The Viper was rushed to St James's Hospital and armed detectives were immediately assigned to protect him. When investigators visited him in the early hours of the morning they were hoping that Foley would be able to give them some information about who had tried to kill him and what the motive might have been. When asked if he knew who had been responsible for the botched hit, Foley said he did but he wouldn't share the information with the cops. He did say the mystery men behind the shooting 'tried their best and they can't fucking get me. I'm too quick for them.'

Gardaí had no idea who was behind the shooting. It was fair to say that Foley had amassed a fair few enemies over the years and there were many suspects in the frame. The man in charge of the investigation into the attempted murder, Denis Donegan, had been a detective sergeant in charge of a Tango Squad unit and he had known Foley for years. Donegan was now a detective superintendent operating out of Crumlin Garda Station, and he urged Foley to help him and his colleagues to solve the shooting. Foley liked Donegan on a personal level and often spoke to him, but he would never under any circumstances cooperate with a garda investigation.

With Foley refusing to cooperate, there was little that detectives could do. They arrested a Sinn Féin member from Crumlin in connection with the shooting, trying to establish if the IRA was behind it, but he was released without charge. Donegan and his detectives also knew that the Foley gang had fallen out with Chris Casserly's mob, with each side accusing the other of being the informants responsible for the seizure of drugs shipments. They did not rule this out as a possible motive, and Clive Bolger later said in an interview with the *Sunday World*, 'Martin fell out with them [Casserly's mob] over something and they decided to kill him.'

Except they didn't kill him. Foley spent a week or so in hospital and emerged with a pair of crutches but little other evidence of his injuries. He immediately moved out of his home on Cashel Avenue and went to ground for a few months.

Shavo Hogan called to see his best friend every day and the pair spoke probably a lot about the old days. Foley and Hogan must have reminisced about the robbery of Russborough House in 1986. They blamed Martin Cahill for all the trouble the robbery caused them and for the repeated botched attempts to sell the Dutch masterpieces.

Hogan was desperate to secure a nest egg for his wife and three children because he was due to face trial later in 2000 over his arrest in March 1999 in possession of 28 kg of cannabis. As they spoke about the Russborough heist, Hogan suggested they rope some of the many up-and-coming criminals from Crumlin into hitting the house again. Only this time they would be sure to do things properly. Conveniently, in the fifteen years since the daring heist, the security at the County Wicklow mansion had not been significantly upgraded. Best of all, neither man would have to be anywhere near the property when the robbery took place.

Foley had is own reasons for wanting to hit Russborough House a second time: he had received a letter from the Criminal Assets Bureau. They had carried out an investigation into The Viper's criminal activities and were of the opinion that he had earned a considerable income from the importation of drugs. Foley was hit with a bill of £172,586 in unpaid taxes, based on his criminal activity and social welfare claims. That was just the half of it though. A further £159,000 was added in interest and penalties. The Viper was left with no choice but to pay CAB off. A major heist would take the financial pressure off, so Foley and Hogan used Foley's enforced rest to hatch a new plot.

On the afternoon of 26 June 2001 a stolen Mitsubishi Pajero jeep rammed into the front door of the Russborough House and a gang of young criminals made off with two paintings worth in the region of £2.5 million. One of the paintings, Gainsborough's *Madame Baccelli*, had been stolen by the Cahill gang during the original heist but it had been recovered and re-exhibited. The other painting, Belotto's *View of Florence Towards the Ponte Vecchio*, was described by the National Gallery as priceless. There was nothing stylish about the robbery. It was a straightforward smash-and-grab, but an effective one nonetheless. Foley and Hogan were less concerned with the intricacies of planning than The General had been, but the raid went off without a hitch, so it was a good day's work. Foley's young nephews, Ian and Gareth Quinn, along with Kevin Lynch, from Tallaght, had been involved in the robbery, as had John Kearns, a security worker from Terenure.

Having successfully carried out the heist, the gang faced the same problem as Cahill had a decade and a half before: how to get rid of the paintings. Paddy Shanahan, the Cahill gang's art expert, had been murdered. Shavo Hogan was a suspect in that killing, and he and Foley didn't exactly mix in the world of art dealing. Even if they had contacts in the art world, the two paintings would have been next to impossible to fence. Art risk consultant Graham Saltmarsh said: 'It's very, very difficult to understand what these guys think they are going to do with these pictures. They are never going to be able to sell them on the open market.'

The two criminals decided that their best chance for making money out of the robbery was the old tactic of approaching the insurance company and telling them that they had information about the paintings and could possibly broker their safe return – for a sizeable reward of course. However, fate intervened.

At 9.15 p.m. on 14 July 2001, Shavo Hogan and his wife, Lilly, left their home to go for a drink in the Transport Club in Crumlin. Hogan had moved from Walkinstown because he felt he was vulnerable there and he now lived just across the road from the working man's club where he often went for a pint. Hogan was about to park his Mitsubishi Mirage outside the club when he saw a man, dressed all in black and wearing a balaclava, rush towards the car. The man was carrying a sawn-off shotgun. Hogan shouted 'Don't get out,' at his wife and just then a shot was fired through the driver's window, shattering it. A second armed man then appeared and opened fire. Hogan knew a thing or two about survival, and he immediately put the car into reverse and desperately tried to get away. Two or three more shots were fired at the car and Hogan shouted at Lilly to get out of the car and take cover. With Lilly out of the car Hogan continued to reverse and ended up on a football pitch, one hundred yards away from where the shooting had begun. Hogan lay seriously injured in his seat, having been shot twice in the heart and lungs. He had saved his wife from injury but he was unable to save himself. A black Mazda

323, which had been stolen in Drumcondra, was used as a getaway car. It was found abandoned half a mile away from the murder scene.

Forty-eight-year-old Hogan was officially pronounced dead an hour later. He had died of shock and blood loss. A total of eight shots from a shotgun and a .45 calibre semi-automatic handgun had been fired during the incident. A heartbroken Lilly Hogan later said in her statement: 'We were bent right down in the car. He screamed at me, "Lilly get out," and I said, "I can't." The car seemed to be speeding around the car park. There may have been one, two or three more shots; I'm not sure.'

The murder was captured on CCTV cameras at the Transport Club and gardaí instantly knew that they were dealing with professional assassins. However, because Hogan had fallen out with so many people in the course of his long criminal career, it wasn't clear who was responsible. It was well known that he was on an IRA death list, so this seemed the most likely explanation.

Martin Foley was devastated by the death of his best friend and drug-dealing partner. It was a bitter blow, both personally and professionally. Hogan's death coincided with Foley deciding that the life of a drug dealer was no longer for him. He was still limping after being shot the year before and he was also a potential target for the Provos, who would no doubt be encouraged to go after him by the ease with which they whacked his partner.

With Hogan now dead Foley would have to rely on the young criminals who had aligned themselves with him. But these youngsters were mere pups compared with the wily Hogan. They might have carried out the Russborough House robbery without any major problems but they still had a lot to learn. Foley decided that his medium-term future would not be in drugs. As soon as he could he would go legitimate, or semi-legitimate anyway.

Around five hundred people turned out to pay their respects to Hogan at his funeral mass at St Agnes' Church in Crumlin village. The church is located directly across the road from Crumlin Garda Station and officers looked out the windows at the rogues' gallery of criminals and gougers who turned up to say their farewells. Prominent, of course, was Martin Foley, who helped Lilly and her three children organise the funeral of his slain pal. The service opened with the hymn 'Here I Am, Lord', before John Lennon's 'Jealous Guy' was played. Hogan was described as a 'kind family man who adored his grandchildren'. This was news to the detectives who had chased him for twenty-five years or more. Curate Alan Mowles told Lilly, her sons, Keith and Tony, and her daughter, Lisa, that there was 'hope beyond the grave' and that God would forgive anyone their sins. Dozens of floral tributes lined Hogan's plain oak coffin, including a large arrangement that read 'Shavo'. After the funeral four stretch limousines made their way to Mount Jerome Cemetery in Harold's Cross for a private burial. Martin Foley was one of the pallbearers. The funeral party then made its way to the Red Cow Inn for drinks in memory of the criminal.

Although the criminal fraternity shed tears over Shavo Hogan's death, gardaí did not. They remembered the dead man as a ruthless criminal who had given them the runaround for years. The closest officers got to a breakthrough was when Lilly Hogan visited them in the weeks after the murder and revealed that in the months before Hogan was shot he had a number of run-ins with the man who had

been arrested outside the Cherry Tree pub in Walkinstown
in April 2000 and who had admitted that he was keeping
tabs on Hogan. Most of these encounters involved the Sinn
Féin member 'eyeballing' Hogan and trying to intimidate
him. During one incident three months before he was shot
dead, Hogan was driving up Clogher Road in Crumlin when
the neighbour pulled up beside him on a motorbike and
formed his hand into the shape of a gun and mimed shooting
Hogan. Lilly Hogan also said her husband had several run-
ins with other Sinn Féin/IRA members in the Transport
Club and that a number of heated arguments broke out.
She later named four men she believed had murdered her
husband. They were all either Sinn Féin or IRA members,
and several of them had been in the Concerned Parents
Against Drugs movement in the 1980s and had marched on
Hogan's home. The man suspected of pulling the trigger
was the same criminal who had been arrested after falling
off the motorbike and dropping his gun outside the Cherry
Tree pub. A total of nine suspects were arrested during the
investigation. They were all known Republicans and not one
of them would cooperate with gardaí. Foley had managed
to fend off the Provos. His best mate had not been so lucky.

Foley still had the Russborough House paintings on his
hands but he was no longer so motivated to sell them
now that Hogan was gone. He did make a couple of half-
hearted efforts to try to get the insurance company on
board. Eugene 'Dutchie' Holland, who was responsible for
murdering Veronica Guerin, told the gang that they would
be better off burning the paintings because they would
bring them nothing but bad luck. Gardaí knew that Foley's

Young Turks had carried out the robbery and that they had also been active in other armed robberies throughout the country. A special taskforce was assigned to monitor the key members of Foley's new gang, the hope being that they would be caught in possession of the stolen paintings, which would be a public relations dream.

The garda spying paid off towards the end of 2001, when Foley's nephews, Ian and Gareth Quinn, along with Kevin Lynch, from Tallaght, and John Bishop, from Clondalkin, were observed stealing several high-powered cars and meeting to discuss a robbery that they were about to attempt. Undercover gardaí from the National Surveillance Unit (NSU) monitored the men's every move and on Friday 7 December 2001 they met close to Dublin Airport, where the three stolen cars were parked up. The Emergency Response Unit (ERU) was on standby to intervene when the robbery took place.

The convoy of stolen cars travelled to the midlands and stopped in Abbeyleix, in County Laois. At 4 p.m. the NSU observed the men moving into the car park at the side of the AIB bank and the order was given to two units of the ERU to intercept the gang. When the ERU moved in, the gang desperately tried to escape by ramming through a garda car that was blocking the car park exit. An ERU officer fired shots in an attempt to disable the raiders' engine. In the confusion, Detective Sergeant John Eiffe of the NSU was hit in the chest by a round fired from an ERU shotgun that had ricocheted off one of the stolen cars. The father of four tragically lost his life.

The four gang members were taken into custody. Proposals were then secretly made to gardaí about the possibility of the Russborough paintings being handed over in exchange for the criminals being given leniency when it came to sentencing for the robbery. Having lost one of their own in the incident, gardaí were in no mood to negotiate and the offer was rejected.

Gardaí eventually recovered the stolen paintings in South Dublin in September 2002. A couple was later jailed for possession of the paintings and they told the court they had been ordered to hold them by 'people you don't say no to'. It was officially said that members of the Garda Arts and Antiques Unit had found the paintings as a result of an ongoing investigation, but there is little doubt that gardaí were tipped off about their whereabouts.

In November 2002 Ian Quinn, Kevin Lynch and John Bishop were convicted of conspiracy to rob the AIB in Abbeyleix and were each sentenced to ten years. Gareth Quinn went on the run and failed to show up for his trial. The two Quinns and Kevin Lynch were arrested and questioned over the Russborough House robbery but, despite gardaí recommending that they should be charged with the crime, no charges were ever brought against them. However, in February 2003 twenty-six-year-old John Kearns pleaded guilty to the theft of the two paintings and was jailed for six years, although this was later reduced to four years, on appeal.

The second Russborough House robbery ultimately turned out to be a disaster for Foley. One of his nephews had been sent down for a lengthy stretch, while another was on the run. To rub salt into the wound, he had not made a penny from the heist. The curse of the Beit paintings was still alive and well.

❖   ❖   ❖

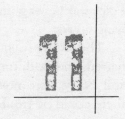

At War With Wigsy

THE SHOOTING OF MARTIN Foley outside Terenure College swimming pool triggered a major falling out between The Viper and his young protégé, Clive Bolger. While Foley was convalescing and contemplating his mortality, he left Wigsy Bolger in day-to-day charge of the gang. Shavo Hogan was becoming more and more preoccupied with his upcoming trial on the drugs charges, so he also took a hands-off role, spending most of his days with his old friend.

Foley and Bolger had been as thick as thieves for years and they were great friends. But the men fell out when Foley accused Bolger of double-crossing him while he was recovering from the shooting. Bolger apparently told Foley that he had stopped dealing drugs and was taking a break from the trade until Foley was fit enough to return to work. However, Foley heard from others that Bolger was continuing to deal with gusto and was keeping all the proceeds for himself. Bolger denied this, but Foley believed that he had been stitched up by his former friend and he disowned him. The legendary miser had been told that Bolger had made €200,000 while he was recuperating, and

Foley was never going to take the loss of that sort of money lying down.

The strong friendship was replaced by an equally strong hatred, and both men plotted attacks on the other. Bolger and Foley were powerful as individuals and gardaí knew there could be trouble, so they started keeping tabs on the men to try to prevent any escalation.

Bolger seemed to be in fear of Foley and he moved address on several occasions because he thought The Viper's henchmen were looking for him. And he was right. During one ugly incident, one of Bolger's best friends was taken to a car valeting business in the middle of the night by three of Foley's associates and tortured for information about Bolger. His pal was strung up with a power hose and stabbed in the leg with a screwdriver. When he was eventually released and admitted to hospital, detectives paid him a visit, but he was afraid to make a statement.

In February 2001 Bolger called the gardaí after Foley and an associate called to his apartment in Blanchardstown, West Dublin. Gardaí called to see Bolger and he told them that the dispute between them began when he said he wanted to withdraw from their criminal schemes and Foley didn't take the news well. He was forced to move out of the apartment and went to live in Dunboyne, County Meath. On 3 April eight masked men tried to force their way into the house in Dunboyne, but Bolger saw them from an upstairs window and dialled 999. Gardaí scrambled to the house but the masked thugs had fled by the time they arrived. Bolger told the gardaí that Foley was responsible for the incident. 'Martin was behind that attack on my house. I have no doubt that I was going to be done that night. I heard later that he bragged that he had trained me too well,' Bolger said.

The following month Foley was arrested in a hotel in Dun Laoghaire when armed members of the Emergency Response Unit swooped as he was lying in bed with a woman he was romantically involved with. The officers placed a hood over his head and he was forced to wear a forensic suit while they investigated an anonymous report that he was in possession of a firearm. A sawn-off shotgun and ammunition were found in Foley's car but he claimed that Bolger had set him up and he knew nothing about the weapon. Forensic examination of the vehicle revealed that the boot had been tampered with and forced open, and Clive Bolger and a female friend were spotted in the area while the raid was taking place. Foley was never charged but it was just another ugly incident in an increasingly bitter and dangerous feud. Foley later said: 'I know who planted the gun in my car. It was Bolger. The police had to do their job. They were very fair to me and treated me fine despite our past differences.'

When Shavo Hogan died, Foley was isolated and he knew that because he was effectively at war with Bolger, he would need reinforcements and support to make sure he was equipped to deal with the violent dispute. As well as this, Foley needed to keep the drugs business going, although he still planned to quit as soon as he could. Foley was a cult hero for many of the young criminals across South Dublin. They heard the stories of The Viper and The General pulling off daring and outrageous armed robberies and they looked up to the veteran crime lord. Foley was happy to 'mentor' some promising young hoods from the local area, knowing that it was wise to keep in with the next generation of gougers.

It wasn't only the local criminals who respected Foley. He was well regarded in the community and often acted as an arbitrator in disputes. People regularly came to him for help if they had problems with crime or other issues. Foley was usually happy to help and he always remembered that in order to thrive in crime, you needed ordinary people onside as much as possible. His nephews and their friends had already been put to good use by Foley and Hogan, and he was a keen watcher of up-and-coming criminal 'talent'.

There was a group of school friends from Crumlin and Drimnagh whose behaviour was worrying gardaí. The likes of brothers Declan and Aidan Gavin as well as Brian Rattigan and 'Fat' Freddie Thompson had, with Foley's blessing, started dealing drugs and they were doing very well for themselves. Declan Gavin was the leader of the mob and he and his brother were very close to Foley, clearly in awe of his greater experience. They lived on Mourne Road, not far from Foley's house, and were regular visitors to the Foley home. Foley happily met with the Young Turks and offered them whatever advice and help he could.

The gang suffered its first setback in March 2000 when Declan Gavin and two other criminals, Graham Whelan and Philip Griffiths, were caught with a £1.3-million haul of drugs at the Holiday Inn on Pearse Street in Dublin city. It was a major blow, but while Whelan and Griffiths were charged with possession of the drugs, Gavin walked free. The gang split in two, with one faction accusing Gavin of being a rat. This accusation led to the murder of Declan Gavin in August 2001, when he was stabbed to death by Brian Rattigan outside a fast food restaurant in Crumlin. Rattigan took control of one side of the gang, while 'Fat' Freddie Thompson took over from Gavin as leader of the other half of the gang.

The Crumlin/Drimnagh feud was born with the murder of Declan Gavin and it would claim sixteen victims over the next decade. Martin Foley stood by on the fringes as the feud kicked off, keeping both sides sweet, but he was closer to the Thompson faction because of his friendship with Declan and Aidan Gavin. Foley often called in reinforcements from the Thompson side when he felt that the row with Clive Bolger was escalating or whenever he saw that his opponent was weak and could be targeted.

Gardaí had received intelligence reports that Foley had planned to attack Bolger when he was due before Dublin District Court on 28 February 2002. Informants told gardaí that Foley's men planned to either shoot Bolger or petrol bomb his car when he arrived. A large team of Emergency Response Unit gardaí were drafted into the area and they set up roadblocks and cordoned off streets to prevent a bloodbath.

Gardaí noticed two up-and-coming criminals from Crumlin acting suspiciously outside the court. Twenty-one-year-old 'Fat' Freddie Thompson was in a car with his friend, Darren Geoghegan. The two were arrested for questioning but were not found to be in possession of anything they shouldn't have been. Gardaí were just glad that the two young criminals were off the streets while Bolger was in court. Martin Foley was also spotted in the area, being driven by a young acolyte. In the end the day passed without incident.

On 5 March 2002 Foley saw a suspicious car drive past his house on Cashel Avenue at around 11.30 p.m. There were three people in the car and they were all wearing masks. Foley feared that he was about to be shot again.

Then a high-powered motorbike sped up the road, and a young criminal who was with Foley at the time opened fire on the driver and his passenger. He missed and the bullets hit a neighbour's house.

Gardaí were informed and they rushed to the scene, but nobody was prepared to make a statement because they were too afraid of The Viper and his criminal cronies. It is not known for certain if Foley was going to be targeted that night, but gardaí suspected that Bolger was behind the incident.

On St Patrick's weekend in 2002 the Foley versus Bolger dispute took another nasty turn when a new attempt was made on Wigsy's life. A car pulled up outside the house of a female pal of Bolger's at around 11.45 p.m. on the Friday night, in the remote Glenasmole area of Tallaght. A gunman got out and opened fire into the house, thinking that Bolger was inside. A total of four shots were fired through a bedroom window, the sitting room window and the front door. Luckily Bolger and his pal had gone away for the weekend, because the indiscriminate nature of the shooting could easily have resulted in somebody being seriously injured or killed.

Later that year, in June, Bolger walked into Crumlin Garda Station and said that Foley and his associates had targeted him at the Traders Pub in nearby Walkinstown. He said The Viper was sitting in the front seat of a parked car and was carrying a pistol and that some of Foley's young criminal allies had tried to barricade him into the pub's car park so that he could be trapped and shot dead. However he refused to make an official statement about the incident. The following month a .38 pistol that had been stolen from a policeman in Northern Ireland was discovered in the front garden of a house close to Foley's. Although detectives had their suspicions that Foley might have hidden the weapon there as a form of protection, there was nothing to physically link him to it and he was never charged in connection with the find.

On another occasion Clive Bolger was driving through Crumlin with his girlfriend when he looked in his rear-view mirror and saw Martin Foley in a car behind him, driven by one of his nephews. There ensued a game of chase around the streets of Crumlin until Bolger sped towards Crumlin Garda Station and saw that the back gate into the yard was open. He made for the safety of the car park and jumped out, telling startled gardaí that Foley was out to get him.

Gardaí also learned that Clive Bolger had been back in touch with Chris Casserly and had been travelling back and forth to Spain with him to discuss resuming their drugs shipments. It was also claimed by sources that a former provisional from Belfast had agreed to travel to Dublin to take Foley out, but nothing ever came of this alleged plot.

Two drug dealers who were operating for Bolger and Casserly had shots fired at them by members of the Foley gang and it was claimed by sources that a former IRA man from Belfast had agreed to travel to Dublin to take Foley out, but nothing ever came of this alleged plot.

In the autumn detectives learned of yet another plot to murder Foley. A refuse collection truck had apparently been stolen and was to drive to Cashel Avenue on the day the rubbish was normally collected. However, instead of bin men there would be assassins on board the truck and their job would be to murder The Viper. Gardaí spent weeks carrying out surveillance in the area and the ERU was also deployed to the streets, but the gang may have got wind that their plan had been compromised, as it was never brought to fruition.

One would imagine that the war with Clive Bolger would have taken up all of Foley's time and attention, but he could not help but get himself into trouble and he became embroiled in a nasty dispute with a neighbour. He appeared before Dublin District Court in April 2002, charged with damaging Tina Doyle's car with a steering lock on 7 August 2001.

In the time leading up to this latest incident Foley's two daughters, Amy and Rachel, had allegedly been receiving obscene phone calls and letters. Their father decided that the culprit was seventeen-year-old Paul Hynes, Tina Doyle's nephew. The court heard that Foley walked up to Ms Doyle's car brandishing a steering lock and proceeded to smash up the vehicle. Hynes had been sitting in his aunt's Citroën Saxo but fled when he saw the enraged Viper approaching.

Tina Doyle said in evidence that she knew nothing about a row between the two men and was shocked when Foley approached her car and started banging it and roaring and shouting. 'He was like a raving lunatic,' she said. She claimed that he damaged the window rim of the door and scraped the roof and the sunroof with the makeshift weapon. Her two young children had been sitting in the back of the car during the ugly incident and had witnessed everything. They were in great distress and didn't know what was happening. Tina Doyle said she was left terrified by the whole ordeal. Paul Hynes claimed he saw nothing after he jumped out of the car and legged it.

Foley took the stand and admitted that he wanted to give Hynes what he described as 'a clatter' but denied that he was armed with the steering lock. He said his two teenage girls had been subjected to a barrage of obscene phone calls from Hynes 'saying what he would like to do with them'. Foley claimed, 'It was so bad that we had to get the phone disconnected from the house. I had wanted to speak to Mr Hynes about the letters and calls and I got me chance when I saw him in Tina Doyle's car. I jumped out of my car and ran at the passenger window. He ran off.'

Judge James McNulty found Foley guilty of the criminal damage. The judge noted that Foley had not been convicted of any crime in twelve years, but with thirty-eight previous criminal convictions he had to decide whether the defendant had 'reverted to old ways'. He jailed The Viper for three months but suspended the sentence.

The court was not told that the attack on Tina Doyle's car was also linked to a dispute between Foley and Doyle's former partner, Bobby Tohill.

Tohill, who was from Belfast, was a former senior member of the INLA, but had been shot in 1994 for stealing weapons. The pair hated each other when they were neighbours on Cashel Avenue and were frequently at loggerheads. Tohill had initially been a suspect when Foley was shot in 1996, although Brian Meehan had actually been responsible.

Shortly after The Viper was convicted for damaging Tina Doyle's car, Tohill broke his silence about the row: 'The Viper was shot and I was blamed for it by the gardaí. They had been building a file on me but when they came to raid my house they missed me. When I came back a few weeks later The Viper had got out of hospital. As soon as I went back, his associates attacked me on the street. I fled to the border with a broken jaw and shoulder and two hundred quid in my pocket.'

Tohill claimed that he had tried to persuade the IRA to take revenge on Foley but they turned against him and threatened to shoot him instead. Foley appealed the criminal damage conviction. Tina Doyle later had a dead hamster posted through her letterbox.

In August 2002 Clive Bolger turned up north of the border and was spotted driving a black Mercedes in Newry, County Down. Bolger had spent a lot of time in the northern city and had once been romantically linked to a female associate of a local drug kingpin nicknamed 'The Border Bandit'. When Bolger started to frequently visit the city, towards late 2002, local police became very concerned because of his feud with Foley and because he was regarded as a major drug dealer down south. The PSNI feared that he was going to team up with gangs along the border and build his business there because his dispute with The Viper was affecting his profits in the Republic.

Foley was back before Dublin District Court in September 2002, when he pleaded guilty to making a false declaration that his car was off the road between June and October the previous year. The court was told that The Viper had signed an official form on 23 November 2001 to say that his car had not been in use earlier that year. However, gardaí had seen him behind the wheel of the car on 14 July and 4 August. Judge Gerard Haughton fined Foley €200 for the false declaration and €300 for not displaying a valid tax disc.

In January 2003 Pauline Foley tragically died of cancer. It was a terrible shock for her husband, who despite the ups and downs worshipped Pauline, who was just fifty years old.

Foley was distraught that the love of his life was gone. The couple had two teenage daughters and Martin would now have to bring them up without any help, which was no doubt daunting. On 19 January 2003 the *Sunday World* ran a story about Pauline's untimely passing and used photographs, as had several other newspapers, of the funeral. They showed The Viper in an emotional state outside the church after Pauline's funeral mass, accompanied by his daughters.

The funeral mass at St Agnes' church in Crumlin was packed to capacity and among those present in the church was a lady friend of Foley's who had gone to pay her respects. The *Sunday World* said that this young woman was understood to be expecting a baby but it didn't allege that Foley was the father. Foley went absolutely ballistic when he read the article and got in touch with his solicitor on Monday morning, demanding that action be taken against the newspaper.

Foley didn't realise, or he chose to ignore, that anybody can be photographed at any time in a public place, regardless of the occasion. Whether he liked it or not, Foley was a well-known figure and the public wanted to read about him and the sad loss of his wife. There was ultimately nothing, by legitimate means anyway, that Foley could do to stop this. Nevertheless on 23 January his solicitor wrote to the *Sunday World* claiming the article was 'grossly insensitive and invasive' and alleging it had 'stooped to a new low' by picturing the criminal with his daughters. It invited the newspaper to produce the pregnant woman or he would consider 'among other steps, referring the invasion of our client's privacy to the Human Rights Commission for investigation'.

Foley's solicitor did in fact write to the Irish Human

Rights Commission on the same day as he wrote to the *Sunday World* and said: 'We would be grateful if you would let us have copy application form in respect of an invasion of human rights which we would like to bring to your attention.' On 31 January the Irish Human Rights Commission wrote back to Foley's solicitor: 'You may write directly to the Commission about the matter. There is no application form.' It seems that Foley then changed his mind because there was no other correspondence received about his complaint.

A good example of the type of mischievous behaviour designed to frustrate authority, so beloved of Foley, came on 5 March 2003, when the trial of a man charged with assault causing harm to a garda, came to court. Twenty-eight-year-old Kenneth O'Callaghan from Rathmines was accused of spitting blood in the face of Garda Colm Gallagher in May 2001, causing the officer to develop a nasty eye infection. However, the case collapsed because of Foley.

Sergeant James Judge approached Judge Michael White to report that he had seen The Viper wink at a juror and speak to him in the lobby outside the court. The garda said that Foley approached the juror and said, 'You are a juror' and when the man nervously moved on, Foley said, 'Not any more.' The juror was asked to explain what happened and he said that he knew one of Foley's daughters, and although he was not acquainted with the criminal, he did know him to see. Judge White said that he had no option but to discharge the jury over what had taken place. A new jury had to be sworn in.

Foley was back in court the following month but was

cleared of driving his car without insurance. Dublin District Court heard that Foley had been observed the previous April by Garda Michael Ryan in Crumlin driving a 93 D car that did not have valid insurance. Evidence was heard that Foley had switched his insurance policy to a 97 D car the previous month. Foley's insurance broker was called to give evidence on behalf of the prosecution and he said that Foley's policy entitled him to drive any car, provided he was not the owner and it was not a hired vehicle. However, Garda Ryan admitted there was no record that Foley was the owner of the 93 D car, which meant, Foley's solicitor argued, that he was insured to drive it. Judge Geoffrey Browne agreed and dismissed the case.

The death of Pauline Foley caused something of a ceasefire between The Viper and Clive Bolger. Foley realised that life was short and had to be appreciated. The feud settled down and a truce of sorts was declared. However, there were further incidents from time to time and both men still despised each other.

One such incident occurred in May 2003, when the army bomb disposal team had to be called to Crumlin Garda Station after Foley walked in with a suspicious package that gardaí feared was an explosive device. He said it had been sent to his house two days previously and he didn't know what to do with it. He decided that bringing it to the gardaí was the wisest course of action.

The package was immediately taken out to the station yard and when the Explosive Ordinance Disposal team arrived at the scene it was decided that a controlled explosion should be carried out. It transpired that the package was a hoax. The 'bomb' was a video cassette with a shotgun cartridge attached to it.

Foley and Bolger remain at loggerheads to this day. Bolger says that Foley has become paranoid and no longer trusts anyone. He says that he won't take out Foley but he predicts that his old pal will undoubtedly get into trouble and step on the wrong toes: 'Martin will self-destruct along the way and he won't need any help from me.'

It turned out that Wigsy Bolger was spot on.

A New Low

MOST CRIMINALS CAN'T STAND media attention. They despise being publically recognised because it puts unwanted attention on their illegal work and inevitably leads to even more unwanted attention from the boys in blue. Foley was no different. Because he was so long in the criminal game and had a nickname that was snappy and that people remembered, he expected the odd article about him to be published.

However, he couldn't understand why the *Sunday World* was 'picking on him' and the relentless coverage of his affairs was driving him mad. The *World* and Paul Williams, its crime correspondent until 2010, had been writing about The Viper for years and he hated seeing himself in the newspaper and having his record dragged up again and again.

Foley was still furious over being pictured with his daughters at his wife's funeral, so when he opened up the *Sunday World* on 26 October 2003 he must have choked on his corn flakes. The paper had published extracts from

Paul Williams' latest book, devoting a twelve-page pull-out to some of Ireland's biggest criminals; four pages were dedicated to Martin Foley.

Both gardaí and Paul Williams knew Martin Foley was very upset that Williams had included a chapter on him in the book, and detectives had received intelligence from informers that Foley's mob was planning to 'teach Williams a lesson'. Three days after the serialisation in the *Sunday World* a close associate of Martin Foley poured acid on Williams' car outside the journalist's home, causing extensive damage to the vehicle.

Two days later, on Halloween night, a phone call was made to Dublin Fire Brigade from a public telephone box on Wellington Lane in Templeogue. The caller said that there was a fire raging in Williams' home. Two fire engines had to rush to the journalist's house on the busiest night of the year for the emergency services. There was no fire and the hoax put ordinary members of the public at risk because the fire brigade was tied up with a fake call.

Gardaí knew that Martin Foley's cronies were behind the hoax and when they retrieved the recording of the 999 call, several gardaí were certain that they recognised the voice as that of one of The Viper's closest criminal pals. However, there was not enough evidence to bring charges.

At 1.12 a.m. on 14 November 2003, a man was captured on CCTV cameras outside Williams' home. He took some sort of device from a shoulder bag and placed it underneath the car that was parked in the journalist's driveway. It was a replacement car given to Williams while his own car was being repaired following the acid attack. When the device had been left under the car the man got into a waiting car and was driven away.

Gardaí later determined that Martin Foley and one of his associates were at that time in an apartment in Terenure, listening to the garda radio via a scanner. The two men who had been involved in placing the device soon joined the others at the apartment, expecting to hear over the airwaves that the device had been discovered and the gardaí alerted.

But nothing happened. One of the young criminals phoned a garda he knew and told him there was a rumour doing the rounds that a bomb had been left at Paul Williams' house. The thug also sent the cop a text message, saying, *You did not hear this from me. I can't say where it came from but it's 100 per cent. Text me back to let me know you got this.*

Around the same time a call about a bomb at Williams' home was made to a newspaper. Gardaí were notified about the alleged bomb at 2.45 a.m. and two officers immediately rushed to the house to check out the threat. The gardaí checked under the car and saw what looked to be a viable explosive device. They told Williams that he and his family would have to be evacuated and the Army Bomb Disposal Squad were called in to examine the device. The family was taken to Crumlin Garda Station.

When the army arrived they used a bomb disposal robot fitted with an X-ray machine to go under the car to investigate. It was about 4 a.m. by the time a preliminary examination of the device led experts to fear that it was primed and ready to explode. A decision was taken to evacuate the entire street while a controlled explosion was carried out. One hundred and fifty men, women and children were woken and brought to a local school, where they were given blankets and told to wait while the bomb disposal team did its job.

At 4.30 a.m. the device was blown up and then taken

to Cathal Brugha Army Barracks for analysis. It emerged that the suspect device was placed in a tin box with circuit boards and everything that would normally be in a genuine bomb – except explosives. The box contained dough so that when it was X-rayed it would appear that the device was fitted with explosives.

Gardaí later determined that Foley had been picked up by taxi with an associate at around 4 a.m. from the Terenure apartment and driven back to Crumlin. As the driver innocently took his fare home he probably wondered what all the commotion was about, as gardaí from across the city rushed to Paul Williams' house with their blue lights flashing.

The hoax bomb made headlines the following day and gardaí privately said that there was little doubt that Foley was behind it.

Criminals close to Foley leaked information that the Irish National Liberation Army (INLA) had been responsible and even named several skilled bomb makers as being responsible for assembling the device. Investigators soon ruled out the involvement of the Republican organisation, though, and focused their attention on Martin Foley and three of his closest associates, who had all been with him in the apartment in Terenure.

In the immediate aftermath of the bomb scare Paul Williams believed that the INLA was responsible. He never imagined that Martin Foley, a so-called Ordinary Decent Criminal would have the gumption to target him for simply doing his job.

There was political outrage after the hoax bomb incident. Labour's justice spokesman, Joe Costello, said it was a 'sinister attempt to intimidate a courageous journalist who had done much to expose the leaders of criminal gangs. This must be a very worrying development for Paul Williams and his family, but it also has serious implications for society generally. The clear message from those responsible is that "if we can so easily place a hoax device, we can easily place a real bomb." This incident once again points to the power of these gangs and their belief that they can operate with little fear of being called into account.'

Minister for Justice Michael McDowell strongly condemned the incident but rejected Williams' suggestions that government-imposed cutbacks were responsible for the gardaí being pulled from his protection detail. McDowell said this was an operational matter for the garda commissioner. Nevertheless in the immediate aftermath of the hoax Williams' security was reinstated.

Led by the *Sunday World*, the media went on the offensive. The 23 November edition of the Sunday newspaper ran the front page headline WE KNOW YOU DID IT, with a pixelated photo of Foley, although anyone who knew him would have little trouble recognising the criminal. The sub-headline was NET IS CLOSING ON THE THUG WHO WAS BEHIND THE ATTACK ON WILLIAMS.

The front page included a quote from Justice Minister Michael McDowell, who said that the outrageous attack on the journalist and his family 'throws [down] the gauntlet to all who value liberty, freedom of expression and the right of our citizens to go about their legitimate business'. McDowell vowed to give gardaí extra resources to 'tackle the new generation of low-life thugs who hope to replace the Gilligans and Generals of yesteryear'.

Reporter Eamon Dillon wrote:

The *Sunday World* knows who plotted the recent

elaborate hoax bomb in an effort to intimidate Paul
Williams. A group of criminals pooled their resources in
several recent attempts to silence our reporter. A garda
source yesterday revealed that "strong evidence" had
emerged linking the threat with a major Dublin criminal
boss and a former terrorist ... The main suspect has
had several run-ins with Williams over articles in the
Sunday World. Gardaí believe he may have teamed up
with a rogue former INLA member to "scare" Williams
into stopping his exposés. A garda source said: "Gardaí
have uncovered strong evidence linking these two
individuals to the threat on Williams. What has emerged
is not circumstantial and is very concrete. Gardaí know
who assembled the device. They are treating the threat
against Mr Williams very seriously." Detectives from the
gardaí's Special Detective Unit are protecting Paul's home
in South Dublin twenty-four hours a day and patrol cars
are regularly circulating the property.

The *Sunday World* can reveal today the full extent of
the efforts by low-life scumbag gangsters to intimidate
our man. These have been going on since the beginning
of the summer. In early June, gardaí uncovered a plot
by an INLA cocaine-dealing gang to attack Paul and his
family over a story that appeared in the *Sunday World*.
The gang concerned has close links to the Keane crime
family in Limerick. Following an exclusive investigation by
Williams into an associate of Sean 'The Fixer' Fitzgerald,
a file was sent to the DPP.

Death threats were issued against Williams, telling
him he was going to join Veronica Guerin in the grave.

In the past six weeks garda intelligence has also
picked up reliable information that Williams was to be
lured to a quiet place and abducted. The plan was to
carry out the vile deed in a rural area when he was home
visiting relatives. His home town of Ballinamore, County
Leitrim had been monitored in the middle of October
by the gang. Gardaí also believe there was a plan to lure

Williams to a Dublin pub and to bundle him into a car to torture and/or assault him.

Matters dramatically escalated when a thug employed by the gang poured acid over his car. The incident was followed the night after with a call to Rathmines Garda Station saying the attack on the car was just the start and he would be firebombed out of his home. Gardaí immediately placed armed protection on his home at night and the following night two fire engines were sent to the house after a fire was falsely reported there. The plan was to further intimidate the journalist and his family.

Then came the incident in the early hours of Friday morning when the elaborate hoax bomb was found under Paul's car.

Over the next few weeks several articles appeared in national newspapers about Foley's links to the hoax bomb and he was eventually named as being involved in the plot. The plan was a serious tactical error on Foley's part. It put him back in the headlines as a notorious criminal and it also ensured that gardaí would be monitoring him like never before.

Pointing the finger of blame at the INLA was another mistake. It put in jeopardy the early release under the Good Friday Agreement of several high profile INLA terrorists. This led to criminals like the notorious psychopath, Dessie 'The Border Fox' O'Hare, going ballistic, leaving Foley and his gang open to attack. Gardaí were very aware of this possibility and they had several conversations with Foley about his personal security and the need to watch his back. Foley had already made himself very unpopular with his fellow crooks, as the three failed murder bids on his life had confirmed, and now he was courting further danger.

The Garda investigation into who had planted the hoax

bomb continued, and on 23 February 2004 detectives moved to arrest Foley and quiz him about the incident. A twenty-seven-year-old man and Foley were lifted during dawn raids and held under Section 4 of the Criminal Justice Act. Foley was held for twelve hours at Crumlin Garda Station. He protested that he was innocent and said he knew nothing about the bomb hoax. Foley's devoted crony said the same thing. The man had once worked as a clamper and had been arrested for viciously assaulting an innocent motorist who had the cheek to query why his car had been clamped. This man acted as 'muscle' for Foley in case anyone tried to mess with him.

The week before Foley and his mate were arrested, the two other men who were present in the apartment in Terenure on the night of the hoax had also been nabbed. They knew the drill and said nothing to gardaí. Foley had been targeted on the same day as the pair of his goons, but he was in Prague for a romantic Valentine's Day break with his new girlfriend, Sonia Doyle.

Ultimately nobody was ever charged over the planting of the hoax bomb. However, the controversy surrounding the targeting of a journalist meant that the spotlight was on Martin Foley like never before. Whereas previously it was only the *Sunday World* focusing their attention on his activities, it was now open season on The Viper. The attention drove him mad and as usual he went running to his solicitor.

On 5 March 2004 Foley's solicitor wrote to Maurice Manning, president of the Irish Human Rights Commission (IHRC), after an article about Foley appeared in the *Irish Daily Mirror* on 20 February, just a few days before Foley was lifted. The article was under the headline VIPER BOMB

Hit Is Foiled, with the sub-headline Foley's enemy caught building deadly device from IRA plans. The piece stated:

> An enemy of Martin 'The Viper' Foley has been caught building a bomb aimed at killing the underworld boss, the *Irish Daily Mirror* can reveal. The device, constructed from IRA blueprints, was to have been planted at his home, security sources say. One added: 'This device was intended to kill and maim. If it had gone off bits of Foley would have been found all over Dublin.' It would have levelled much of Cashel Avenue, in the Dublin suburb of Crumlin where Foley lives.
>
> It is suspected a one-time associate of The Viper planned to kill his former boss after falling out with him over a failed drug deal. The man was arrested in possession of bomb-making materials, including ammonium nitrate, and was last night being quizzed by detectives. The suspect is being questioned at Blanchardstown Garda Station under the Offences Against the State Act and can be held for up to 72 hours. The security insider added: 'A man was caught red-handed with the bomb, which was at an advanced stage. There is no doubt that the target was Martin Foley's house. Anyone inside would have been killed by the blast. There is also every chance that many other people living nearby would have lost their lives as well … this is another one of Mr Foley's lives gone. He is a very lucky man that this bomb was not planted at his home. If it had been we would be talking about him in the past tense.'

In a letter to the IHRC Foley's solicitors wrote:

> We act on behalf of Mr. Martin Foley who has consulted us in respect of an article carried in the *Irish Daily Mirror* on the 20th February last. You will see that the article contains a number of defamatory references to our client, but of particular concern, dehumanises him in the fashion in which they jovially describe talking of Mr Foley in the 'past tense'. Our client is also concerned at

the manner in which the article seeks to strike terror into the persons of Cashel Avenue, suggesting that a massive bomb was about to be placed at Mr. Foley's home which could have caused untold loss of life and damage to property ... This is one in a long series of articles, carried in what might be referred to as the tabloid media, vilifying Mr. Foley. The newspapers have calculated that Mr. Foley is not a person who is in a position to bring expensive proceedings for defamation on each and every occasion that false material is printed of him. It appears to us that this is a matter that warrants the intervention of the Human Rights Commission to investigate the circumstances in which significant commercial interests seek to achieve substantial profits to increase newspaper sales and can do so without any effective sanction being available to Mr. Foley. We would welcome an opportunity to meet and discuss this matter with a representative of the Human Rights Commission.

After sending this letter to the IHRC, solicitors for Foley wrote to the gardaí to ask them about their investigation concerning the man who had been held at Blanchardstown Garda Station in connection with the bomb-making attempt. Foley's solicitors later told the IHRC that 'correspondence which has passed between ourselves and An Garda Síochána [has been] most unhelpful.' He also said that the response of the *Irish Daily Mirror* was 'to say the least contemptuous'.

On 27 April 2004 an IHRC caseworker met with Foley's solicitor to discuss his concerns and the solicitor complained that the article breached Foley's human rights under the Human Rights Commission Act 2000. While he was there he took the opportunity to complain about the story published in the *Sunday World* in January 2003, in which Foley and his daughters were photographed at his wife's funeral. He also complained about a front-page article in the *Sunday World* the weekend before his IHRC meeting, headlined Sɪɴɴ Fᴇ́ɪɴ's Dʀᴜɢ Cᴀsʜ. This article revealed how Sinn Féin's party coffers were being swelled with cash from the proceeds of crime carried out by IRA members and that Foley was one of the drug dealers paying the terrorist group protection money.

> Today the Provos and Sinn Féin cannot afford to put drug dealers out of business because they are actually living off the proceeds of the rackets. One of their benefactors is the country's best known drug baron, Martin 'The Viper' Foley who, by his own admission, has been paying off the Provos for the past few years rather than suffer the same fate as his best mate Seamus 'Shavo' Hogan who was murdered three years ago. Foley, a notorious miser, decided to help the 'cause' after a senior Sinn Féin representative visited his daughter's school. During the visit the Sinn Féiner/Provo told the kids, including the Viper's daughter, that the drug problem was 'being taken care of' in the area. Astonishingly the Shinner told how Shavo was out of the way and then he named two other local drug dealers, Foley and another man. The Viper got a fright when he heard about the comments and ran to the police to complain about the Shinner. Local gardaí then foiled what they believed to be an attempt by the Provos to shoot the Viper. Since then Foley has been paying up to help fund the Sinn Féin election machine and he has had no more trouble from the Provos.

The day after the meeting at the Irish Human Rights Commission, Foley's solicitor wrote to the organisation about what had happened the previous day:

> Firstly many thanks for meeting with me on 27th April to discuss the request being made by Mr. Foley of the Human Rights Commission to carry out an inquiry under Section 9 of the Human Rights Commission Act 2000. We discussed the above three articles which

are examples of the type of publicity which Mr. Foley
has attracted in recent years from sections of the print
media, principally from the *Sunday World*. The general
thrust of the coverage is to portray Mr. Foley as a career
criminal who is engaged in ongoing criminal acts. This
is frequently reported in the context of reporting the
fact that he has twice previously been the subject of
attempted assassination. In our submission there is
by virtue of the publicity of this kind a clear risk to Mr.
Foley's life being created in potential violation of his
Article 2 rights. Secondly there is material published on
Mr. Foley which is grossly invasive of his family and family
rights. A particular example is the *Sunday World* of the
19th January 2003 purporting to report the funeral of
his late wife Pauline, whilst at the same time containing
deeply offensive and untrue allegations in relation to Mr.
Foley's private life and a claimed 'pregnant girlfriend'. A
particular source of complaint in relation to this article is
that the photograph of the cortege appears to have been
taken from the adjacent garda station in circumstances
where an organ of the State is directly contributing to the
violation of Article 8 rights that occur.

As indicated it is the view of the writer and of Mr.
Foley's other professional advisers that it is not open to
him to take satisfactory and effective legal proceedings in
respect of these publications.

Under the law as it presently stands, Mr. Foley's
clearest course of action would be to bring proceedings
for libel. To succeed in these proceedings Mr. Foley
would need to demonstrate not only that the matter
published was untrue but also that his reputation had
been damaged in consequence of the publication. Having
regard to Mr. Foley's acknowledged general reputation
this would be a most unlikely outcome, but that is not to
say that he should be left without any protection for his
fundamental rights.

[...] We would urge that the Commission accept that

the matter complained of is neither trivial nor vexatious having regard to the seriousness of the matter published. As recently as 25th April after our meeting had been scheduled, a further dangerous matter was published concerning Mr. Foley – in the knowledge that Mr. Foley is powerless to take conventional proceedings in respect on that matter. The article published in the *Daily Mirror* is one which would not only strike terror into Mr. Foley and his family, but into those of his immediate neighbours also.

As indicated to you some years ago I was called upon to represent Mr. Anthony Cawley who at that time was being caricatured by the media as 'The Beast'. Whilst Mr. Cawley had committed serious sexual crime, and was serving sentences in respect of those crimes, what was not publicised was that he himself as a child had been a victim of the most horrific neglect and abuse whilst in the care of the State. He too was powerless to take conventional proceedings against the newspapers and as is a matter of public record took his own life, on the eve of a well promoted intended publication making further reference to him. That sad event was prior to the incorporation of the European Convention on Human Rights into domestic law and our client had not the protection of the Human Rights Commission. It is hoped that the Commission will address the urgent need for the provision of an effective swift remedy to avail persons who wish to deal only with the truth and accuracy of matter published concerning them irrespective of previous general reputation.

It is unclear whether Foley's solicitor was suggesting that Martin Foley was on the brink of suicide because of what was being written about his criminal activities but it is certainly clear that his client was desperate for the IHRC to step in and somehow stop newspapers from investigating him. The solicitor's admission that because of Foley's criminal actions he had no reputation in the eyes of the law and would find it hard to sue for defamation was significant. Foley was clearly hugely frustrated and was exploring every avenue available to get the newspapers off his back.

The Viper liked to blame the press for his problems but the simple fact is that he was more often than not the author of his own misfortune. When evidence was heard at Tallaght District Court in November 2004 about an ugly incident involving Foley, it was clear why the media were investigating him.

Foley appeared at the court, charged with a breach of the peace following an incident outside a pub in which the criminal threatened to kill a bar manager. Evidence was heard that on 8 December 2003 Foley forced his way into McGowan's pub in Churchtown, South Dublin despite having been refused entry. He was told he would not be allowed in but he became very agitated and barged passed the bouncer, Emmet Quinn. Quinn tried to calm Foley down but he only became angrier. He told the bouncer, 'Get your hands off me. Do you know who I am? I am The Viper.'

A customer gave evidence and said he had been very frightened during the nasty incident and that one member of Foley's party had been very abusive. Garda Jeff Kenny said he was called to the pub at 12.20 a.m. and that Foley had made various threats to kill staff working in the pub.

A defence witness, Michael Keating, gave evidence that the bouncer had initially let Foley and his pals in, but then changed his mind. He said he did not find Foley's actions to be aggressive and denied a claim by State solicitor Donal Forde that he was making up his evidence.

Judge Gerard Haughton convicted Foley on the basis that the State had proved beyond reasonable doubt that Foley had entered the pub using force. He gave the criminal the option of doing one hundred hours of community service or serving a two-month jail term. Unsurprisingly Foley took the community service, but he was back before the court in February 2005 after he had failed to carry it out. Judge Haughton jailed him for the original two months and Foley was taken down to the court cell and held for an hour before being released pending an appeal. It is believed that Foley then saw sense and agreed to do the community service immediately to avoid being sent to Mountjoy.

The Viper had become etched in the national consciousness and even ordinary people who knew nothing about gangland were aware of Martin Foley. An example of this occured in December 2004 when a parcel containing a T-shirt, a CD and a pen was delivered to Cypress Grove in Templeogue. The person sending the package had inadvertently written 'Viper's Grove' on the envelope, and the recipient panicked, fearing that it might have been meant for Martin Foley, who lived in nearby Crumlin. The Templeogue resident brought the parcel to Rathfarnham Garda Station and officers decided to call in the army bomb squad just to be sure.

On 7 December 2004 Foley's solicitor wrote another letter to the IHRC about an article published in the *Sunday World* two days previously. The article was headlined FOLEY'S A DEAD MAN WALKING. The solicitor concluded the letter by saying, 'We are anxious to establish what steps the Human Rights Commission propose to take in relation to "reporting" of this kind.'

But Foley was about to take his own radical step, and go head to head with the *Sunday World*.

Taking on the World

On 16 December 2004 Martin Foley took the extraordinary step of going to the High Court to seek a restraining order to prevent the *Sunday World* from publishing articles about him. This was a new departure and it showed just how desperate Foley had become. Foley's solicitor filed an affidavit claiming that extracts of Paul Williams' book *Crime Lords* that had been published in the newspaper on 5 December were 'sensationalist' and 'profoundly irresponsible'.

Barrister Rossa Fanning, acting for Foley, secured leave from Ms Justice Laffoy to apply for an injunction restraining the *Sunday World* from 'publishing any material concerning Mr Foley which encouraged, advocated, promoted or predicted, explicitly or by necessary implication, an attempt to endanger Mr Foley's life and health'.

Foley's solicitor filed a further affidavit on Foley's behalf, giving the reasons why he was seeking the injunction.

The quotes from Foley's solicitor below are not necessarily in the same sequence as they appeared in the original affidavit.

The Plaintiff has been the recipient of much adverse publicity from several sources, but particularly from the *Sunday World* newspaper over a lengthy period of time. Solicitors' letters have previously been sent to the publication complaining of unsubstantiated allegations that have linked the Plaintiff, quite incorrectly and unfairly, to various criminal activities and enterprises, these allegations accordingly being grossly defamatory of him and his reputation. However, it is accepted for the purpose of the present proceedings at least, that the Plaintiff is a citizen whose reputation and character is blemished and who for that reason is unlikely to have an effective remedy available to him in the law of defamation even when matters that are materially untrue and highly prejudicial are published about him. I say and believe that conscious of the difficulties in this regard facing the Plaintiff and knowing he has no effective conventional legal remedy the Defendants have exploited the situation to their commercial advantage by repeatedly publishing sensationalist material concerning him to boost their newspaper circulation.

Foley's solicitor went on to say that Foley objected to the article published on 5 December 2004 across two pages of the *Sunday World*. This was the article headlined FOLEY'S A DEAD MAN WALKING, and with the sub-headline VIPER ISN'T TRUSTED BY OTHER GANG MEMBERS.

The solicitor wrote:

I am instructed by the Plaintiff that he denies all of the allegations made about him in the body of the lengthy article ... The article concludes with what cannot be other than a prediction of his demise by violent methods. An unnamed retired detective is quoted as saying, 'I have always predicted that Foley will not die in his sleep and have told him this on many occasions. The only thing that amazes me is that he has lived for so long.'

[...] The Plaintiff is deeply concerned to read in a Sunday newspaper that has a particularly wide circulation amongst his friends, family, associates, neighbours, acquaintances and general social class that his violent demise is effectively being predicted in a banner heading. In the context of he being a person who has already had the misfortune to be the subject of three violent attempts on his life, this aspect of the article is either intended to provoke a further attempt on his life or is reckless and irresponsible as to this possible effect. The banner headline in particular is in all the circumstances, amongst the most profoundly irresponsible journalism and editorship of a widely circulating national newspaper that I could conceive of.

Whilst the Plaintiff has an admittedly blemished reputation, I say and believe that no citizen can be left without a legal remedy in circumstances where the very continuation of his or her life is put in question by such articles.

[...] The article also makes, to the best of my knowledge, and according to my instructions, an entirely new allegation about the Plaintiff. It alleges that he has acted as a police informer in respect of the activities of criminals and persons engaged in drug dealing. In the relevant part the article states: 'The Viper's charmed existence in terms of dealing with the IRA and other gun attacks has been reflected in his dealings with the police. He has successfully avoided a long-term stay in prison. Foley's ability to avoid being caught has caused unease among many police officers, especially among those whose job it is to watch The Viper. Several reliable sources both in the Garda Síochána and in the underworld, believe that The Viper is being protected by a senior member of the force. The theory is that Foley passes high-grade information about the activities of other drug dealers to this officer. In the last 12 months since the bomb hoax Foley has miraculously managed to avoid at least three major drug busts where large amounts of cocaine and other narcotics were seized. In each case Foley had, astonishingly, left the scene where the drugs were found just a short time before the police came knocking.'

It is impossible to overemphasize the damage that this aspect of the article is capable of doing. The Plaintiff is accused of being an informer of An Garda Síochána in respect of the activities of drug dealers, although it is clear from the terms of the article that the allegation is based on speculation rather than evidence. I say and believe that the allegation necessarily presents a real and substantial risk to the safety and life of the Plaintiff as the sort of people involved in the activity of drug dealing would very likely be indifferent to the right to life, privacy and bodily integrity of the Plaintiff were they to believe that he was providing material to the police about their activities. The Court can take judicial notice of the unhappy trend of a large amount of so-called 'gangland killings' in recent times that evidence the very real nature of the threat that this aspect of the article poses to the Plaintiff's safety and life.

[...] I might add that I consider it absolutely extraordinary that the excerpt from the article quoted above discloses sources from An Garda Síochána as being at least partially the foundation for the allegation that the Plaintiff is a police informer. Clearly, neither I nor the Plaintiff have any idea of whether members of An Garda Síochána were in fact sources for this story. However, an issue as to negligence and misfeasance in public office must surely arise if it is the position that servants or agents of An Garda Síochána are willing to speculate to members of the media about such a matter.

[...] On receipt of instructions from the Plaintiff early last week, my firm wrote by letter dated 8 December 2004 to the editor of the newspaper ... The letter complained that the edition in question was in the nature of irresponsible and sensationalist reporting, pointing out that the Plaintiff had not been charged much less convicted of the many criminal enterprises with which the article sought to implicate him. The letter complained that the article had the effect of inciting hatred against the Plaintiff and created a risk to his personal safety and even to his life itself.

The solicitor's affidavit was effectively accusing the *Sunday World* of lining up Martin Foley to be killed. Despite the fact that he admitted his client was a criminal who had been shot three times before, he wanted to prevent the newspaper from writing anything about Foley. Everybody has the right to sue a newspaper if they feel they have been defamed, but Foley's solicitor admitted that no libel action brought by Foley could succeed, because he has no reputation.

The *Sunday World* responded robustly to Foley's solicitor, and on 13 January 2005 Colm McGinty, editor of the *Sunday World*, responded with an affidavit drawn up by the firm Fanning and Kelly. The affadavit stated:

The *Sunday World* has always adopted a policy of exposing and reporting on the criminal underworld and its principal figures.

[...] The article of the 5th December 2004, focuses on the Plaintiff's reaction to Mr. Williams' previous book entitled 'Crime Lords' which was published in August 2003. The first book contained a chapter devoted to the Plaintiff which gave a detailed account of his criminal activities. The Defendant stands over the truth of this work in its entirety. Notwithstanding all the material published by the Defendant and Mr. Williams featuring the Plaintiff he has never issued defamation proceedings. The Plaintiff has never seriously disputed that he is the notorious gang boss known as The Viper. I believe that when the Plaintiff learned of his inclusion in the first book the Plaintiff embarked on a campaign of intimidation against Mr. Williams. The campaign of intimidation included placing a hoax explosive device beneath Mr. Williams' car in November 2003. At the time this incident attracted enormous publicity from all parts of the media.

In these proceedings Mr Foley's solicitor, on behalf of the Plaintiff, complains about two aspects of the article on the 5th December 2004. First, the Plaintiff claims the article seeks to provoke another attempt on the Plaintiff's life and secondly, the Plaintiff complains that he has been identified as a Garda informer. In respect of the former ... I say and believe that it is important to look at the full wording of the paragraph in question. Mr. Williams writes that:

'The Viper is not the type of hood who will simply retire and fade away to obscurity. A retired detective who has known the colourful gangster for almost 30 years commented, "No that's not for Martin. He doesn't have the cop on to know when to quit and he can't help himself getting into trouble. I have always predicted that Foley will not die in his sleep and have told him this on many occasions. The thing that has amazed me is that he has lived for so long."'

The portion in question is an understandable comment by a person familiar with the Plaintiff's activities and the previous attempts on the Plaintiff's life. It is not in any way an attempt to provoke a further attempt on the Plaintiff's life. On the contrary the retired Garda Detective states that as the Plaintiff is a violent criminal and given that his fellow criminals have already tried to kill him, if the Plaintiff continues to engage in criminality he is likely to be the subject of further violence and attempts on his life.

As indicated by Mr. Foley's solicitor there have been three attempts on the Plaintiff's life. The Plaintiff has also been abducted by the IRA. These incidents have all stemmed from the Plaintiff's involvement in criminal activities. The Plaintiff is a person who orchestrates and deals in terror and violence. It is therefore not surprising that his life has been threatened in the past and may again be threatened in the future. Any threat to the Plaintiff's life is wholly attributable to his continued involvement in crime and association with other members of the criminal class.

I say that the same quote was originally published in the first book published in August 2003. The quote was also included in the serialisation of the first book in the 26th October 2003 edition of the Defendant's newspaper. The Plaintiff never complained about the extracts prior to now nor does Mr. Foley's solicitor refer to any attempts on the Plaintiff's life since the allegation was published in October 2003.

With regard to the second complaint, Mr Foley's solicitor objects on the Plaintiff's behalf, to the Plaintiff being identified as a Garda informer ... Mr Williams states that the theory is that the Plaintiff is being protected by a senior ranking officer of An Garda Síochána in exchange for information about the activities of other drug dealers. It is also stated that this theory has been the subject of speculation by other members of An Garda Síochána and members of the criminal underworld. In support of this theory Mr. Williams refers to the fact that on at least three separate occasions in the past 12 months the Plaintiff has avoided arrest following major drug raids carried out by An Garda Síochána. On each occasion the Plaintiff left the scene a short time prior to the arrival of the Gardaí.

Although I do not believe that anyone could justifiably complain about a statement that they were providing information to the Gardaí in respect of criminal activities, this is not in fact what the article says. Mr. Williams clearly states that there was a theory that the Plaintiff was being protected by a senior Garda officer. This was based on observations made by the Plaintiff's associates

to Mr. Williams and from information Mr. Williams has
received from members of An Garda Síochána.

[...] Contrary to the suggestion in Mr. Foley's solicitor
Affidavit, I believe that the publication of the article of
the 5th December 2004 and other articles concerning the
Plaintiff's activities is in the public interest. The public is
entitled to know about persons such as the Plaintiff, and
his involvement in drug dealing, violence and crime. It is
also entitled to know about the efforts of the authorities
to deal with the Plaintiff's activities.

As part of his case Foley's solicitor sought to have the
Sunday World release records of an interview with a criminal
who provided the newspaper with information about
Martin Foley and his criminal activities. The newspaper
naturally refused to hand over anything that had come
from a confidential source. The paper argued that it was
unreasonable of Foley and his solicitor to claim that the
Sunday World was putting Foley's life in danger by running
an article about him, and at the same time demand that the
paper reveal the identity of a whistleblower.

The Irish Human Rights Commission, which had
been looking into Foley's claims that his human rights had
been violated by three newspaper articles, was obviously
surprised by the injunction attempt. On 21 December 2004
the commission wrote to Foley's solicitor, saying: 'Following
our meeting of 27 April 2004, at which we discussed, inter
alia, your client's contention that certain newspaper media
reporting had negatively impacted on his human rights,
I understood you would confirm with the Commission
whether Mr. Foley wished to request an enquiry under
Section 9(1)(b) of the Human Rights Commission Act,
2000, into the matter. In the light of your recent letter, you
might now advise the Commission whether this is indeed

the case. However, from a recent *Irish Times* report, I note that you may have instituted legal proceedings on behalf of your client in respect of the *Sunday World* newspaper article of 5 December 2004 to which you refer in your recent letter. Perhaps you might advise the Commission further in this regard.

'If it is the case that you have instituted legal proceedings, you will be aware of the provisions of the section 9(4) of the Act which may require the Commission to postpone considering a request for the enquiry if the Commission considers that 'the matter in relation to which it is requested under subsection (1)(b) to conduct an enquiry relates to or is concerned with ... legal proceedings that, in its opinion ... are likely to be ... instituted or ... have been ... instituted'.

It is unclear if any IHRC probe ever got under way. Nothing ever appeared on the organisation's website or in any other area of the public domain to suggest that the IHRC made any mention of or ruling on Martin Foley's case.

On 18 January 2005 the gag attempt came before the High Court under Mr Justice Peter Kelly. Predictably, Martin Foley didn't turn up for the two-day hearing, but the court was packed to capacity with journalists eager to report on the unusual case.

Senior Counsel Michael O'Higgins, representing Foley, told the court that he was seeking a declaration that the *Sunday World* article had breached his client's right to life under the Constitution and the European Convention on Human Rights because it had exposed him to the threat of violence and had infringed his right to privacy. He said, 'Mr Foley is here because a national newspaper is carrying out its business in a way likely to exhort psychopathic elements to feel indisposed towards him.'

O'Higgins argued that outing Foley as a garda informant posed a 'real and serious' risk to his life and that this exposed Foley to psychopaths in the criminal underworld, if they believed the article.

O'Higgins said that the claim that his client was paying drugs money to Sinn Féin was also likely to put his life at risk from the 'political enemies of the IRA'. He said the claims had been embarrassing to Sinn Féin and potentially life threatening to Foley. 'The Republican movement has shown it has veering methods of dealing with embarrassment,' O'Higgins told the court. Some were legal while other less subtle methods included punishment beatings and execution. The senior counsel said that Foley was seeking an order preventing the *Sunday World* from publishing further articles about him because, as a convicted criminal, his chances of successfully taking a defamation case were slim. O'Higgins said that every citizen had the right under the European Convention on Human Rights to prevent publication of articles that caused 'a real and substantial risk'. He said, 'It doesn't matter whether Mr Foley was the biggest blaggard or thug; that's not the issue.'

The *Sunday World*'s senior counsel, Eoin McCullough, said Foley did not have an arguable case. He said that he could not claim to be living in fear because of the *Sunday World* articles, given that he had already survived three assassination attempts. McCullough said that Foley hadn't sworn his own affidavit in his attempt to get an injunction, instead getting his solicitor to do it for him, thus avoiding cross-examination. 'If people had given evidence, he's opened to being cross-examined as to how he would realistically say he had any fear of what the *Sunday World* was writing, when unfortunately there have been previous attempts on his life in the past,' he said.

McCullough said that if a journalist had established that Foley was a garda informant, it was in the public interest that it be revealed and that Foley had no right to prevent the publication of true information about him.

After listening to the arguments of both sides, Mr Justice Kelly reserved his judgement. On 28 January 2005 he delivered his written verdict. The judge said that the case came down to whether Foley's right to privacy and to seek an injunction was greater than the right of the media to freedom of expression, which is guaranteed by the Constitution.

> There are a number of matters which appear to me appropriate to take into account … First, all of the material which has been complained of is already in the public domain. Much of it has been in the public domain for a very long time. In the case of what I have described as the first complaint it was published in book form in August, 2003. It was repeated by the newspaper in October, 2003. Despite what is now said by the plaintiff he took no proceedings of any sort in relation to those publications. In my view it is altogether too late to seek an injunction restraining further publication of this material. It also calls into question the genuineness of his alleged belief concerning this material, particularly when he has avoided swearing any affidavit himself in these proceedings.
>
> Similar observations can be made in respect of the second complaint, which deals with material first published in April, 2004.

Mr Justice Kelly then summed up his judgement:

> In the present case it appears to me that the evidence falls short of what would justify me in curtailing the freedom

of the defendant to state facts and express opinions upon the plaintiff and his activities.

As I have already pointed out, I can find no evidence of any express exhortation or positive encouragement to persons to do violence to the plaintiff.

The three previous attempts on his life long antedate the publication of any material by the defendant which the plaintiff has identified as offensive. That fact is supportive of the view that any risk to the plaintiff's life or well-being comes not from any publication by the defendant but rather from his own involvement in criminal activities and the criminal underworld.

As the evidence stands I am satisfied that I would not be justified in restricting the defendant's right between now and the trial of this action to write of or concerning the plaintiff provided of course that they do not exhort anybody to do violence towards him. They have not done so in the past and there is no evidence that they intend to do so in future.

Whatever about the issues that fall to be determined at trial the evidence before the court does not justify the curtailment of the defendant's rights which the plaintiff seeks.

Furthermore the information in question is in the public domain and the bringing of this action with its attendant publicity has given it a much wider circulation. An injunction restraining this defendant from repeating it would have little value. The plaintiff has of course by bringing this action obtained prominence for his denials of the allegations with which he takes issue.

I am also satisfied that the order which is sought is altogether too wide. If it were to be granted in the terms sought the task of the defendant in attempting to ascertain what would be permissible material to publish and what not would be very difficult indeed. Even if I were minded to grant an injunction I would not do so in those terms.

> Accordingly the application for injunctive relief is refused. I will however direct an early trial of this action and will hear counsel on the question of the delivery of accelerated pleadings and the fixing of a trial date.

It was a spectacular victory for the *Sunday World*, and for newspapers in general, in their efforts to shine a spotlight on criminal activity.

The court bid was an expensive error on The Viper's part. Mr Justice Peter Kelly ordered that the criminal would pay the newspaper's costs, which, in addition to his own legal costs, would have amounted to something in the region of €200,000. He knew that it would be too expensive for the *Sunday World* to pursue its costs from him because he would never pay them anyway, so they would end up in court for years trying to get blood out of a stone. He had to pay his own legal bill, though, and must have rued his costly mistake.

Two days after the verdict was given, the vindicated *Sunday World* published a comment piece entitled VIPER WON'T GAG US with the sub-headline WE'LL CONTINUE TO REPORT ON GANGSTERS AND THUGS.

> Martin Foley's life's already in danger from his own criminal activities.
>
> That was the damning verdict from the Viper's failed attempt to gag the *Sunday World* last week. Foley – a career criminal with a string of convictions and several attempts on his life behind him – had the nerve to claim this newspaper was endangering his life.
>
> [...] Foley has chosen to make crime his way of life and as a result of his activities three attempts have been made on his life. To try and claim the *Sunday World*

could add to the danger he has already put himself in is laughable.

On Friday, Mr Justice Peter Kelly in the High Court agreed with us. He pointed out the right to freedom of expression was provided for in the Irish Constitution and the European Convention of Human Rights. Mr Justice Kelly ruled there was little value in granting an injunction when stories of the Viper's drug dealing were already in the public domain for a number of years.

Foley doesn't like what we do. He whines and whinges even though he knows what we write is true. For more than 15 years we've highlighted his criminal career and have no doubt made it difficult for him to commit crime. It's not something we're about to stop or apologise for.

Nobody asked Foley to become involved in drug crime or to cause offence to supporters of terrorist organisations. If he chooses to associate with terrorists and gangsters he can expect his life to be in danger. The *Sunday World* is not responsible for Martin Foley's choices in life.

Foley also claimed that irrespective of whether it was true or not, writing that he was a Garda informer was a danger to his security. Now hold on, no law-abiding citizen can justifiably complain that by providing information to help Gardaí fight crime they are putting their lives in danger … This paper has never endangered Martin Foley's life, but we do know what it's like to feel your life is under threat.

Mr Justice Kelly said that the *Sunday World* did not exhort any person to cause hurt to Foley. The only exhortation the *Sunday World* will make to Martin Foley is to give up yer aul' sins:

STOP drug dealing;

STOP intimidating people; and

STOP your life of crime.

Trying to Go Straight

THE DEATH OF HIS wife and the responsibility of raising his daughters alone, the feud with Clive Bolger, the publicity surrounding the fake bomb and the subsequent failed action against the *Sunday World* had left Martin Foley jaded. He had escaped death on three occasions and had seen his best friend killed by an IRA bullet. Foley wasn't stupid and he realised he should get out of the drugs business while the going was relatively good, otherwise he would probably be shot again by one of his many enemies.

Also, at fifty-three Foley wasn't exactly a spring chicken, and drug dealing was a young man's game, as the likes of 'Fat' Freddie Thompson and his other young friends in Crumlin and Drimnagh were proving. By the mid 2000s if you wanted to prosper in the drugs game, you had to be prepared to murder people to protect your territory, and that had never been Foley's style.

Foley had most likely put away a lot of money over his thirty years of criminal activity, so he was happy to hang up his drug-dealing hat and act as a father figure to the next generation of thugs.

The Viper's exit from the drugs game wasn't entirely out of choice, however. Christy Kinahan, the main man now behind most of the drugs coming into the country was a long-standing enemy of Foley and he wouldn't do business with him in a million years. After John Cunningham was arrested in March 2000, his friend Kinahan took over the cartel. He moved his drug-dealing base from Amsterdam to Puerto Banus, on the Costa del Sol, but still used all the old contacts that had been made by Cunningham.

Christy Kinahan was born in 1956 and grew up in the Oliver Bond flats complex in Dublin's city centre. He received his first criminal conviction in 1979, and in 1987 he was jailed for six years after being caught in possession of heroin worth over £100,000. Soon after his release, he was caught with £16,000 worth of stolen cheques that had been taken in an armed robbery at a North Dublin bank in 1993. He fled to England but returned home four years later and was given a four-year jail term.

After spending eleven out of fifteen years in prison, Kinahan decided to leave Ireland for the continent and go into the drugs business on a large scale. He fancied himself as a bit of a gentleman and used his time in prison to educate himself. He learned several European languages and earned a degree in sociology. Kinahan was so determined to complete his education that he turned down the chance of early release in order to finish his degree.

When he was questioned by gardaí, Kinahan would try to impress the officers by talking about Machiavellian theories, to show off how smart he was. He was nicknamed 'The Dapper Don' because he quickly shed his working-class Dublin accent for a more cultured one, and was always seen in the best of clothes made by top tailors. One of his favourite outfits was a white silk suit paired with a panama hat.

From 2000 onwards Kinahan was actively targeted by police forces in Ireland, Britain, Belgium, the Netherlands, France and Portugal. He also featured in intelligence reports carried out by the US Drug Enforcement Administration, and he was one of Europol's top targets. He cultivated associates in the Russian mafia, Israeli drugs gangs, and Colombian drug cartels. By the mid 2000s the vast majority of drugs sold on Irish streets originated through Kinahan, often imported with legitimate goods such as flower pots and pitta bread. The sheer size of Kinahan's business is illustrated by the fact that between 2002 and 2010, various police forces across Europe seized in excess of €50 million worth of Kinahan's product.

When John Cunningham completed his Dutch prison sentence in November 2004, he was extradited back to Ireland and sent back to prison to serve the remainder of his term for the Guinness kidnapping. He was released after a matter of months and he moved to Puerto Banus, where he re-established himself as The Dapper Don's trusted business partner. The pair had learned their lesson and now operated on a strictly hands-off basis, letting their minions take the risk, while they pocketed the rewards.

The problem for Martin Foley was that Christy Kinahan hated his guts. The pair had fallen out when John Cunningham was arrested by Dutch police in March 2000 and Foley had ripped Cunningham and Kinahan out of the £90,000 that was to be used to pay for a drugs shipment. Foley claimed the money had been stolen from the cab of a truck driver in Paris and kept the loot for himself. Kinahan let it be known that he would get his revenge on Foley one day and he vowed that he would never work with him again. A drug dealer without drugs wasn't a whole lot of use to anybody.

In November 2004, the month before Foley took his case against the *Sunday World*, Viper Debt Recovery and Repossession Services Ltd was quietly registered in the Companies Registration Office in Dublin. Martin Foley was the sole shareholder and sole director of the company. Foley described himself as a sales rep on the company documentation and listed the headquarters as his home on Cashel Avenue in Crumlin. Foley also appointed himself the company secretary. The Viper had clearly gone into the debt collection business, an industry with the reputation for attracting dodgy characters who ruthlessly pursue the debts of those who have fallen on hard times. It is an industry rife with bullying and harassment and it is not subject to any regulation whatsoever – the perfect environment for The Viper.

Foley reckoned he could turn his notoriety to his advantage and use his fearsome reputation to make money. It was a shrewd decision because within a few years the debt collection business would be one of the few thriving industries in Ireland, after the dramatic collapse of the Celtic Tiger economy.

Foley charged customers a commission of between 15 and 20 per cent of each debt he collected, meaning the more money that was owed, the greater his incentive to recover the debt. He started off slowly and didn't do much business in the first year or so, but Foley was happy that he looked legitimate and he reckoned that once he got a bit of publicity, customers would flock to him.

Foley stayed in the shadows and tried to grow his new

business. He spent a lot of time in the company of Aidan Gavin and Freddie Thompson, but the new breed of criminals wasn't paying a great deal of attention to Foley's words of wisdom.

The murder of Declan Gavin, in 2001, had started a bloody tit-for-tat war and 2005 was the worst year of the feud. In March 2005 John Roche, who was a member of Brian Rattigan's gang, was shot dead in Kilmainham by the Thompson mob. In November of the same year, Thompson gang members Darren Geoghegan and Gavin Byrne were shot dead in a stolen car in Firhouse, South Dublin. Darren Geoghegan in particular had been close to Martin Foley. Gardaí believed the pair had been murdered by their own gang over an internal dispute about money.

Less than forty-eight hours later Noel Roche, whose brother had been shot six months previously, was executed as he drove through Clontarf after a Phil Collins concert at the Point Theatre.

The three murders caused outrage. They indicated that crime in the capital was getting out of control and there were fears that innocent citizens would soon get caught in the crossfire. Foley knew that gang members executing each other in public would only lead to a garda crackdown. He knew the three men who had been murdered and, bizarrely, made a brief appearance on *Prime Time* on RTÉ to make an impassioned plea for the feuding thugs to 'stop the madness' and halt the violence. The real reason for going on the show, however, was to refute claims that he was a mentor to the criminals. 'That is absolute rubbish. I've never heard such crap. I was reading a while ago how I was apparently taking them out to camps to teach them how to pick up a gun. That is fucking rubbish; I've never been involved with any of them,' he said, before adding that a life of crime was 'no way to live'.

The irony of Foley's self-serving comments was not lost on gardaí. He had been regularly spotted in the company of young gang members and they were sure that he was friendly with them. To claim that he had taught the youngsters how to shoot may have been a tad hysterical, however.

The Viper found love again with Sonia Doyle, from Rathfarnham in South Dublin, who was twenty-three years his junior. The pair became very close very quickly and were soon inseparable according to pals of Foley, who said she was a very nice woman and that they made a lovely couple. The pair had known each other for years and had become involved in a relationship not long after Pauline Foley died.

The lovebirds were caught up in an embarrassing situation in the summer of 2003, when they went for a spin in a speedboat off Dun Laoghaire, in Dublin. Maybe Foley was trying to impress his new girlfriend with his skills as a mariner, but he was left red-faced when he couldn't start the engine of the high-powered speedboat and began drifting out to sea. He eventually had to call the Coast Guard to come to the rescue and the couple was picked up over a mile off the coast, dangerously close to a major shipping lane.

The lovers were towed back into Dun Laoghaire harbour and gardaí had a good laugh when they heard about Foley's bad fortune. They advised him to stick to dry land in future. More seriously, gardaí were concerned at that time that criminals were using boats and jet skis to pick up drugs shipments at sea, although the only thing

Foley had in his speedboat was a picnic lunch.

Foley was again left red-faced in January 2006, when he appeared in the debt collection journal, Stubbs' Gazette, as owing €5,673.11 to Massey Brothers funeral directors. Foley had not paid the bill for Pauline's funeral three years previously, despite asking the State for a grant of €2,500 to pay for the burial. Foley had claimed he was broke and couldn't afford the funeral and he had applied to the Department of Social Welfare for help in paying the bill. Gardaí and even Foley's fellow criminals couldn't believe the cheek of him. Everyone knew he was well able to afford to pay for his wife's funeral.

Foley went mad when he read the report of the debt in the *Sunday World* and he told another newspaper that the article 'made a show of him' and that he had since settled his bill with Massey Brothers.

Pauline's family was furious about the revelations and one of her sisters said, 'We know that our sister had saved up for her own funeral and that he (Foley) sold off her car when she died. The money was there in a Credit Union account. We cannot believe that the miserable bastard would leave the bill unpaid. We are going to get the cash together ourselves and pay for it ourselves. Pauline had a hard enough life with him without this.'

Foley tried to improve his image by inviting a newspaper photographer into his home to take pictures of the latest addition to his family. He kept American Pitbull Terriers, and one of his dogs, Jessie, had just given birth to four puppies. As ever, Foley had an ulterior motive for the invitation: he wanted to advertise that the dogs were for sale for €1,000 each.

The Viper was in the news again in February 2006 when

he was prosecuted at Dublin District Court for driving with a bald tyre and for having a faulty brake light. You would think the former tyre fitter would know the importance of having good grip on the road. Foley denied that the tyre was bald and asked the garda to test them. Although the officer had no tyre gauge when he stopped Foley, Judge Patrick Clyne took the side of the law and convicted the accused.

Martin Foley has been a thorn in the side of gardaí for over three decades and he likes nothing better than getting under their skin. In September 2006 the criminal actually attempted to join the Garda Reserve, which was being set up by Justice Minister Michael McDowell. Despite having over forty criminal convictions, Foley filled out a tongue-in-cheek application to join the part-time force, much to the consternation – and amusement – of gardaí in Crumlin, who received his application.

Foley was one of over six thousand people who applied to join the Garda Reserve. Although McDowell wanted diversity in the ranks of the Reserve, he drew the line at allowing career criminals to join.

The following month, Chief Superintendent Felix McKenna, the head of the Criminal Assets Bureau (CAB), retired after a long and illustrious career in the force. In an interview with journalist Nicola Tallant, McKenna gave an insight into some of his biggest cases during his decade at the helm of CAB. He said that one of the highlights of his career was accepting a bank draft from notorious robber Gerry 'The Monk' Hutch after CAB presented him with a demand for back tax. 'Sitting at a table opposite Gerry Hutch and his people, and coming to an arrangement with him, was a time that the CAB really turned a corner. When it got out that Hutch had paid up, lots of other criminals contacted us. It is an amazing phenomenon of an Irish criminal that they will barter their way out of any situation. It is safe to say that a settlement is reached in excess of 50 per cent of all proceeds of crime applications that we lodge before the courts.'

McKenna also mentioned one of his old sparring partners, Martin Foley, who was hit with his tax assessment in May 2001. McKenna explained how Foley walked into the CAB offices on Harcourt Square in Dublin with €35,000 cash in a plastic bag. The wily old Chief Superintendent eagerly accepted the cash, not bothered how it was brought to him, but when he opened the bag he noticed that the notes were damp. 'It came from the canal bank – where all good criminals go with their money,' he joked.

Foley was at the centre of another controversy in January 2007, when photos of him doing the full monty while on holidays with fellow criminal Derek Hutch were leaked to the *Sunday World*. A member of the public handed in the saucy snaps of Foley and Hutch, a brother of 'The Monk', Gerry Hutch, dropping their pants in an Irish bar in an undisclosed location abroad.

The source said he sent the pictures to the newspaper because he was disgusted that boys and girls as young as six watched in horror as Foley and Hutch stripped until they were completely naked. He said, 'It was disgusting how these sick bastards entertained themselves. They were swaggering around with a few birds and letting it be known that they were tough Irish hoods so no one would mess with them. They had no problem taking off all their clothes in public in front of young children. It was a great laugh for them to put police helmets on their heads and then use them to cover their private parts after their strip. No one wanted to protest at the event because there was a lot of people from Dublin who knew this pair and a number of other criminals. If you opened your mouth then you'd probably end up in hospital.

'At least they wouldn't get away with this behaviour back in Dublin. I didn't want anyone to have these pictures until a decent period of time had passed. I have to admit that I am afraid of the likes of Hutch and Foley and the scum they hang around with. The reason I am handing them over now is that I want the public to know how so-called Ordinary Decent Criminals like these could not care less about stripping in front of young children.'

Foley was still smarting from the picture of his bare bum being splashed across a newspaper when he was again summoned to appear in court. However, this time he enjoyed a rare court victory when his case was struck out. Foley was accused of failing to produce his insurance certificate and driving licence within ten days of being stopped by gardaí in Chapelizod in March 2006.

A week before the case went to court Foley did call to Crumlin Garda Station and hand over his licence and insurance certificate, which proved he was actually allowed to be on the road when he had been stopped. His defence counsel told Judge Patrick McMahon that because he had proved that he had the relevant documentation before the case proceeded, it should be struck out.

Judge McMahon said that because he was satisfied that Mr Foley had presented his documents to gardaí, he was prepared to strike out the charges, so The Viper left the court a free man, with no new conviction to his name.

Foley could easily have been forgiven for thinking that he had turned a corner in his life. He was the owner of a burgeoning business, he had found love again, was doing a very good job bringing up his two girls, and for once he was not falling out with people who might try to shoot him.

'Dean Did It'

TOWARDS THE MIDDLE OF 2007, 'The Dapper Don', Christy Kinahan, began to consider retiring from the drugs game and returning to Ireland to enjoy his vast ill-gotten fortune. Kinahan had made tens of millions from drug dealing but he was a home bird at heart and he missed the old country.

Kinahan had fallen out with Martin Foley in 2000, and despite having the wherewithal to have The Viper shot, he did nothing for all that time. Many gangland players were surprised that Kinahan had not tried to either get Foley to pay the £90,000 they had fallen out over, or make him pay some other way. So The Dapper Don decided that he would not be able to return to Dublin with his head held high unless he had Foley murdered, sending out the message that he was back and was not to be messed with.

Kinahan decided he would have one of Martin Foley's own confidantes do the deed and he chose Fat Freddie Thompson, whom the Viper had mentored since he was a young buck climbing up the criminal ladder. Kinahan was well placed to order Thompson to do his dirty work. Thompson had become embroiled in an ugly dispute with the INLA and its dangerous leader Declan 'Whacker' Duffy. Duffy and his terrorist pals had been putting the Thompson gang under pressure to pay protection money from the proceeds of their drug dealing, but Fat Freddie was having none of it and he got into a fight with one of Duffy's lieutenants in a pub in Dublin's inner city.

In November 2007 a passing garda spotted a young INLA volunteer, Denis Dwyer from Tallaght, walking briskly up Camden Street. The apprentice plumber was carrying a sports bag with what looked like the barrel of a gun sticking out of it. He was stopped and searched and found to be in possession of an AK-47 assault rifle along with twenty rounds of ammunition. The gun had just been transported from Limerick and was to be used in a hit attempt on Thompson, who was drinking in a nearby pub.

Freddie was warned by gardaí from Crumlin and Kevin Street – for the umpteenth time – that his life was in danger, and he wisely decided to leave the country while he was still able. Spain was the obvious destination for Thompson. He sourced his drugs through Christy Kinahan, and Thompson's right-hand man and enforcer, Paddy Doyle, had been permanently based there since November 2005, when he left the country having murdered Rattigan gang member Noel Roche. Paddy Doyle was living in a three-bedroom luxury apartment in a gated community in Cancelada, near Marbella, and he was more than happy to let Fat Freddie join him there.

There are several reasons why the Spanish Costas are so attractive for Irish drug dealers. There has long been a perception that the Spanish police are somewhat lax and simply do not have the will to crack down on the drug importers and exporters who give the country a bad

name. It doesn't help that the country's coastline stretches
to 4,900 km, which means that drugs can be smuggled in
by boat from South America, via countries like Morocco
and Algeria, without much fear of seizure, because it is
impossible to police that much coastline.

Southern Spain is the European centre for large-scale
drug importation. The imported drugs are broken up in
Spain and then smuggled to other European countries.

The Costa del Sol is not known as the Costa del Crime
for nothing. In the early 1980s it developed its reputation
when an exodus of major criminals from Britain fled there
because of the complicated extradition laws. The British
criminals set up their drugs businesses in Spain and were
soon followed by their Irish counterparts. There are so
many Irish criminals operating out of the country that a
garda detective sergeant is permanently based in Madrid to
act as a liaison between the two police forces.

The Spanish lifestyle suited Freddie Thompson. Every
day Paddy Doyle and Freddie would work out in the gym,
have a long, boozy lunch in Marbella or Puerto Banus
and then meet other criminals to arrange shipments back
to Ireland. The evenings involved heavy cocaine-fueled
sessions and prostitutes, and the pair mixed with other Irish
criminals based in Spain, including Gary Hutch and Peter
'Fatso' Mitchell.

Christy Kinahan saw the life of luxury that Thompson
was living in Spain and felt that he was only able to enjoy
such a lifestyle because he, Kinahan, was supplying him
with drugs. He was happy to do business with Thompson,
but he always left other Irish criminals in little doubt that
he was the boss, and let them know that what he could
give with one hand, he could just as easily take away with

the other. So when Kinahan went to Thompson just before Christmas 2007 and said it was payback time, Thompson had no choice but to agree. His position was not helped by the fact that he owed Kinahan a fortune after a drugs shipment had been seized by gardaí, leaving him without the cash to pay up.

Kinahan told Thompson that he wanted him to organise the murder of Martin Foley as a personal favour to him. Thompson wouldn't be paid a cent, but his debt would be reduced. You would think that Thompson would have balked at having the man who had taught him the ropes killed, but he knew he had no choice, and he couldn't let any fondness he had for Foley get in the way.

Martin Foley had no idea about the plot to kill him that was being hatched. He was busy with his debt collection business and was making a small fortune on jobs up and down the country. He continued to work out in the gym every day and the fifty-six-year-old was probably as fit as he ever had been. He had also taken up yoga, believing it was good for his flexibility. Foley was also a keen cyclist, and Sonia Doyle and he would go for a forty-five-minute spin around Crumlin a couple of mornings each week.

So it was business as usual for the veteran crook on Saturday 26 January, 2008. He arrived at the Carlisle Health and Fitness Club on Kimmage Road West shortly after 1 p.m. and met with Thompson gang member Dean Howe. Twenty-four-year-old Howe from Clanbrassil Street in Dublin 8 was well known to gardaí investigating the deadly Crumlin/Drimnagh feud. Howe was a second cousin of Freddie Thompson and had hung around with him and other senior gangsters since he was a kid. Although he had only minor criminal convictions, he was regarded as being a trusted member of the gang.

Martin Foley and Dean Howe lifted weights and used the treadmills. At around 2.30 p.m. Howe announced that he had to leave unexpectedly and he quickly left the gym without even taking a shower. Foley thought nothing of it and, after showering and getting changed, he too left the gym shortly before 3 p.m. He put his gym bag into the boot of his green Audi A6 and drove the car towards the exit of the gym car park.

Foley stopped at the junction of Kimmage Road West and as he looked left and right to make sure there was no oncoming traffic, a man wearing a balaclava and brandishing a gun ran towards him. Foley barely had time to register what was happening before the gunman opened fire with a Glock 9 mm semi-automatic pistol. The shooter was less than three feet away from Foley when he pulled the trigger and within a couple of seconds, seven rounds had been discharged, all of them hitting their target.

Foley was hit in the hip, spine, kidney and three times in the shoulder. One round bounced off his skull near his right eye, miraculously causing little or no damage. None of the rounds hit Foley's arteries or vital organs. His legendary survival instincts kicked in and he crouched under the steering wheel and managed to continue to drive the car, making it far harder for the assassin to finish him off. The gunman fired four more shots but the Audi sped across the road and crashed into a garden wall, attracting the attention of passing motorists and pedestrians. The gunman fled in a waiting white Ford van, thinking that one of the shots was bound to be fatal.

Several people witnessed the murder attempt and the emergency services received multiple 999 calls. An ambulance was on the scene within five minutes, and as The Viper lay slumped on the floor of the car, losing a lot of blood, he told the paramedic, 'Dean did it, Dean did it.'

Foley was conscious enough to remember how his friend had left in a hurry not long before the incident and he immediately fingered Howe as the one who had set him up. Foley then lapsed into unconsciousness and was rushed to St James's Hospital in a critical condition.

Doctors were unsure if Foley would survive the five-hour operation to remove the bullets that were lodged in his body. There was also the chance that he could be paralysed because of the injury to his spine. He had now been hit by a total of eighteen bullets, surely a gangland record.

While doctors battled to save Foley's life, dozens of gardaí descended on Kimmage Road West and a fingertip search was carried out to try to find evidence to link somebody to the crime. The high-profile investigation was led by Detective Superintendent Denis Donegan from Crumlin Garda Station, who probably knew Foley as well as any member of the force from his time in the Tango Squad. He regularly spoke to The Viper, urging him to change his ways and go on the straight and narrow before it was too late. The pair got on quite well but Foley very rarely listened to anybody's advice. Donegan's deputy, Detective Inspector Brian Sutton, who had experience with Foley from his time in the GNDU, was put in day-to-day charge of the investigation.

The two senior detectives knew that even if Foley pulled through, the chance of him cooperating with their investigation was slim. The best hope they had of solving the case was with forensic evidence that would nail the gunman.

Everyone who was in the gym at the time of the shooting had to remain there for several hours and each person was interviewed by gardaí as they left, to see if they had noticed anything suspicious while Foley had been working out.

An hour or so after the incident the Ford van that had been used as a getaway vehicle was found a short distance away, on Wainsfort Road in Terenure. The gunman and the getaway driver had then escaped in a waiting Opel Vectra. Crucially, they made a mess of burning out the van, and when it was recovered there was a significant amount of evidence in it. The Glock pistol, which had an empty magazine, was found on the floor of the front passenger seat and a balaclava was also recovered from the van.

Gardaí initially had no concrete idea of who was responsible for the murder attempt. They knew that Foley was aligned to both the Thompson and the Rattigan gangs and they thought that perhaps one of the mobs got jealous. But Foley had crossed so many criminals over the years that any number of people could have been involved. Detectives famously joked that the Carlisle shooting was like the *Simpsons* episode 'Who Shot Mr Burns?' because there were so many potential suspects. However, when the paramedics told gardaí that Foley had mentioned Dean Howe's name, underworld touts were soon spilling the beans about Christy Kinahan's plans to come home and reassert himself in Dublin. Detectives knew that Foley and Kinahan were enemies but they didn't know that The Dapper Don had finally decided to take revenge.

Word soon spread across Dublin that Martin Foley had been shot, yet again, and within an hour the crime scene was like a circus. Journalists and passers-by gathered to try to get an insight into what had happened, all the while wondering if the legendary Rasputin-like criminal had finally met his maker.

The showband singer Dickie Rock, who lives nearby said in the aftermath of the incident, 'I came out for a wall to see what happened. It can happen anywhere. It doesn' matter where you live these days. I feel sorry for him; no human being deserves that.' Another local, Brian Kelly heard the shooting. He said, 'At five past three I heard five shots. It sounded like a handgun. Bang, bang, bang, bang bang – really quick. Then five minutes later the sirens were blaring and they took him away. I'm a regular in the gyn and I'd always see him there. They must have known hi routine, because he always goes on a Saturday.'

The fourth assassination attempt was a massive new story and it dominated the front pages of the newspaper for days. Well-known former Garda Detective Inspecto Gerry O'Carroll, who had been based in Crumlin for year and knew Foley very well, wrote a column in the *Evenin Herald* about his old nemesis two days after the inciden and predicted that if Foley recovered he would not make complaint to gardaí.

After Foley's lengthy and delicate operation, doctor said he had a 65-75 per cent chance of surviving. The were especially worried about an infection in his liver Twelve days after he was shot The Viper finally woke up He couldn't speak for several hours but he eventually began to recover and doctors were happy with his progress. Two days after he regained consciousness he was sitting up in bed and eating unassisted.

Detective Inspector Brian Sutton and Detectiv Sergeant Barry Butler called to St James's Hospital to se the patient and they were astonished by how well he looked

Sutton was a key figure in trying to broker a peace deal between the feuding Rattigan and Thompson gangs, along with local clergy and families of some of the feud victims. Sutton and Butler reminded Foley that he had implicated Dean Howe just moments after being shot and they asked him if he was prepared to make a statement. Foley shook his head and said that he could remember nothing of what happened to him. He chatted to the two detectives but he would not help them with their investigation.

Word spread that Foley would live to collect another debt and Christy Kinahan was furious that the murder had been botched. Kinahan was a far bigger player than Foley, but The Viper still had the ability to strike back. Whether he had the stomach to take on Kinahan was another question.

The Dapper Don blamed Freddie Thompson for the debacle and he was humiliated in front of other major Irish criminals at a party in Kinahan's mansion, when he was made to clean the leaves out of the swimming pool like some domestic servant.

There was good news for gardaí when the forensic laboratory came back with a DNA sample from both the gun and the balaclava. If they arrested the shooter and got his DNA, they were certain he would be convicted in court. Gardaí had seen Dean Howe around Dublin in the days after the shooting but held off on arresting him until the DNA results came back.

On 3 May gardaí made their move when the Emergency Response Unit (ERU) raided the house Howe shared with his girlfriend in the city. They found a high-tech CCTV camera system in the property, recording everyone who came or went. Howe was taken to Crumlin Garda Station and quizzed for forty-eight hours. Gardaí asked him why

Martin Foley had called out his name when he thought he was dying. Howe shrugged his shoulders and said he didn't have a clue. He made no admissions in custody and was not in the least bit helpful. A DNA sample was taken from him and he was released without charge.

Ten days later his brother Morgan was also arrested for questioning. Morgan Howe said he had no idea why The Viper had fingered his brother and said he knew nothing about the attempted murder, apart from what he had read in the newspaper. After giving a DNA sample he too was released.

The son of Eamon Daly, one of Foley's oldest associates, was also arrested as part of the investigation. Eamon Daly Jnr lived just a few doors down from The Viper and he had known Foley all his life. What Foley or Daly's father made of him being caught up in the garda probe was anyone's guess, but it's probably safe to say that things were awkward for a while if the two bumped into each other when they were bringing in their milk in the morning.

Dublin gangland is very incestuous. Everybody knows everybody else, with many players being related through intricate family relationships. Crumlin is no different. Associations went back forty years and generally criminals stuck by each other through thick and thin. But the generation of young gangsters who came up behind Foley and Daly were different in that they didn't have the same sense of loyalty that the older men did. Foley's contemporaries would have raised their eyebrows when they learned that the Howes and young Daly had been lifted for questioning about the gym shooting.

A total of six people were arrested as part of the investigation. Among those detained was Graham 'The

Wig' Whelan. Whelan, who was born in 1982 and is from Clonard Road in Crumlin, was one of Dean Howe's best friends. Whelan had been arrested in the Holiday Inn in March 2000 along with Declan Gavin, when they were found with a £1.3 million shipment of heroin and ecstasy. It was this drugs seizure that had led to the beginning of the Crumlin/Drimnagh feud, when Whelan was charged and Gavin was not. Whelan was sentenced to just six years in prison for his role and when he was released he became a key player in the Thompson gang. Whelan was very close to Freddie Thompson and detectives believed he may have been the point man in Dublin who set up the Carlisle shooting and hired the hitman. But while he was in custody Whelan said nothing and he was released without charge.

All those who were detained had DNA samples taken from them and the gardaí's real aim was to cross-check the suspects' DNA against that found in the getaway van and on the gun and balaclava. Unfortunately for detectives the gunman's DNA profile did not match any of the six men and the case hit a wall.

Gardaí are still hopeful that charges will be brought in the case. Sooner or later the shooter will be arrested, probably for a totally unrelated matter, and they will get a DNA match. The situation was frustrating for gardaí, though, who believed that if a DNA database existed, they would surely have got their man and wouldn't have had to wait for a breakthrough.

On 23 February, exactly four weeks after being shot eight times, Martin Foley told his doctor that he was ready to go home. He had been able to walk unaided around the hospital

grounds for the previous few days and was slowly getting his strength back. He said he wanted to recover in his own bed, and he was allowed to leave. The staff at St James's Hospital could not believe how quickly he had recovered but said that he would have to rest for three months to allow his body to recover from the shock and trauma. Foley nodded his head in agreement. When he arrived home to Cashel Avenue there was an unmarked garda car discreetly parked up the road to make sure nobody tried to finish the job.

One of the first things Foley did when he was back on his feet was contact gardaí and arrange to collect his car. The Audi was peppered with bullet holes but Foley brought it to a panel beater who did an excellent job repairing it. Foley didn't like to spend more money that he absolutely had to and still drives the Audi today.

Foley soon found out why he had been shot but he decided he would not retaliate. His options were limited and he didn't have much choice other than to reach out and make peace with Christy Kinahan. He also forgave Freddie Thompson, although he no doubt felt betrayed by the man he had trained.

Just a week after The Viper had survived the murder attempt, Paddy Doyle was assassinated in front of Fat Freddie. Freddie and Doyle, along with Gary Hutch, were driving in Doyle's €70,000 BMW jeep in Estepona in Spain when a man opened fire, causing the vehicle to crash. The three jumped out and made a run for it but Doyle was singled out and shot in cold blood. Gardaí believe that the Turkish mafia was responsible for the murder but Spanish police suspected that Christy Kinahan was behind it. With his chief enforcer out of the way, Freddie Thompson was extremely vulnerable and he would need the protection of The Dapper Don more than ever.

Just five weeks after returning home Foley went back to the gym and was lifting weights and swimming lengths of the pool. Staff and other gym members couldn't believe their eyes as The Viper went through his old workout routine. He did not have any minders with him and it was almost as if the shooting had never happened. Within a month, he was back to his five- or six-day-a-week fitness regime. He smiled and waved at friends and well-wishers who said it was great to see him back and looking so fit and healthy. He really was a medical wonder.

Forever in Your Debt

AFTER FOLEY WAS SHOT outside the gym in Kimmage, he decided that it would probably be wise to concentrate on his debt collection business on a full-time basis. There was no way that even his body would be able to cope with another murder attempt, so he decided to get out while the going was still good.

Foley was in a good position. The Irish economy went into recession in 2008, putting hundreds of thousands of people on the dole queue, leaving ordinary people struggling to make ends meet. Debt collection became one of the country's few thriving industries. The Viper took on several employees and had more work that he could handle. Predictably, wherever Martin Foley went, controversy followed and he quickly became the best-known and most-maligned debt collector in Ireland.

Because he was so busy, Foley realised that he would need someone to help with the day-to-day running of the company. He chose his close friend, Troy Jordan, who was born in 1970 in Tallaght, but was living in a fancy house in Allenwood, County Kildare. Jordan was regarded as one of the most senior gangland leaders, with links to mobs throughout Ireland. He had been a long-time associate of John Gilligan and even grazed his horses on Gilligan's massive Jessbrook estate. He is believed to have met and become friendly with Foley through 'Factory' John.

Before becoming a director of Foley's company, Troy Jordan was unknown to the general public and he went about his criminal business free from media interference.

Although the general public might not have had any idea who Troy Jordan was, he was well known to members of An Garda Síochána and especially to detectives attached to the Garda National Drugs Unit (GNDU), who had him on their radar since the mid-1990s. During the investigation into the murder of Veronica Guerin, in 1996, Jordan was discovered to be one of Gilligan's customers. He was purchasing large quantities of hash every week for resale and his business grew even larger when the Gilligan gang were all handed lengthy sentences for organising and carrying out the murder of the journalist.

Taking advantage of his newfound wealth and status, Troy moved to an eighteen-acre estate in Allenwood, with dog kennels and stables. It was very difficult for gardaí to monitor the sprawling, remote estate and practically anything could go on there unbeknownst to the authorities. The estate was raided by GNDU officers on several occasions, but Jordan was never found with any drugs and still has no convictions for drugs offences.

Despite leading a lavish lifestyle Jordan has never paid taxes and he was hit with a €1-million bill from the Criminal Assets Bureau, which he contested in court. The married father of two has a love for high-powered cars and dabbles in second-hand car dealing.

Jordan has been very lucky when it comes to criminal convictions. In 2005 he was jailed for eighteen months for cruelty to animals, after he was nabbed at an organised dogfight, but the conviction was overturned on appeal. He frequently goads the gardaí about their lack of success in putting him behind bars. On one occasion when he was stopped by gardaí close to his home, he shouted, 'See my arm you midget, that would break your fucking back. Get a warrant; raid my house. Fuck off, wanker! All you ever got me for was dog fighting.'

Like Foley, Jordan has been accused of being a garda informant because of his lack of convictions. But his attitude towards officers he meets does not suggest he is a man who likes the force. Foley would have a cup of tea with a garda he knows and happily chat with him, but Jordan has no time for cops.

Jordan was on very good terms with the INLA and had known many members since he was a youngster growing up on the streets of Tallaght. His brother, Arthur, was suspected of being a member of the INLA. When Arthur died in a motorbike accident in 2003, he was awaiting trial at the Special Criminal Court for the possession of weapons and ammunition. The INLA seemed to trust Jordan and he had the reputation of being a trustworthy, diplomatic type who could work with several gangs at once, even if the mobs were feuding with each other.

Jordan was arrested as part of one of the biggest murder investigations in recent years. In November 2006 Latvian mother of two Baiba Saulite was smoking a cigarette at the front door of her home in Swords, when a masked man calmly walked up and assassinated her in cold blood. The twenty-eight-year-old's two sons were asleep in their bedroom and were awoken by the gunfire. Jordan was arrested on suspicion of supplying the handgun that was used in the brutal slaying.

Gardaí suspected that he gave the weapon to the gang led by Martin 'Marlo' Hyland, a Finglas-based criminal and a massive importer of drugs. Jordan had been a close associate of Hyland and liked to keep him onside and help him out when he could. Hyland owed money to Limerick-based criminals who were members of the McCarthy-Dundon gang and it was agreed that the debt would be reduced if Hyland got one of his men to murder Saulite.

The man who wanted the Latvian killed was her estranged husband, Hassan Hassan, a crooked Lebanese car importer and general Mr Fixit in the crime world. He had been involved in a bitter custody dispute with Baiba. He also took out a contract on her solicitor, John Hennessy. Hassan shared a cell in Mountjoy with one of the Limerick criminals and together they hatched the plot to murder Saulite.

Jordan didn't know anything about the murder plot and was just doing some friends a turn by supplying the gun. When he heard about what happened to Saulite he went ballistic and had a major falling out with Hyland, accusing him of misleading him and dragging him into a murder he wanted nothing to do with.

Just three weeks after Baiba Saulite's murder, Marlo Hyland was himself shot dead in his sister's home in Finglas. Two gunmen walked into the house and fired at him as he slept in an upstairs bedroom. The killers had been surprised to find a young apprentice plumber, Anthony Campbell, doing a job on a downstairs radiator and, fearing that he would be able to recognise them and identify them to gardaí, they shot him dead.

Hyland was killed by members of his own gang, who suspected that he had been a garda informer for years. The man who masterminded his death, Eamon 'The Don' Dunne, took over the gang, and in a four-year period he ordered the murders of at least seventeen men. Dunne was shot dead in April 2010. He was whacked because the murders he ordered brought unprecedented garda attention on gangs operating in the capital.

Although Troy Jordan had been close to Marlo Hyland he also made sure that he kept on the good side of his ruthless successor. It was such calculated decisions that made Jordan so successful. Choosing him to be part of his debt collection company looked like a smart move on The Viper's part. With his reputation and connections, it was obvious that Jordan was not to be messed with.

It wasn't long before Foley's thriving business attracted media attention. In February 2009 a man calling himself 'John' rang Joe Duffy's *Liveline* radio programme and spoke about why he had hired Foley to collect debts on his behalf, despite knowing that he was regarded as one of the country's most notorious criminals. He was responding to complaints by several callers about the conduct of members of Foley's debt collection team. One woman said, 'There were about four or five of them and I felt intimidated when they surrounded my car. It seemed like they were up to no good. The whole thing left me very upset.'

'John' provoked outrage when he said that he would have no problem in going out for a pint with Foley. He told Joe Duffy, 'I was owed by between nine and eleven people about €330,000 and a good friend of mine told me about Martin Foley and I got in contact with him. I asked him was he legit in his business. He showed me his credentials and I was happy enough that he was above board. When I asked these people to pay me back, they told me to get lost with myself. But after putting it over to Martin Foley I got half my money back. He called himself and he has seven or eight of the companies paying up so far. When I told them I was going to hire Martin Foley it made no difference but when he went round they agreed to pay. I thought he was a decent enough skin that you could go for a drink with.' 'John' said that he had paid Foley an up-front fee of €1,000 and was also giving the criminal 20 per cent of every debt he successfully collected.

The following Sunday the *Sunday World* revealed 'John' to be Noel O'Reilly, the owner of O'Reilly Oil in Graiguecullen, in County Carlow. The newspaper approached the fifty-five-year-old businessman and asked him to justify hiring the thug to collect money for him.

O'Reilly said he only approached The Viper as a last resort and that he was 'sick to his stomach' over the controversy it had brought him. The owners of a local family business that went into liquidation owing O'Reilly Oil €100,000 made a formal complaint to the gardaí, claiming that Foley and his partner, Sonia Doyle, had threatened and intimidated them when the couple called to their home the previous December. Noel O'Reilly said, 'It is a road that I never went down in my life. I never threatened anyone in my life. It is unfair [to me]. If I had the help that everyone else has, none of this would even happen. We do have feelings and bad health goes with all of this, especially when you have never been down this road before. Businesses should not have to resort to thugs like Foley. I had no choice but to get my money back and I did everything in my power to ask people to give me the money they owe me. He [Foley] was successful and he collected €160,000 of €329,000 that I was owed. I won't be using his services any more because I have enough money to keep my business going. People were prepared to pay straight away. I am only owed money now by that one family.

'It cost me €100,000 to pay the bank and Foley. There are several people in Carlow who have hired his services because they are all in deep trouble. There is no help out there for the self-employed. If there was someone there to help me like every other organisation there to help the unemployed then I would not have went to Foley.'

The businessman then said that if there are official doubts about the suitability of Martin Foley to be a debt collector, he should be stripped of his licence. 'If the government and the Department of Justice are saying that this man is a thug and on the other hand are giving him a licence, it doesn't make sense. Why don't they either go one way or the other and just say that this man doesn't deserve a licence and he's not getting a licence? Why does the regulator allow people like Foley to practise?'

O'Reilly said he was aware of the backgrounds and reputations of Martin Foley and his fellow director, Troy Jordan, and when asked about how he felt about employing them to act on his behalf, he replied, 'I feel horrible, absolutely horrible. I am finished with them now.'

The interview with Noel O'Reilly was hugely revealing because it essentially showed just how much Foley and his company were making from debt collecting. O'Reilly admitted that Foley had collected €160,000 on his behalf, so Foley would have pocketed a minimum of €32,000. He was making more than the average industrial wage for just one job, and judging by the number of times he was popping up around the country, his debt collection business was proving to be a very lucrative one.

On 30 April 2009 building projects manager Greg Kavanagh went to the High Court to seek an injunction against developer Dara O'Neill, who had hired Martin Foley to collect a debt on his behalf. Kavanagh told the court that a man who identified himself as Martin Foley from The Viper Debt Recovery and Repossession Agency arrived at his family home on 15 April with another man called Barry. He said they were there to collect a debt on behalf of Dara O'Neill. Mr Kavanagh said he felt threatened by the pair and feared for his own safety and also the safety of his family. He told Foley that he did not owe O'Neill a penny and that he was actually owed money by O'Neill for project management work he carried out for him. Foley warned him that he would be calling back 'and that I had better pay,' Kavanagh said. He went on to tell the court that on 28 April he received a phone call from Barry, who said he was working on behalf of Dara O'Neill and that he had better fix him up immediately 'and if I didn't he would organise a gang of men in a van to come and get me'.

Kavanagh said he was now very afraid there 'may be violence which may result in personal injury and/or death'. He claimed that people acting on behalf of O'Neill had previously broken into his office, assaulted him and tried to assault a female member of his staff before being removed by gardaí. He also alleged that on the night of 7 April 2009, four unidentified men arrived at his family home, took him out of the house and assaulted him. He said three of the men held him down while a fourth put a gun in his mouth and advised him to pay what he owed. These men were never identified. Mr Kavanagh was granted a temporary injunction preventing and restraining 'his [O'Neill's] servants or agents, or anyone entering in concert with them from interfering with, threatening or using violence against him [Kavanagh] and members of his family.'

Dara O'Neill was not represented at the hearing, but the following week he went before Ms Justice Mary Laffoy and strongly denied that he had anything to do with any threats allegedly made by others to Greg Kavanagh. He said, however, that he was prepared to give an undertaking that he would not interfere with or threaten Mr Kavanagh or members of his family.

In May 2009 Foley and several of his employees turned up to a creditors' meeting of renewable energy retailer Solire, who owed around €800,000 to unsecured creditors. The meeting, at the Amber Springs Hotel in Gorey, County Wexford descended into farce and the solicitor who had been appointed liquidator of the company walked out. The meeting heard that Caroline Godkin, from Bridgetown in Wexford, had hired Foley to collect an €8,000 debt owed to her by Solire. This amount was at the lower end of the scale, which meant Godkin had little chance of recovering her money.

One of the creditors told the local newspaper that he was shocked to see the well-known crook from Dublin. He said, 'The Viper and his four henchmen came in and sat in front of Barry [Doyle, a director of Solire], asking a lot of direct, personal questions. Things started to get heated up and Foley did not get the response he was looking for and kept on asking questions.' This was too much for the solicitor, who left the meeting and said he no longer wanted to be involved in the liquidation process. It is likely that he knew exactly whom he was dealing with and didn't like the prospect of working with The Viper.

Caroline Godkin told the *Wexford People* that Martin Foley's company had been recommended to her and that she was unhappy with the way she was treated by Solire after she had paid the company for a heating system that was never installed. She said, 'I chose a small, local Wexford company to keep employment in this county. I paid that money in good faith and I have nothing to be ashamed of.' The frustrated woman said she hired Foley after she had spent a lot of time chasing the renewable energy company. 'I have no more time for phone calls or chasing this company, so I hired a very effective debt recovery company.' She added that Foley's company had never been prosecuted and said, 'If the biggest issue people have from that meeting is who I hired, they are very misguided.'

Politicians had been reading the media reports about the activities of Foley and his cronies and following the various High Court injunction cases, and they were becoming very uneasy. Fine Gael's justice spokesman, Charlie Flanagan, led the charge against Foley being allowed to operate in the debt collection business. In May 2009 he used Dáil privilege to blast The Viper and his dubious tactics. He said, 'One particularly well-known criminal drug trafficker – I am reluctant to name names when people are not here, but I will – Martin Foley, glories in his criminal connections. He has used his criminal moniker as part of his debt collection company's title, Viper Debt Recovery and Repossession Service Ltd. He has his white van and travels up to people's doors, sometimes at night. He parks the van in such a way that people see the livery on the side of the van, and in case anybody does not recognise him or know who he is, he asks, "Do you not know who I am? There is my van. Look at my name. Now do you know who I am?"

'There have been widespread reports about The Viper's debt collection activities in the Midlands and the South East, and yet the authorities are doing little to relieve the burden and stress on the individuals who have had occasion to meet this man in recent times. I have drafted a bill which is aimed at protecting debtors from people like The Viper.'

Under Flanagan's proposals debt collector licences would be granted only to individuals who had been vetted by gardaí and had their criminal records checked. Debt collectors would also be required to have a tax clearance certificate and complaints about debt collectors could be made to the Financial Regulator. The plans included a clause that stipulated that the Financial Regulator and the person owing the money would have to be informed if the debt was being sold on to a third party such as Martin Foley's company.

On 23 July 2009 another debt collection case came before the High Court. A couple applied for an injunction against a County Roscommon contractor who had hired Viper Debt Recovery and Repossession Services Ltd to collect a debt for them.

Martin Canny, a retired surveyor, and his wife, Teresa Hand-Campbell, a school principal, claimed that intimidating thugs from Foley's company had been harassing them. The couple sought the injunction against Richard Kenny, who had carried out gardening work on their land. The court heard that the couple denied that they owed Kenny €13,250 and there was a separate court case about this alleged debt.

In her affidavit Ms Hand-Campbell said there was a knock on the door of her home on 13 July at around 3 p.m. She was in the house with her ten-year-old daughter and when she opened the door she saw two men in a white van with 'Viper Debt Recovery and Repossession Services Limited' printed on the side in large lettering. Ms Hand-Campbell said that one of the men looked quite threatening and that the other had a clipboard and documents in his hands.

The man with the documentation handed her a business card and told her that they worked for Martin Foley of Viper Debt Recovery. He said they were there to collect €13,500 that was owed to Richard Kenny. She told them that the matter was in the hands of their solicitors. Foley's employee said, 'I doubt that,' and asked for her solicitor's number. He then asked for her husband's number, to which the school principal replied that her husband was visually impaired and should not be harassed.

Ms Hand-Campbell asked the men to leave immediately. As they were leaving, one of the men turned and said, 'We will be back later and again tomorrow, without a doubt.' The woman felt intimidated and she phoned the gardaí in Roscommon, who told her to ring them if the men returned.

Ms Hand-Campbell told the court that Mr Kenny would not let the matter of the disputed debt rest and he wouldn't call off Foley. When asked why she wasn't seeking an injunction against the well-known criminal, she said she was intimidated by his reputation but was seeking an order restraining his company from acting for Richard Kenny.

Ms Justice Mary Laffoy granted a temporary injunction restraining Kenny or anyone acting on his behalf from watching or following the couple. The following day Richard Kenny appeared before the court and denied that he or

'Fat' Freddie Thompson was mentored by Martin Foley but organised for him to be shot in January 2008.

Fat Freddie was extradited to Spain in October 2011 to face questioning about his role in Christy Kinahan's drug empire.

John 'The Colonel' Cunningham with his wife, Mary.

Cunningham being led away by Spanish police in May 2010 after he was arrested as part of Operation Shovel, which smashed Christy Kinahan's drug dealing operation.

Dean Howe (left) and Graham 'The Wig' Whelan are part of 'Fat' Freddie Thompson's gang. Both men were arrested as part of the garda investigation into the failed murder attempt on The Viper in January 2008.

© *Sunday World*

Paddy Doyle was mentored by Martin Foley. He was assassinated in Spain in February 2008.

© *Sunday World*

'The Dapper Don' Christy Kinahan came from humble roots in Dublin to become one of Europe's biggest drug dealers.

© *Sunday World*

Kinahan's empire came to a spectacular end in May 2010 when he and the key members of his gang were arrested as part of a massive investigation led by Spanish police.

© *Sunday World*

Martin Foley does the full monty on a holiday in
January 2007.

Foley celebrates his daughter Amy turning twenty-one in July
2010.

Foley is famous for keeping himself in great shape. His fitness helped to save him during the four attempts on his life.

© *Sunday World*

The Viper sits in his van outside the home of somebody he is trying to collect a debt from. Foley's debt collection business has made him a wealthy man.

© *Sunday World*

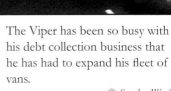

The Viper has been so busy with his debt collection business that he has had to expand his fleet of vans.

© *Sunday World*

Foley photographed in garda custody.

Foley loses his cool when confronted by journalist Donal MacIntyre in August 2012.

Detective Superintendent Brian Sutton is in charge of policing in the Crumlin area and led the investigation into the shooting of The Viper outside Ben Dunne's gym, in January 2008.

© *Mark Condren*

anyone on his behalf had been intimidating the couple. However, he agreed that he would obey the injunction and that nobody would approach the couple or look for payment of the disputed debt on his behalf. He handed in a letter to the court stating that although he had hired The Viper's company, he had since asked Foley not to act on his behalf. Ms Justice Laffoy said it was very important that he understood the terms of the injunction and that if he broke any of the terms the Campbells could return to court and apply to have him jailed for contempt.

It wasn't just the politicians who were speaking out against the unregulated debt collection industry. Influential legal reform groups were also having their say. A Law Reform Commission report in October 2009 called for criminals to be barred from becoming debt collectors:

> A major concern arises from the fact that Irish law does not place restrictions on those who may act as a debt collector, with the consequence that those guilty of criminal offences or other prior misconduct are not prevented from carrying on collection activities. The Commission therefore believes that a licensing system should be introduced for the debt collection industry. All those engaging in debt collection activities should be required to obtain a licence. Concerns have been raised about the use of deceptive and unfair practices by private debt collectors, as well as of debtor harassment. In 2009 High Court injunctions were obtained against creditors and their debt collector agents restraining them from activities such as interfering with, threatening or using violence against debtors, as well as restraining them from trespassing on debtors.
>
> The Commission believes that a strong case exists for the introduction of a licensing system for debt collection.

The laissez faire attitude in Ireland towards debt

collectors is in stark contrast to the UK where anyone wanting to work in the area is required to go through a thorough application and vetting process with the Office of Fair Trading. Once officials are satisfied that the person is of good character then they are issued with an official licence and subject to regular checks. If not, then they are not allowed to officially work in the field.

In early 2010 Foley split with his business partner since 2006, Troy Jordan, who left The Viper's company to set up his own business, the suspiciously familiar sounding Troy Jordan Debt Recovery and Repossession Agency. When asked by a newspaper if his company was separate from Martin Foley's business Troy said, 'Yes, I can confirm that my relationship with Martin Foley is finished.'

Gardaí had no idea why the pair ended their successful business relationship. Jordan refused to shed any light on the subject, saying he had no other comment to make except that his business was legitimate. Jordan's company website says, 'We specialise in pre-court debt recovery as well as post-court-judgement debt enforcement. We get real results. When letters are ignored and cheques bounce, it's time for a face-to-face visit from a debt collector. Our agents are very persuasive and your debtors will soon discover that a debt collector is not as easy to ignore as a letter or phone call.' Whatever the reason behind the split, the two men seemed to have parted amicably and are still said to be on good terms today.

As the worst recession in living memory tightened its grip on the country, gardaí were getting calls from concerned members of the public who had the bad luck to come across Foley. Business was so brisk that Foley expanded his fleet of vans from one to five. Despite the roaring trade he was doing, Foley's accounts for 2010, which were filed towards the end of 2011, showed that his company somehow managed to lose €18,000. Foley claimed that his turnover was just €22,252, against administrative costs of €40,590 leaving him with a net loss. This was in sharp contrast to the €27,316 profit he made the previous year. Records showed that the firm employed just two people, including Foley, which was down one person from the year before. Foley and his fellow director, Sonia Doyle, claimed salaries of €20,000 each, which was up from €12,285 in 2009. He failed to file any company accounts between 2004 and 2009 and was lucky that the company was not struck off.

In May 2010 Foley turned up at Terenure Garda Station, in South Dublin, having made an appointment to meet with detectives who were investigating claims that the debt collector had tried to intimidate a businessman in Dundalk, County Louth into paying him money. Foley and a close associate were interviewed for over two hours and, predictably, denied any wrongdoing, claiming that the company never broke the law in any way. Almost as predictable was the fact that Foley walked out the front door of the station after the questioning without being charged with any offence.

In October 2010 Sinn Féin TD for Kerry and former IRA man Martin Ferris came out against Martin Foley after The Viper was spotted around the county trying to collect debts. Ferris said the people Foley was targeting were very frightened and were under severe financial pressure because of the recession. He said that the mere appearance of the criminal was enough to spread fear. Criticising the government for not introducing legislation to properly regulate the industry, Ferris said,

It has come to my attention that some people are employing the services of known criminals as debt collectors to pursue people in this constituency. One of these criminals is Martin 'The Viper' Foley, who has been in the debt collecting business for quite a while. Unfortunately there is little regulation and no code of conduct for debt collecting in this State, so anybody, including known criminals, can set up legitimate debt collecting companies and are free to use whatever tactics they can get away with. I have received a copy of one letter sent to a businessman in North Kerry stating that his details had been passed on to The Viper Foley's company. This person, whose business has collapsed, has a young family and is extremely fearful about what might happen.

I am sure there are other families out there who are in a similar position and I want to make it clear to them that Sinn Féin will stand with them against any form of intimidation by these people. This is another legacy of this government's reckless policies over the past decade. We have the ESB and Bord Gáis threatening to disconnect people's electricity, we have banks threatening people's homes and we have The Viper Foley collecting debt without fear from the law.

Deputy Ferris's speech was undoubtedly passionate, but the same man had served a ten-year jail sentence for importing 160 guns and over 70,000 rounds of ammunition on board the *Marita Ann*, at Fenit, County Kerry. In 2005 Ferris was also named by Justice Minister Michael McDowell as being a member of the IRA Army Council. Mr Ferris failed to see the irony of a man with his history lecturing against criminality.

In another case, in Bunclody, County Wexford a man said he was on holidays with his wife in November 2010, when he got a phone call from his son to say that a man who claimed to be from The Viper's debt collection business had called to the door, looking for payment of a bill of over €6,000 for work that had been carried out on the man's farm. The man's son told The Viper's representative that he was on private property and asked him to leave or he would call the gardaí. The debt collector, named in court as Kevin Ryan, allegedly shouted as he got into his van, 'I'll be back and I'll get you.'

Ryan allegedly later telephoned and said he had been hired to do a job and wanted the full €6,000 that was allegedly owed. The son said Ryan vowed to 'come and see me again and it wouldn't be fucking pretty'.

A few days after this incident the man being pursued for the debt rang Foley's company and said he would not deal with debt collectors. He is then alleged to have received a phone call, during which the caller told him, 'You got the guards on one of our lads yesterday and the best thing you can do is leave the bleeding country. The next time I see you it won't be on private property.'

In court the man who hired Kevin Ryan to collect the debt on his behalf said he wasn't aware of any threats and that Ryan hadn't mentioned Martin Foley to him. It appeared that such was The Viper's reputation that other debt collectors were using his name to inspire fear in those they went after. In fact Ryan was not on Foley's staff and had no relationship with him.

In July 2011 the country's most notorious debt collector came face-to-face with the country's most notorious chef in a confrontation that left diners shocked and amazed.

Conrad Gallagher is a controversial character with a long and chequered financial history. Although he is undoubtedly one of the greatest chefs of his generation, his ability to run a business and pay his bills is more questionable. During the 1990s he ran popular high-end restaurants in Dublin, including Peacock Alley, Christopher's and Lloyd's Brasserie, and he even cooked for Bill Clinton at the White House on St Patrick's Day in 1996. However, all of Gallagher's businesses have eventually closed after running up sizeable debts. Gallagher had recently taken over the popular Dining Room restaurant at the La Stampa Hotel, on Dublin's Dawson Street, when Foley sauntered in and asked a waiter if he could speak to the owner.

The fiery Donegal chef came out of the kitchen, where he was in the middle of a busy lunch service, and was confronted by The Viper, who told him who he was and said he was there to collect a debt for a food supplier who hadn't been paid.

According to witnesses there was an angry confrontation between Gallagher and Foley. Gallagher was reportedly not at all intimidated by Foley, and told him to get out of his restaurant and that he wouldn't be paying him a penny. Sources say that the supplier was owed €16,000 and that the debt stretched back several years. He felt he had no option but to hire Foley because he couldn't get Gallagher to pay up.

Gallagher dialled 999 and two uniformed officers came and arrested Foley and took him to Pearse Street Garda Station. He was searched and released without charge, and because Gallagher decided not to make an official complaint, the investigation went no further.

The temperamental chef is known to have a hard neck and, with a straight face, he told a newspaper, 'There are several people in this building that he [Foley] could have been in to see. The whole thing was very upsetting for my family, my wife.' In January 2012 it emerged that Gallagher was up to his old tricks after he closed his restaurants and left the country, leaving behind an unpaid tax bill of €160,000 and debts in the tens of thousands.

◆ ◆ ◆

In July 2011 one of Foley's employees was jailed for seven years for stabbing his girlfriend's brother eight times while out of his mind 'on a cocktail of drink and drugs'. Kenneth Nolan from Rutland Grove in Crumlin had long been suspected by gardaí of being a violent enforcer, used by Foley to intimidate people into paying debts that Foley had taken on. He had featured in several complaints made about Foley's company and gardaí say he was a dangerous psychopath who was unpredictable and could turn violent without warning.

Frightened debtors who were pursued by Foley told gardaí that Nolan would stand and stare menacingly at them and warn them that there would be 'serious consequences' if they didn't pay up. He was well known in Crumlin for his violent ways and had been arrested on over a dozen occasions for serious offences. He was always abusive and aggressive while in custody.

Nolan's victims were afraid to make statements to gardaí, for fear of the retribution he would exact. Because of this the thirty-five-year-old only had a handful of convictions, for minor offences. This was perfect for Foley – one of the reasons he employed Nolan was because he could not be accused of having a serious criminal working for him; Foley liked to keep up the charade that he was a legitimate businessman and that he had no association with crime.

However, this lie was exposed in court when evidence

was heard that on Father's Day in June 2009 Nolan stabbed Patrick Whelan eight times in the chest. Nolan had tried to get into his girlfriend, Pamela Whelan's, flat, but she wouldn't let him in because he was so drunk. Whelan went mental and punched Pamela, who was the mother of his three children, in the face, chest and side. After threatening to set fire to her parents' house he said, 'I am going to kill your fucking brother,' before storming off.

Pamela tried to ring her brother to warn him but she couldn't get through. Nolan had better luck, though, and asked Patrick Whelan, whom he had known his whole life, to come to his house with sleeping tablets, as he couldn't sleep. When Whelan arrived Nolan attacked him without warning in what a judge described as a wholly gratuitous incident.

Whelan suffered a collapsed lung and nearly died on the operating table, but doctors managed to save his life. Nolan was charged with attempted murder but pleaded guilty to assault causing serious harm before the trial got underway. He blamed the amount of drink and drugs he had taken on the day of the attack, but Judge Paul Carney said that 'the voluntary consumption of drink and drugs form no defence and no mitigation'.

Foley was not in court to see his loyal worker caged, but friends said that he regarded Nolan as a good employee and he wasn't ruling out hiring him again after he had served his sentence.

In October 2011 this author interviewed a group of businessmen from County Carlow who vowed that they would not be intimidated by Foley and his cronies, after

Tom Nolan Jnr, a local business tycoon, hired The Viper to collect outstanding debts when his father's company went out of business. Several small electrical contractors complained that they had been targeted by Foley and his employees for sums as low as €5,000. At least five small business owners received visits from the debt collectors, who told them they had been hired by the wholesalers to collect money. Carlow Electrical Wholesalers (CEW) went out of business in July 2011, but the owner's son was still trying to get money out of people who had done business with his father for over thirty years.

Contractors complained that they were being intimidated into handing over money that they didn't have and they came together to offer each other support in dealing with Foley and his heavies. One CEW customer owed €80,000 to the company in 2009 but had worked hard to bring the bill down to just over €20,000. He was paying the debt off each month without fail, but Nolan set Foley on him with no warning. Two employees turned up at his business premises and said they were there to collect cash on behalf of Tom Nolan Jnr. The man, who works with his elderly father, told them he would not deal with them and sent them on their way. However, a secretary working for Foley rang and said if the man didn't settle the outstanding debt they would continue calling to see his father and would deal with him directly and make sure he paid. This author heard the veiled threat and when the secretary was asked if she was threatening the man, she replied that the company operated within the law but that they would not go away until they were paid in full.

The man bravely said that he would refuse to be intimidated by Foley or his employees, despite the company vowing to approach his elderly father. He said, 'My company has been badly hit by the recession, as has Tom Nolan's, who has been forced to shut up shop. For the last ten years we gave him around €30,000 worth of business a month, but a few people we did jobs for closed and didn't pay us, so we fell behind. At one stage we owed Nolan €80,000 and paid upfront for materials and paid the debt off each month. We had it down to around €20,000 and were working to get it down to nothing. Two men who worked for The Viper called and spoke to my elderly father. They said they wanted the money and would be back until they were paid.

'They were careful not to threaten violence but there was clear intimidation. They were rough sorts with lots of tattoos. We are honest business people trying to keep afloat in a recession and won't be intimidated by men like Foley who are involved in serious gangland crime. After I sent them away I got a call from a secretary and she said that if I wouldn't deal with them then my father would have to. It is shocking altogether. I contacted Tom Nolan Jnr and he said it is out of his hands. We have worked with his firm for over a decade. It is disgraceful. I don't care what happens, I won't be giving in to these bullying tactics, even if Foley does call back.'

Tom Nolan Jnr had no comment to make when he was asked why he had hired Foley to collect on his behalf. After Tom Nolan was exposed in the *Sunday World*, Martin Foley and his cronies were not seen again in Carlow.

Because of the amount of money Martin Foley is making out of debt collecting – despite what his accounts might suggest – there is little prospect of him leaving the lucrative business any time soon. He would argue that he operates within the law, does not threaten anyone and has never inflicted violence on anyone. The truth is that he doesn't have to. His presence and reputation and the unspoken threat of violence are enough to bully ordinary people into paying up, for fear of what could happen to them. It is typical bullying behaviour.

The only thing that could force him out is regulation of the industry, and this does not seem likely to be introduced in the short term. Despite the good work of .Charlie Flanagan and Fine Gael in drafting legislation, when the Fine Gael/Labour coalition came to power in 2010 there was no further talk of regulation. However, if the court injunctions and media highlighting of the dubious methods and tactics used by Foley's company continue, politicians will have little option but to act to clean up the industry.

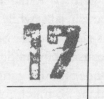

Getting Even

MARTIN FOLEY HAD SURVIVED the January 2008 murder attempt ordered by Christy Kinahan against all the odds. Although he had to swallow his pride and make peace with The Dapper Don, he was obviously bitter about what had happened and had neither forgiven nor forgotten.

The Viper has outlasted many who had plotted his downfall in the past and Kinahan proved to be no different. Foley must have smiled to himself on 25 May 2010, when Kinahan finally got his comeuppance. Hundreds of Spanish police launched a pre-dawn operation aimed at ending the activities of the Irish and British godfathers who were operating out of Marbella and Peurto Banus. By lunchtime thirty-four people in Spain, Ireland and the UK had been detained as part of the massive international operation. Ten Irish nationals were put behind bars in Puerto Banus, including Kinahan, his two sons, Daniel and Christy Jnr, and his right hand man, John 'The Colonel' Cunningham. The arrests were the culmination of Operation Shovel, a two-year investigation that involved police forces across Europe.

Christy Kinahan and his cohorts were thrown into Spanish jails while the investigations were completed. It was clear that the Spanish police had done their homework because they raided dozens of businesses suspected of laundering the gang's drugs money. The Dapper Don was making so much money from drugs that he had to clean it up and make it legitimate, so he devised a clever scheme to put his cash into a massive property portfolio and business empire in Brazil. When the Spanish started to look through the thirty-one companies linked to Kinahan, they were amazed to find a portfolio containing over half a billion euro worth of property located in a number of exclusive resorts in the South American country. The Resort du Mar, Taiba Sands and Malibu Golf Suites are located in Fortaleza, Paraiba and Uruau, along the northeast coast of Brazil, on forty-four hectares of white sand. The three resorts include hundreds of luxury villas, hotels, swimming pools, golf courses, bars and top-class restaurants. The area is known as the St Tropez of Brazil and boasts year-round sunshine.

Spanish cops secured an order from a judge to freeze the assets of the thirty-one companies in Kinahan's empire. Properties in the Brazilian resorts were marketed as good investments by a Spanish company called Green Land Securities, of which Daniel Kinahan had been a director.

When Kinahan was photographed being led into a Spanish court in handcuffs and ankle chains it was a humiliating and stunning fall for the man who had been at the helm of a massive empire that had been built up in less than a decade.

Kinahan's Irish mob was so powerful in Spain that a senior government minister there dubbed them the 'Irish mafia'. They played second fiddle to no other group. The court heard that as well as money laundering and drug dealing, Spanish police were also probing the murders of Paddy Doyle in February 2008 and the disappearance and presumed murder of Irish drug dealer John 'The Mexican' McKeown in January 2007. The Kinahan gang was also linked to a failed assassination bid on former close associate Peter 'Fatso' Mitchell. Gardaí estimated that Kinahan had been responsible for flooding Ireland with close to a billion euro worth of drugs and that his personal fortune was in excess of €150 million.

Kinahan's two sons, along with John Cunningham, were released on bail shortly after their arrest, but The Dapper Don was forced to languish in a Spanish jail until November 2010, when he was finally bailed.

It is estimated that the Spanish probe could take until 2014 to complete, but Kinahan's empire now lies in ruins, well and truly smashed by the massive investigation.

To make matters worse for Kinahan, in the summer of 2011 he was extradited to Belgium to serve a four-year sentence for money laundering. He is still in prison and his son Daniel is now in charge of the family business. Although the gang is still heavily involved in drug importation, it is far less powerful than it once was and it is unlikely to ever recover.

While the Spanish authorities were confiscating the assets the Kinahans acquired with the proceeds of drug dealing, Martin Foley was making more money than ever, and it was all legitimate. Well, as legitimate as Foley gets.

In July 2010 Foley's daughter Amy celebrated her

twenty-first birthday and her dad was at the party, obviously proud as punch. He presented her with a birthday cake, which was decorated with a picture of her in an Irish dancing costume. The veteran criminal was photographed laughing and clapping as a male stripper strutted his stuff in front of Amy, a qualified dance teacher. Foley looked on and took the antics of the stripper in good spirits but Amy later posted on her Facebook page that although he seemed to be enjoying the stripper, he was really mortified. Foley took to the dance floor and boogied the night away, celebrating Amy's coming of age.

Foley could not be faulted for the job he did in raising his two daughters. Their mum had died six years previously and it can't have been easy for him to bring up two teenage girls as a lone parent. The fact that they both turned out to be lovely, law-abiding adults who held down steady jobs showed that Foley was determined that they did not go down the road he had gone down. He had always been a devoted family man and even the most cynical of gardaí admit that they had to raise their hat to his parenting skills.

July 2010 was a mixed month for Foley, though. The week before the birthday shindig this author reported that the Criminal Assets Bureau had launched a fresh investigation into Foley and were anticipating hitting him with a hefty bill for non-declaration of income tax. Senior gardaí were alarmed with the reports that Foley's debt collection business was causing headaches for ordinary decent people, and CAB was ordered to look into his affairs with a fine-tooth comb. Detectives were very sceptical about the accounts filed by the company, and because Foley was heavily involved in criminality, they knew he had the assets to pay any judgement against him.

The garda PULSE computer system was used to collate sightings of Foley, and it soon became clear that either he or his representatives had been spotted in counties up and down the country, trying to collect debts. This busy schedule didn't tally with the tiny amounts of money that had been declared in his annual accounts.

There was more good family-related news for Foley during a Christmas 2010 romantic getaway to Puerto Rico, in Gran Canaria, when he proposed to his long-time girlfriend, Sonia Doyle. Despite the age gap, Foley got down on one knee and asked for Sonia's hand in marriage, presenting her with an expensive diamond ring. Sonia was said to be delighted with the proposal and she immediately accepted. Foley had originally intended to turn on the romance and propose in Paris, but the snowy conditions led to the cancellation of the flight and he instead opted to pop the question in sunny Puerto Rico.

Even though he was now a legitimate businessman, Foley still hated the media and could not help but try to bring them to task when he felt he had been wronged. In March 2010 the Press Ombudsman, Professor John Horgan, gave a ruling about a complaint he had received from Foley against the *Evening Herald* about an article published in the paper on 8 December 2009. Foley's solicitor went to the Ombudsman and made a rake of complaints about the *Herald* scoop, which reported that Foley had been arrested the night before, lurking outside journalist Paul Williams' house. Foley's gripe was that the newspaper had reported as fact that he had been arrested by armed detectives and handed over to members of the Garda Special Branch for questioning, while also having his car searched. Foley maintained that these facts were unconfirmed. The newspaper meanwhile stood over the story and said every word of it was true.

The Viper claimed that seven statements made about him in the story were untrue and when his solicitor was asked to further support his client's claim, according to the Ombudsman, he 'submitted a letter that repeated and amplified the original complaints but did not supply any additional information to support that the statements were inaccurate'. Because the two sides were so opposed Professor Horgan could not rule on the accuracy issue.

Bizarrely, Foley's solicitor claimed that because the *Herald* story had mentioned Williams as being a *Sunday World* crime correspondent it should have mentioned its 'conflict of interest' because both newspapers were owned by the same company. Not surprisingly this argument cut no mustard with the Ombudsman. Professor Horgan found against the paper on a technical issue over one complaint, but Foley's other gripes were dismissed.

Foley was still a prolific whinger when it came to articles about him. He takes offence to what he sees as slights against his character and fires out legal letters like confetti at a wedding. Just two months after complaining to the Press Ombudsman about the *Evening Herald*, Foley turned his attention to the *Irish Daily Star Sunday*, his complaint centring on an article the newspaper published in February 2010, which was illustrated with a photograph of Foley outside a Dublin gym. He complained that the piece was in breach of the principle of fairness and honesty and that it also amounted to an invasion of privacy. His solicitor claimed that Foley 'neither consented to nor was aware that the photographs published in the article were being taken'. In order for his fairness and honesty argument to have succeeded he had to prove that the photos were obtained through either misrepresentation or subterfuge or that he was snapped in a private place. Because he was photographed in public his complaint was not upheld. His claim about a breach of privacy also failed to impress, as did his contention that the publication of the photograph hurt the feelings of his family.

In April 2011 Martin Foley's best-friend-turned-sworn-enemy, Clive Bolger, became embroiled in a bitter dispute with a former pal Shane Lyons. The row started when Lyons was released from a spell on remand in prison to find that Bolger had looted his house after Lyons had given him the key to make sure the property was safe.

The dispute was so bitter that gardaí were forced to warn both men that their lives were in danger and give them personal security advice. Forty-one-year-old Lyons was a former dodgy second-hand car dealer and a convicted drug trafficker. He had spent six months on remand in prison after savagely beating his girlfriend. When Lyons realised that he would be doing a stretch inside he handed over the keys to Bolger, whom he trusted absolutely. Bolger was a tricky character and the row with Foley had never really ended so he was under a permanent threat. He took advantage of the plush pad in leafy Rathfarnham and threw wild parties there.

When Lyons finally stepped out of Cloverhill Prison he expected the house to look as immaculate as when he had left it. Instead he found that the house had been cleaned out.

Lyons was so angry that he broke the number one rule of gangland by going to Rathfarnham Garda Station and making a statement about the theft. He said Bolger was responsible and that he had tried in vain to get him to pay up. Bolger was asked about Lyons' accusations and denied all knowledge of any wrongdoing. Officers privately heard that Bolger had accused Lyons of double-crossing him and claimed he was owed tens of thousands of euro. Bolger kept his head down and stayed in a safe house in Tallaght in case his former chum tried to make him pay for the theft with his life.

With Christy Kinahan and Clive Bolger in difficulty, the icing on the cake for Foley came in October 2011 when 'Fat' Freddie Thompson found himself in a major pickle with the Spanish police, who wanted him extradited for questioning about the Kinahan empire and the murder of his friend and enforcer, Paddy Doyle.

Foley hadn't forgiven Thompson for betraying him by organising to have him killed on Kinahan's instructions back in 2008. The Viper had always been happy to offer Thompson help and advice and the only thanks he got was eight bullets to the body and a narrow escape from death.

From 2008 onwards Freddie Thompson moved between the UK, Spain and the Netherlands. He initially left Ireland because of his war with Declan 'Whacker' Duffy and the INLA, but then legislation was introduced to allow for gang bosses to be arrested and tried before a non-jury court. Thompson was one of the main targets who gardaí wanted to prosecute under this legislation, so he was afraid return to Ireland. Martin Foley was also investigated with a view to bringing possible charges against him under the new legislation, but this never happened.

In the summer of 2011 Freddie was forced to move home because his family was being targeted by rival criminals led by Gerard Eglington. Eglington was a thug who had been in a stolen car that was involved in an incident on the Stillorgan dual carriageway in April 2003, in which two gardaí were killed. Because Fat Freddie had been away for so long, Eglington and his cronies had been trying to take over running crime on his patch.

In March 2011 the Eglington mob bumped into Freddie's brother, Ritchie Thompson, when they were on a night out in the Karma Stone pub in Dublin city centre. An associate of Eglington approached Ritchie and said that they didn't want trouble, so Thompson relaxed and got on with his night. However, when he went outside to smoke a cigarette, a car full of Eglington gang members arrived and viciously beat Ritchie, breaking his leg. His shocked wife, Catherine, tried to intervene and she was viciously slashed with a broken bottle and needed seventeen stitches.

When Freddie heard about the unprovoked assault he went ballistic, but because he was in exile abroad there was little or nothing he could do about it personally. He had his associates try to assassinate Eglington on three separate occasions but they failed each time.

Eglington's crew didn't sit back and take the attempts to kill him lying down. They continued with the campaign against members of Thompson's family. In May 2011 a viable pipe bomb was thrown into the back garden of Freddie's mother's house. Mrs Thompson was an innocent woman and the fact that she was being targeted in order to get at her son was like a red rag to a bull for Fat Freddie. Ritchie Thompson was a criminal and was regarded as fair game, but targeting innocent family members was against gangland rules.

Freddie felt he had no choice but to come back to the country and face down his enemies. Gardaí greeted

Freddie's return with dismay and flooded the streets of Dublin 8, Crumlin and Drimnagh with armed officers, so sure were they that blood would be spilled. However, luck was on their side; the request from Spanish police to extradite Thompson arrived on 14 October. Detectives wasted no time in arresting Thompson and bringing him before the High Court, where he was remanded in custody until the paperwork arrived from Spain. This was a huge relief to officers.

On 28 October Freddie was transported to Dublin Airport under garda escort. He was flanked by nearly a dozen armed officers as he was taken aboard an Iberia flight to Madrid.

There were real suspicions among Freddie's rivals – and indeed members of the Kinahan organisation – that his extradition was a sham designed to protect him from accusations that he was an informant who had provided valuable information about the Kinahans. The fact that the extradition warrant contained precious little in the way of incriminating evidence only added to the suspicions, as did the fact that Freddie Thompson did not object to being extradited.

After being quizzed by the magistrate for just a few hours, Freddie was released without charge. Maybe Martin Foley would have liked for Thompson to be locked up for good because of his role in the attempt to shoot him, but Freddie is now permanently exiled. Whether this puts his enemies out of danger or not is another matter.

On 24 September 2012 Gerard Eglington was shot dead in cold blood at his Portarlington home, while his eleven-year-old stepdaughter and four-year-old son were in the house. Gardaí immediately pointed the blame towards the

Thompson mob. It seems Martin Foley would be wise to keep his wits about him.

The majority of the media coverage of The Viper over the last four decades has been overwhelmingly negative, usually with just cause. However, in November 2011 he made headlines for all the right reasons.

Foley was driving his infamous company van on St Agnes Road in Crumlin Village when he saw nineteen-year-old Ellen Carroll lying on the ground. The teenager's mother, Sheila, was trying to hold up her daughter but it was clear that Ellen was fighting for her life. Foley leapt into action and started repeatedly massaging the young woman's chest because she had stopped breathing. Two passing doctors took over and The Viper volunteered to give the medics and Ellen a lift to nearby St James's Hospital. While one of the doctors performed mouth-to-mouth resuscitation, Foley stopped a garda and quickly explained what was happening.

Gardaí gave them an escort to the hospital and made the five-kilometre journey in no time. Ellen was rushed to the accident and emergency department where doctors battled to save her life. Unfortunately, Ellen, who is believed to have suffered from a heart condition, lost her battle for life a few hours later.

Foley told Michael O'Toole of the *Star* newspaper, 'My mate was driving and I just saw this woman trying to hold her daughter up. It looked really serious, so I jumped out and ran over to her. It was terrible. The girl's mother was in a terrible state and I got a woman to take her into her own house.

'A doctor arrived too and he told me to do twenty

presses on her heart, while he did mouth-to-mouth. I know CPR and just kept doing it. Then we were told that the ambulance would be fifteen minutes and the doctor told me she wouldn't last that long – so he just said drive. We got the girl into the back of my van, as well as two doctors.

'I knew the traffic was too heavy, so I saw this garda up the road and shouted at him for help. Fair play to him – he came down in a garda van and gave us an escort all the way to the hospital. He was great.'

Foley was obviously very upset by what happened to the poor girl and said, 'I thought she was going to make it. She seemed to be doing okay when I left the hospital, but she died later on.'

Very few gardaí have any time for Foley but they say he performed heroics that day and they praised him for his quick thinking.

When Foley was shot in January 2008, retired Detective Inspector Gerry O'Carroll predicted that the criminal's life story would be the subject of a Hollywood movie because it had all the ingredients of a blockbuster. He wasn't exactly right, but the hit RTÉ series *Love/Hate*, which told the story of feuding Dublin gangs, did use the Carlisle gym shooting as the inspiration for a shooting scene. However, unlike the real-life version of the story, the gunman in *Love/Hate* shot his target dead. It must have brought back unwelcome memories for Foley, who claimed to suffer frequent flashbacks and nightmares from his many brushes with death.

In September 2011 Martin Foley complained to the gardaí following an article this author wrote about him in the

Sunday World. The article, headlined DEAD MAN CYCLING, revealed that Foley was taking security precautions after The Dapper Don had taken out a fresh €60,000 contract on him. It stated that he checks under his car each morning for devices, in case he is targeted by yet another hitman.

When the article was published, Foley went straight to Crumlin Garda Station and made an official complaint, saying that the newspaper was putting his life in danger by encouraging a fresh attempt on his life. His solicitor also wrote to the *Sunday World* to complain about the article and he also made a complaint to the Press Ombudsman. Six weeks later a similar story appeared in a new book about the history of gangland. It was yet another example of how Martin Foley picks and chooses when he wants to cooperate with gardaí and of how he simultaneously tries to use the law and flout it. Needless to say the investigation went nowhere.

Martin Foley became involved in the debt collection business to make money, but he also wanted a 'legitimate' job to keep journalists from poking around his business and putting him in their newspapers. The façade that he was not involved in criminality dropped in July 2012 when his home on Cashel Avenue was smashed up by masked men, putting him back on the front pages again. The trouble began when a friend of Foley's contacted him and asked for a lift to Tallaght after a car had been taken from a friend of his. When they found the car, Foley's friend saw a thirty-one-year-old called Glen Keegan in the area and blamed him for the theft. He gave Keegan what sources have described as 'a serious beating' and then ordered The Viper to drive away.

Foley was furious that he had been dragged into a row that had nothing to do with him. His anger was well founded, because a few hours later his home was attacked by three masked men armed with hatchets and baseball bats. The Viper had a steel-and-concrete-reinforced door installed in his house, which meant that even if you managed to break down the wooden front door it was next to impossible to breach the reinforced door, even if six men spent an hour attacking it with sledgehammers. Foley rushed Sonia Doyle to an upstairs bedroom and helplessly looked on as the men smashed all the bulletproof downstairs windows, causing €5,000 worth of damage. The mob then turned its attention to two of Foley's debt collection vans, which were parked on the road, and smashed them up, causing thousands of euro worth of damage to them.

Foley blamed Glen Keegan, nicknamed 'The Little General', for the damage and he demanded €25,000 to cover everything. Keegan came to national prominence in the 1990s when he frequently called radio talk shows from stolen cars he was out joyriding. He was dubbed The Little General because he was a one-man crime wave at the time and was frequently arrested by gardaí. He first came to garda attention aged ten, and was getting arrested for stealing cars by the age of thirteen. He was so small that he had to sit on a cushion to reach the steering wheel. He used to put on driving 'displays' for youngsters in Tallaght, and he taunted gardaí, who were unable to catch him. Judges sent Keegan to young offenders' institutions, but as soon as he was released he would go back to theft, and he told Social Services he got 'a great buzz' out of it. He escaped from detention on nearly a dozen occasions.

In 1998 Keegan was sent to St Patrick's institution for nineteen months for a string of offences, including stealing cars and other driving offences. He was also banned from driving for fifteen years. Keegan's solicitor said the seventeen-year-old had been badly affected by the death of his father the year before. However, the judge said, 'I am seeing him for longer than this. I knew the defendant before his father died. I remember his father coming in here and making all sorts of excuses for him, saying that the educational system had let him down.'

Gardaí always feared it was inevitable that Keegan would reach the highest echelons of Irish organised crime. But his rise was halted in 2005 when he was nabbed robbing a bank in his native Tallaght, after telling a terrified porter that his wife had been kidnapped and would be killed if he didn't cooperate. Keegan pressed a gun to the head of the porter and ordered him to open the safe and hand over €50,000, but the porter activated a secret alarm. An unarmed garda arrived, tackled Keegan and arrested him. It turned out that the gun had been an imitation. The court heard that Keegan was on a methadone programme and was also using cocaine and was in debt due to his drug abuse. Nevertheless, The Little General was jailed for seven years, his sixteenth conviction.

Gardaí advised Keegan that his life was in danger and they feared that an all-out war would break out between Foley and the young criminal. But Keegan was not afraid of Martin Foley or his reputation. The Viper was under pressure to hit back and save face because he was being slagged that he had become an easy target for lesser criminals and was now over the hill. *Sunday World* journalist Donal MacIntyre tried to interview Foley about his latest scrape and ended up seeing the true face of the bully-boy criminal. MacIntyre spotted Foley and Sonia Doyle stuck in traffic in Walkinstown and the journalist waved to him and

asked if they could have a chat. Foley told MacIntyre and
the photographer who was with him to pull in to the side
of the road. When MacIntyre approached Foley's Audi,
The Viper recognised him and smiled. However, when
he realised that MacIntyre was filming him on his camera
phone he snapped and jumped out of the car and lunged
at him. He grabbed the journalist and tried to wrestle him
the ground. Sonia Doyle tried to calm down Foley but he
insisted on dialling 999. When gardaí arrived, the criminal
claimed he had been 'dragged from the car and assaulted'.
However, when the uniformed officers viewed the footage
MacIntyre had recorded, they realised Foley was lying, and
that he had in fact been the aggressor. Foley then reverted
to habit and told MacIntyre, 'My lawyer is the president of
the Law Society of Ireland. He will have something to say
on this,' before shouting, 'I'm going to get you charged.'

If anyone was going to be brought before the courts
over the bizarre incident, it was Foley. As soon as he cooled
down he realised that he had made a huge tactical error by
losing his head with the reporter, and he was soon on the
phone to criminal colleagues asking how he could redeem
himself. It was hopeless though. His outburst guaranteed
that he was yet again splashed all over the papers. With
his attack on Donal MacIntyre and the violent dispute with
Glen Keegan, it was obvious that for the sixty-year-old,
with age, wisdom had not followed.

Martin Foley did not want this book to be written. When he
learned that Paul Williams had included a chapter on him
in a book he wrote in 2003, Foley embarked on a campaign
of terror to put the journalist off. This time, he went down

he legal route. When The Viper heard rumours that this author was researching a book about him, he had his trusted solicitor write a letter on his behalf. The letter, received on May 2012, said:

> We understand that you may be writing a book concerning our client. We would be obliged if you would confirm whether or not that is in fact the position. If it is the position we would be anxious to be provided with a copy of any reference to our client in the book in order that we may consider whether or not the provisions of the Defamation Act 2009 or indeed the constitutional and convention protections that our client enjoyed are breached by the proposed publication.
>
> We appreciate that you may not wish to disclose the contents of a work in progress at this stage and for present purposes it is simply adequate if you confirm to us that you are in fact engaged in such a work and that you will provide us a copy pre-publication. This will enable us to advise our client and to ensure that any appropriate application to a court can be made at the appropriate time.

The fact that Foley's solicitor was effectively saying that he and his client were considering trying to secure a court injunction to prevent this book being published, before they even knew for sure that it was being written, is extraordinary. I contacted Martin Foley and asked him if he would like to contribute to this book in the interests of balance. He declined. Needless to say neither Foley nor his solicitor received a copy of this book before it was made available to the general public. What he chooses to do now is up to him.

Conclusion

MARTIN FOLEY IS UNIQUE. Criminals like him do not exist anymore and will not exist in the future. His criminal career has spanned four decades; he has been there, done that and stolen the T-shirt. Now in his sixties, Martin Foley is the elder statesman of Irish organised crime, and criminals coming up the ranks today can look at his life of crime and learn not only what to do, but also what not to do. Today most young wannabe godfathers have a maximum lifespan of about five years before they are either murdered or sent down. Foley has been shot four times, hit by eighteen bullets and he has escaped an IRA kidnapping. He has been compared to Rasputin because he has cheated death and defied doctors on countless occasions by recovering from injuries that would have killed the average man. The fact that he has beaten the hitman's bullet so often is no accident. Foley tells friends that he has prepared his body for the possibility that he will be shot at. Most people who are shot do not die from the actual wound. Instead their bodies give in to shock and shut down. Foley managed to condition his body to take the bullets without shock setting in and killing him.

He has always treated his body like a machine and worked out obsessively, building his physical strength. Even today he is as fit as a twenty year old and probably far stronger. He did not neglect his stamina either. He has always run, cycled and done yoga to make sure that he is supple and flexible. This stood him in good stead when he had to twist to avoid a bullet from close range or run through back gardens, hurdling over high fences as a gunman took aim at him.

The fact that The Viper has survived and thrived for so long is also a testament to his cunning and his survival instinct, and there has also been a large degree of good luck thrown into the mix. He has outlasted many of his friends and contemporaries. Martin 'The General' Cahill died staring down the barrel of an IRA gun, as did his best friend, Shavo Hogan. Most of his criminal contemporaries and members of the original Cahill gang spent a significant number of their best years behind bars and were never the same after their long stretches. The longest sentence Martin Foley received was two years. To have a career that has lasted so long and to be hit with just a couple of Mickey Mouse sentences is an excellent record, almost unprecedented.

Foley has never been the most intelligent man, but he is street smart. He never made the mistake many of his friends made in handling their own drugs, so there was never a chance he would be jailed for drug dealing. He also refused to get involved in dealing heroin, because he felt that ecstasy and cannabis were less addictive and do not damage communities in the way heroin does. To most people, a drug dealer is a drug dealer, no matter what they peddle, but Foley always saw himself as being above dealers who sold pathetic junkies their fix, knowing they had probably robbed an old lady to pay for it.

Foley has always been an old-school type of villain. He did not go around shooting people without reason, preferring to resolve disagreements through negotiation, instead of violence. That's not to say that Foley was not capable of extreme violence if he snapped. The case of Detective Garda O'Connell is a good example, and his feud with Clive Bolger also showed that he was not a man to be messed with. He was originally embraced by Martin Cahill as 'muscle' and he had no problem dishing out beatings when he felt the occasion warranted it.

Although he linked up with some of the country's most serious criminals during his long career, Foley was never totally trusted by anyone. He was well liked, but not trusted. He was duplicitous, spread rumours and stories, and generally shot his mouth off. His loose lips almost cost him his life when the Gilligan gang decided to whack him for telling the Provos they were selling heroin. The General suspected that Foley was informing to the guards, and Chris Casserly's gang didn't like the rumours that Foley was mouthing off about them.

Foley has never been able to help himself when it comes to telling stories and he is regularly slagged for being like a gossiping old woman. If he had learned to curb this habit, he might have avoided getting into several scrapes over the years.

It is a tribute to Martin Foley that he has succeeded in reinventing himself in recent years. Most fifty-six year olds would have given up after the fourth murder attempt. But Foley is not most people. He recovered from the Carlisle gym shooting and took stock of his life. He knew there was no future for him in drug dealing, so he threw himself into his debt collection business with gusto.

Viper Debt Recovery and Repossession Services is now probably the busiest company of its kind in the country, and Foley is surely making as much money as ever. That's not to say for a minute that he is totally legitimate. The number of people going to the High Court and talking to journalists about having been intimidated by Foley and his henchmen is disturbing. Foley knows that the average, law-abiding member of the public is terrified of his violent reputation. He trades on his notoriety, and while he and his employees are careful not to physically threaten anybody, their presence is usually enough to scare. The threat of violence is always there in the background.

Foley hates the media, and time after time he has tried to sue newspapers, knowing full well that it will only generate more of the type of coverage he despises. Yet he has shown on several occasions that he is prepared to use the media when necessary. He was a spokesman for the Concerned Criminals movement and is known to discreetly contact favoured journalists when he wants something planted in the media. He is prepared to talk to journalists on occasion, but doesn't like the fact that he is not in control of what they write.

One of the things that Martin Foley takes the greatest offence to is the accusation that he is a garda informant. He vehemently denies this and tells his friends and associates that he hates the gardaí, that he always has and always will. Foley has often been happy to chat to gardaí off the record, but he will never make formal statements of complaint against other criminals. Journalists, obviously, are a different matter.

Martin Foley's attitude towards gardaí mellowed somewhat from the late 1990s onwards. He lost the angry streak that had led him to assault officers on several occasions and he became more reasonable and easier to deal with. He is capable of genuine acts of kindness. When Tony Tighe, the garda who saved him from being kidnapped and possibly killed by the IRA, retired a number of years ago, a bottle of whiskey was dropped into his station. The card wished Tighe all the best for the future and was signed by one Martin Foley.

It is also fairly safe to say that Foley has in the past paid off the IRA to be allowed to continue in business. It was, and still is, routine for the Republican movement to demand protection money from drug dealers. Because Foley had such a chequered history with the Provos, it's hardly surprising that he threw them a few bob to keep them off his back. Paying the IRA was a necessary evil and he had little choice but to cough up.

Even the most grudging garda gives Foley credit for the job he did in bringing up his two daughters. Pauline Foley died when Amy and Rachel were still teenagers and it is no mean feat that The Viper brought up the two girls singlehandedly. Most parents want their children to do better in life than they did and Martin Foley is no different. His daughters have never been involved in criminality and are well-adjusted young women with steady jobs. Nobody could ever accuse Foley of being anything but devoted to his family.

Although Foley was determined to shield his daughters from crime and tried his best to steer them on the right path in life, he did not do the same for many young men from the Crumlin and Drimnagh areas. The opposite is in fact the case. Foley not only actively encouraged the likes of 'Fat' Freddie Thompson, Brian Rattigan and Aidan Gavin to get involved in drug dealing and criminality, he also acted as a mentor to them. He helped them, advised them, listened to their problems and generally helped to turn them into the criminals they are today. Sixteen young men lost their lives in the bloody Crumlin/Drimnagh feud, and if the likes of Foley had dissuaded Thompson and Rattigan from getting involved in drug dealing when they were impressionable teenagers, it is fair to assume that at least some of those pointless murders could have been avoided. That is not to say that Foley can be blamed for the feud, but he was respected by the youngsters and had the power to influence them to some extent. He had demonstrated that he had the power to diffuse potentially incendiary situations when he regularly acted as a go-between or refereed in local disputes in Crumlin. People thought enough of him to go to him and look for help, knowing that he would listen to both sides and make a fair decision. It is a shame he did not take this role more seriously.

So what will the future hold for Martin Foley? On the face of it there is no reason why the sixty-year-old should get into trouble with his fellow criminals in the future. He is long enough out of the drugs business that his past should not come back to haunt him, and he claims to have settled his differences with Christy Kinahan. There is always the potential for his dispute with Clive Bolger to reignite but you would have to question what appetite either man has for that row. It is more likely that if Foley does get into trouble in the future that it will be connected with his debt collection business. Any disputes in this area will hopefully be resolved in the law courts, rather than through a violent feud.

But, as Martin Foley has consistently proven over the

last thirty years, he simply cannot help getting into bother and he has the potential to fall out with his own shadow. Also, he is a money-mad miser who may not be able to help himself if the chance of making a quick buck, legally or illegally, comes his way. Only a fool would bet on Foley not pissing off the wrong person at some point and paying the ultimate price. Whatever happens there will never be another criminal like Martin Foley. He most certainly is the last of the Mohicans.